The Repoliticization of the Welfare State

The Repoliticization of the Welfare State

IAN P. MCMANUS

University of Michigan Press
Ann Arbor

Published in the United States of America by the
University of Michigan Press
Printed and bound by CPI Group (UK) Ltd, Croydon, CR0 4YY

First published July 2022

A CIP catalog record for this book is available from the British Library.

Library of Congress Cataloging-in-Publication data has been applied for.

ISBN 978-0-472-07532-4 (hardcover : alk. paper)
ISBN 978-0-472-05532-6 (paper : alk. paper)
ISBN 978-0-472-90286-6 (OA)

DOI: https://doi.org/10.3998/mpub.12140242

An electronic version of this book is freely available, thanks in part to the support of libraries
working with Knowledge Unlatched (KU). KU is a collaborative initiative designed to make
high quality books Open Access for the public good. More information about the initiative
and links to the Open Access version can be found at www.knowledgeunlatched.org.

The University of Michigan Press's open access publishing program is made possible
thanks to additional funding from the University of Michigan Office of the Provost
and the generous support of contributing libraries.

CONTENTS

Digital materials related to this title can be found on the Fulcrum platform via the following citable URL https://doi.org/10.3998/mpub.12140242

LIST OF ILLUSTRATIONS

CHAPTER 1

The Realignment of Welfare State Politics

A profound shift has occurred in the politics of social spending across advanced capitalist economies. After a substantial period of cross-party consensus on welfare state spending, partisan politics is back. While the severity of the global financial crisis (GFC) called for strong social spending responses to limit the costs of the economic crisis for millions of individuals, there has been growing fiscal pressure for governments to reduce budgets and make deep cuts to the welfare state. These contrasting demands have resulted in intensified partisan divisions over proposals to expand or roll back social spending. Whereas conservative parties have embraced fiscal discipline and welfare state cuts after the crisis, left-leaning parties have turned away from austerity measures in favor of higher social spending. These party positions represent a return of traditional left-right ideological beliefs over social spending and economic governance. This book grapples with the evolving nature of political conflict over social spending and the future of social and economic policymaking in Europe and beyond.

Partisan conflicts over social spending have featured prominently in national politics and public discourse in many countries in recent years. For example, in the aftermath of the GFC, the Conservative Party in the United Kingdom (UK) has undertaken the largest cuts to the British welfare state since the end of World War II. This has led the Labour Party, under the leadership of Jeremy Corbyn, to shift further to the left and call for a limit to austerity, for social spending increases, and to a wider condemnation of neoliberal ideas and policies. Social spending was a major point of contestation in Germany as the Social Democrats made the expansion of generous and universal welfare benefits a key demand as the party negotiated entering into another grand coalition with Angela Merkel's conservative Christian Democratic Party. In 2017, Social Democratic prime minister Stefan Löfven cohosted a European Social Summit in Sweden, the first of its kind

in twenty years, which aimed to promote social equality and greater investment in welfare states across the EU and saw the introduction of the European Social Pillar. The position of Sweden's Social Democrats is in sharp
contrast to the promarket welfare reforms and social spending cuts introduced by the previous center-right Moderate Party–led government. In
Spain, the far-left Podemos party put forth an alternative proposal to the
conservative PP party's 2018 budget, which would increase social spending
by €24.5 billion ($28 billion) to address issues such as unemployment and
gender inequality. After the 2018 election in the Czech Republic, the populist ANO party formed a left-wing coalition government with Social Democrats which has promised to reverse many of the tax cuts and social spending reductions enacted by the conservative Civic Democratic Party. Partisan
debates over social spending have, therefore, not only become highly salient
in the modern politics of advanced capitalist economies but prevalent
across different welfare state types.

This book seeks to answer the critical question: How did the global
financial crisis alter the politics of social spending across advanced capitalist economies? In doing so, it will help to contextualize these contemporary
political divisions over social spending and provide insight into the consequences of this conflict moving forward. As critical junctures, crises can
create windows of opportunity[1] for significant changes in politics and policymaking. This book argues that the GFC acted as such a critical moment
that established a new postcrisis dynamic where the partisan composition
of government once again matters for social spending. In this new postcrisis environment, left-leaning governments are more likely to support higher
levels of social spending, while their conservative counterparts are likely to
prioritize fiscal discipline, which includes reduced welfare state and other
public spending.

This analysis of the politics of crisis and the influence of partisan differences on social spending is critical not only to understanding government
responses after the Great Recession, but also contemporary and future crises.
These new political dynamics, for example, are relevant in the midst of the
current COVID-19 crisis. Whereas governments are adopting stimulus measures and expanding social spending on programs, such as unemployment

---

1. A window of opportunity is a moment in time when there is potential for policy
change. Policy entrepreneurs who recognize such moments may use them to take action
and implement their desired policies (Kingdon 1995).

benefits, to address this public health and economic crisis, fiscal conservatives are raising public debt and deficit concerns, worried about the long-term costs of welfare interventions. This book will provide a framework to understand the politics of crisis and how the partisan composition of government influences social spending responses in the contemporary era.

The following chapters of this book will argue and empirically support the case that a new and lasting postcrisis dynamic has emerged in which political parties once again matter for social spending. At the heart of this repoliticization of the welfare state are contentious ideological disagreements over fiscal discipline, market regulation, redistribution, and the role of government. Surprisingly, partisan divisions over welfare spending have arisen even in countries less affected by economic downturn, such as Sweden and Germany. This indicates that partisan conflict over social spending was not simply an immediate reaction to the GFC but reflects deeper ideological differences which have re-emerged between parties on the left and right. This partisan discord is in contrast to the precrisis welfare consensus that emerged between parties and across countries.

The next section provides a brief history of social spending during two distinct phases of the GFC. It highlights changes in social spending over time and identifies the growing disparities between and within countries as governments struggle to balance national finances with the need for effective social protection. This will be followed by an analysis of the repoliticization of the welfare state after the GFC and the significance of this event as a moment of critical juncture.[2] The chapter will conclude by providing information about the remaining chapters of the book.

A Brief History of the Crisis

Before delving into the specific history of the Great Recession, two important points about the term *crisis* must be addressed. The first point has to do with the particular definition of crisis, which must be differentiated from how the term has been commonly described in the welfare state literature.

---

2. Critical junctures are conceptualized "as moments in which uncertainty as to the future of an institutional arrangement allows for political agency and choice to play a decisive causal role in setting an institution on a certain path of development, a path that then persists over a long period of time" (Capoccia 2015).

The second point has to do with identifying the time frame of the crisis so that clear parameters are set to understand what is meant by the precrisis and postcrisis periods. To begin with, it is important to clarify that the term *crisis* in the context of this book has a precise meaning. Within the literature, there are long-standing references to the multiple crises faced by modern welfare states, referring to shifting labor market and demographic challenges confronting social protection systems as well as the lack of funding for welfare expansion that has persisted since the 1970s. Crisis for the purposes of this book, however, refers specifically to the social and economic challenges that advanced welfare states have experienced as a consequence of the severe and rapid global economic downturn that began in 2008.

The collapse of global financial markets in 2008 triggered one of the worst economic crises in nearly a century, resulting in the loss of trillions of dollars in GDP and millions of jobs worldwide (Atkinson, Luttrell, and Rosenbloom 2013; *Wall Street Journal* 2012a; World Bank 2014). The severity of this crisis should not, therefore, be understated. Its effect on the politics of social and economic policymaking was unprecedented in the modern age. While the EU had seen steady growth in the decade preceding the GFC, GDP plummeted sharply across member states at the start of the crisis (see figure 1). Although the EU had seen some economic recovery after the initial financial crisis in 2008, the region had by 2012 entered into a double-dip recession (see figure 1). At the same time, the unemployment rate rose sharply across the region as firms and other private-sector actors began to reduce large portions of their labor force (see figure 2). The crisis, therefore, represented a serious cross-national threat to economic, political, and social stability. In response to rising unemployment and other growing social concerns, welfare spending increased markedly across the OECD starting in 2008. At the same time, real GDP on average shrank, resulting in growing debt and deficit problems for governments, which increased public expenditures to offset the negative social effects of the crisis and to stimulate economic growth. Across the OECD, social spending-to-GDP ratios grew considerably (see figure 3). Government social spending decision making, therefore, took place within a broader context of austerity and limited budgetary capacity as the crisis wore on. This laid the foundation for greater political conflict over the need to balance fiscal concerns with adequate social protection.

Second, this research defines the crisis as beginning in 2008 and continuing until 2013, although, as the country case studies in this book reveal,

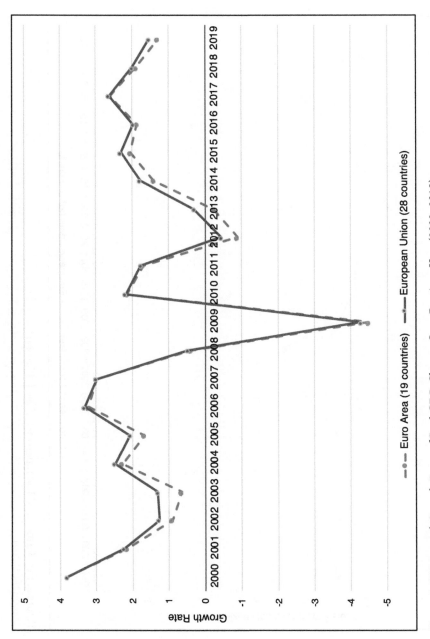

Figure 1. EU Annual Growth Rates of Real GDP, Change Over Previous Year (2000–2019)
Source: OECD 2021

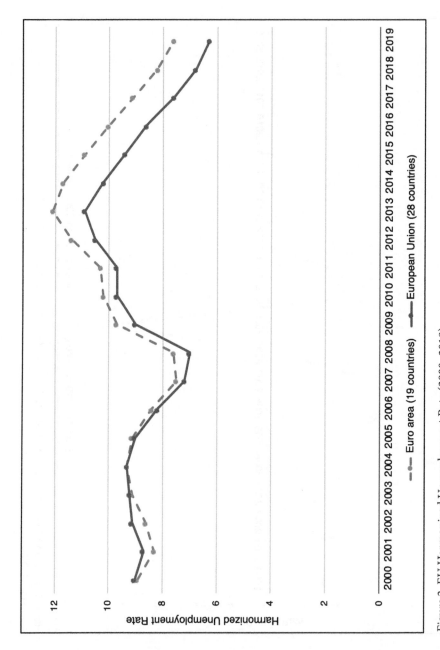

Figure 2. EU Harmonized Unemployment Rate (2000–2019)
Source: OECD 2021

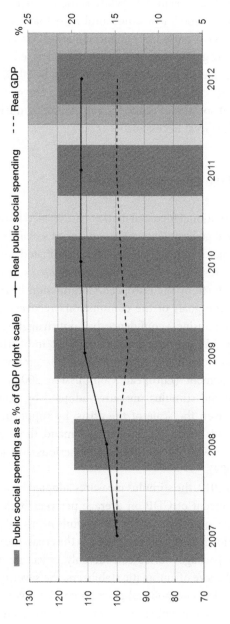

Figure 3. Real Social Spending, Real GDP, and Social Spending as a % of GDP (2007–2012)
Source: OECD 2012

the impact of the GFC on the politics of social spending has persisted across welfare states up to the present day. While some countries witnessed an economic slowdown in 2007, it was not until 2008 that a worldwide economic crisis began. What started as a financial market crisis in 2008 rapidly became a far-reaching global economic crisis characterized by high unemployment and low domestic growth across countries. By 2010, it had turned into a sovereign debt crisis and a larger social crisis. The next section provides an overview of social and economic policymaking during these two distinct phases of the Great Recession.

The First Wave of the Crisis (2008–2010)

The collapse of international financial markets in 2008 led to rapid stimulus responses by national governments across advanced welfare states. Within the EU, member states pursued relatively coordinated countercyclical Keynesian stimulus responses in line with *European Economic Recovery Plan* guidelines put forth by the European Commission in 2008 (Leschke and Jepsen 2012). The goals of the commission's recovery plan were to restore consumer and business confidence, bail out struggling banks, stimulate investment in EU markets, support hard-hit industries, including construction and manufacturing, protect vulnerable groups, create jobs, and lower unemployment (European Commission 2008). While some experts categorized the stimulus measures adopted by governments as extremely modest given the scale of the crisis, by supporting collapsing financial markets and bolstering economic demand these policies have largely been credited with preventing a more serious and lasting global depression (IMF 2009).

From 2008 until 2010, the stimulus measures adopted by member states infused around 1 percent of GDP on average per year back into the EU economy (European Commission 2009a). But while nearly all governments implemented some form of stimulus response to the crisis, the size and content of their bailout packages varied considerably, reflecting different welfare state legacies, the size of automatic stabilizers, the severity of the crisis on domestic economies, and political partisan conflict over discretionary spending. Whereas some member states were able to weather the crisis fairly well, increasing debt and deficit levels limited the ability of other states to provide the level of social support needed to offset negative distributional costs (Watt and Nikolova 2009). For example, whereas Austria, Germany, Sweden, and Finland were able to adopt stimulus measures equivalent to around 3–4 percent of domestic GDP, other states, like Hungary, who were economically harder hit, were unable to increase public spending at all (European Commission 2009a). Differences in the size and content of stimulus responses led to significant disparities in social and economic outcomes across states.

During the first two years of the GFC, unemployment increased by 2.6 percent in the EU and GDP fell by around 5 percent, yet there was significant variation across member states (see figures 1 and 2). For example, while the German economy shrank by 6 percent of GDP, the unemployment rate was lower than it had been before the crisis. In large part, this was due to the comprehensive and well-funded welfare programs designed to protect jobs. By contrast, the Spanish economy contracted by only 4 percent of GDP but experienced an unemployment rate increase of 7.5 percent (Leschke and Jepsen 2012). The downturn was far worse in some parts of eastern Europe. For instance, Baltic states between 2008 and 2009 faced an average increase in unemployment of more than 10 percent and a GDP loss of up to 20 percent (Leschke and Jepsen 2012). This variation indicates that not only did the GFC impact states differently but that the capacity of governments to respond effectively to this economic downturn and provide social protection to their citizens varied considerably.

The Second Wave of the Crisis (2010–2013)

By 2010, it was clear that the GFC was having a destabilizing effect on government finances in the EU, with public debts and deficits rising to unsustainable levels (Theodoropoulou and Watt 2011). Stimulus measures, while helping to offset the initial effects of the crisis, left state coffers drained at the same time that growth and revenue streams were declining in several countries, such as Spain, Ireland, Greece, and Portugal. These problems came to a head in 2010 as a loss of confidence had grown over the Greek economy and the government's ability to pay its debts. This loss of faith in Greece marked the beginning of a larger sovereign debt crisis throughout the EU and a turning point in the GFC. This second phase of the crisis was characterized by a turn away from stimulus and the implementation of austerity measures across several states in an attempt to reduce public spending and increase revenues. Whereas in 2008 and 2009 governments implemented measures to stimulate domestic markets and increase social spending, by 2010, many countries began to make budgetary cuts and structural reforms to encourage growth and reduce public expenditures.

Social spending became the target of drastic cuts in many countries, as welfare states came under severe financial strain. Although many EU member states began to reduce social spending after 2010, as was the case with stimulus measures, the degree of austerity varied widely across countries. In other words, there was considerable divergence in government capacity to balance the need for fiscal discipline while maintaining adequate levels of social protection. Cuts in social spending as a percentage of GDP were the greatest in eastern and southern European welfare states, which were already worse off in terms of economic growth, unemployment rates, and social protection levels. By contrast, social spending cuts were considerably lower in wealthier western and northern Europe welfare states. According to the European Commission's *Stability and Growth Programmes* report, public budgets between 2010 and 2014 were cut by 15–20 percent across most eastern European states, while similar government spending cuts were less than 10 percent in western and northern European countries, including Belgium, Denmark, Finland, Germany, and Sweden (Theodoropoulou and Watt 2011). In some states most hard hit by the crisis, public spending reductions were significantly higher. For instance, spending cuts in Ireland between 2010 and 2014 amounted to around 40 percent of GDP (Leschke and Jepsen 2012). The pressure to reduce public spending and implement welfare cuts was particularly strong in countries that received bailout funds from the EU and IMF. These states included Greece, Hungary, Ireland, Latvia, Portugal, and Romania.

In sum, beginning in 2010, many countries turned away from stimulus and instead introduced fiscal austerity measures aimed at addressing rising debt and deficit problems. The austerity measures adopted by EU member states, however, were uneven, with some countries making much more drastic cuts to social spending than others. Those countries that were most hard-hit by the crisis were typically the least able to respond effectively with countercyclical measures and instead implemented deep social spending cuts. This was problematic as these cuts may have prolonged the effects of the crisis in these countries and had a destabilizing effect on domestic and international markets.

Divergence Between States and Within Countries

The GFC had a profound effect across welfare states. During the first phase of the crisis, social spending rose on average across the EU. There was, however, significant variation in these stimulus measures, with welfare states in western and northern Europe offering higher levels of spending than their counterparts in southern and eastern Europe. Wealthy states, including Austria, Finland, Germany, Sweden, and the UK, for example, each spent at least 2 percent of their GDP on active labor market policies and household benefits (European Commission 2009a). By comparison, eastern European states, including Bulgaria, Cyprus, Hungary, Lithuania, and Romania, each spent less than 0.1 percent of their GDP on these policies (European Commission 2009a). Given the importance that social spending played in reducing the negative effects of the crisis, differences in government responses contributed to an uneven recovery and rising inequality between EU countries.

In addition to cross-national variation in social spending responses to the GFC, some countries experienced rising inequality and declining social solidarity. Social benefits in continental, southern, and eastern Europe welfare states, for instance, tend to favor full-time employees with standard work contracts, leaving part-time workers and other labor market outsiders more vulnerable after the crisis. In fact, outsider groups were disproportionally affected at the start of the GFC, such as younger workers, who faced a sharp rise in unemployment. Austerity measures, which are largely regressive, have further intensified these inequalities. Such widening inequality was more pronounced in countries already struggling the most as they are under intense pressure to cut social spending at the same time that they are faced with rising levels of unemployment and poverty. This dynamic is problematic, as social spending cuts are positively correlated with the risk of poverty and social exclusion (see figure 4).

It is important to note that while the wealth of a welfare state has been an important factor in defining its capacity to respond to the GFC, it is the political composition of government that has been the driving force behind social spending. For instance, there has been substantial variation in post-crisis social spending, even among countries with similar welfare states and economies, that reflects partisan divisions. Governments led by right-leaning parties have tended to favor fiscal discipline and welfare cuts, while

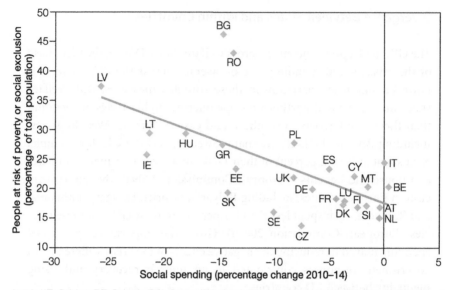

Austria (AT), Belgium (BE), Bulgaria (BG), Cyprus (CY), Czech Republic (CZ), Denmark (DK), Estonia (EE), Finland (FI), France (FR), Germany (DE), Greece (GR), Hungary (HU), Ireland (IE), Italy (IT), Latvia (LV), Lithuania (LT), Luxembourg (LU), Malta (MT), Netherlands (NL), Poland (PL), Romania (RO), Slovakia (SK), Slovenia (SI), Spain (ES), Sweden (SE), United Kingdom (UK).

Figure 4. Risk of Poverty or Social Exclusion (2009) and Planned Changes in Social Spending, 2010–14 (Percentages)
Source: Leschke and Jepsen 2012

left-leaning parties have been less supportive of austerity and have instead stressed the need for higher social spending and greater state intervention. This was not true in the precrisis period and marks a radical shift in social spending dynamics.

The Repoliticization of the Welfare State

In the aftermath of one of the worst economic crises since the Great Depression, the challenges facing welfare states are unprecedented as governments are confronted with the need to maintain responsible budgets while at the same time providing adequate social protection for their citizens. These challenges are compounded by new social risks, such as aging populations, changing labor markets, and rising inequality, which increases demand for social spending despite slow economic growth and high unemployment in many countries. This need to balance social protection against budgetary concerns has led to serious political divisions. Although fiscal concerns remained high, nearly all OECD countries adopted social spending stimulus at the start of the GFC (Armingeon 2012). As the crisis continued, however, national responses differed considerably. To understand why governments adopted such varied welfare responses, it is vital to identify how the GFC has changed the politics of social spending.

Although social spending in the decades preceding the GFC was largely depoliticized, with a widespread neoliberal welfare consensus in place across countries and political parties, this book argues that the crisis resulted in a realignment of welfare state politics and policymaking. As a result of this critical juncture, the partisan composition of national governments has once again become highly influential in determining whether countries expand or cut social spending. Intense political debates and partisan conflict have increased as ideological divisions have grown between parties on the left and right over austerity and the role of the welfare state.

There are several reasons why this realignment of welfare state politics has taken place. First, the GFC powerfully challenged neoliberal ideas and policies, which had been widely adopted across states before the crisis (Glyn 2001; Mishra 1999; Roberts 2013). Indeed, many perceived neoliberal economic policies, such as financial market deregulation, as a main cause of the Great Recession. At the same time, neoliberal-inspired welfare state reforms, which resulted in reduced social spending, benefit cuts, and eligibility restrictions, left many citizens less protected against the negative consequences of the crisis. By undermining the neoliberal welfare consensus that had existed between left and right-leaning parties, the crisis created a window of opportunity for ideological divisions over social spending to re-emerge, thereby increasing the possibility for partisan conflict. Since the start of the GFC, we have seen such an ideological shift as parties on the left and right have turned toward traditional beliefs and policies. Left-wing parties, such as social democratic parties, have renewed their traditional support for the welfare state and have encouraged higher levels of social spending (Bremer 2018; McManus 2019). By contrast, center-right parties have largely embraced fiscal conservatism and lower social spending. This shift in welfare positions is evident in the party platforms and the policies adopted by left- and right-leaning governments. As the political agreement over welfare has weakened postcrisis, the ideological disposition of ruling parties has mattered more for social spending outcomes.

Second, along with acting as a catalyst for ideological change, the GFC created political incentives and opportunities that have reinforced partisan divisions over social spending. As social and economic concerns have become more salient among voters, parties on the left and right have sought to distance themselves from the policy positions of their political opponents on issues such as welfare. Left-wing parties have tended to favor more generous social spending after the crisis than their center-right rivals, as these policies are seen as beneficial to their core constituents made up of lower- and middle-class voters (Ahrend, Arnold, and Moeser 2011; Bremer 2018; Starke, Kaasch, and van Hooren 2014). Right-wing parties, on the other hand, have limited welfare spending to emphasize their commitment to fiscal conservatism and appeal to their middle- and upper-class core supporters. Mainstream political parties have also moved further to the left and right on policy issues, respectively, as voter support for radical left and right parties has increased (Hobolt and Tilley 2016).

In the EU, conservative parties were the clear electoral winners post-crisis, with nineteen of the twenty-seven EU member states led by center-right governments by 2012. This dominance of conservative parties has helped to reinforce a proausterity agenda in Europe both domestically and at the EU level. A coalition of member states led by center-right parties, including Germany, the Netherlands, Finland, and the UK, worked with EU institutions to develop crisis responses that emphasized budgetary responsibility and the necessity of promarket social and economic policies (De Grauwe 2011; EUCE 2013; Regan 2012). The influence of neoliberal preferences can be seen, for example, in the bailout conditions imposed on highly indebted peripheral member states, such as Greece, Ireland, and Italy. This proausterity agenda increased pressure to reduce social spending across welfare states. At the same time that conservative party leadership shaped the postcrisis austerity responses in Europe, center-left parties who had formerly embraced neoliberal welfare policies prior to the GFC have since grown in their opposition to such measures. Left-leaning parties across Europe after the crisis began to challenge conservative social spending cuts and renewed their support for traditional left-wing policies, calling for a stronger welfare state and more, rather than less, social spending.

To summarize, there has been a significant change in the politics of social spending since the onset of the GFC. Whereas partisan differences once held little effect over social spending, the political composition of governments has been a key driver of social spending across different welfare state types in the postcrisis era. This book will analyze this significant shift in welfare state politics that has characterized the past decade. In doing so, it will also provide insights into the politics of social spending in response to contemporary and future crises. The next chapter will examine theoretical arguments and provide empirical evidence for the postcrisis transformation of social spending politics in greater detail.

Chapters of the Book

Chapter 2

Chapter 2 begins by examining theoretical explanations for the influence of political and institutional variables on social spending within the welfare state literature. It starts by analyzing theoretical arguments about the influence of EU membership and policies on the social spending of member states. It then explores the rich literature on the effects of political partisanship on social spending. This is followed by an analysis of how the historical and institutional characteristics of different welfare states influence social spending patterns and play an important role in structuring political conflict within states. The literature review concludes by analyzing how economic crises act as critical junctures that may alter existing social spending dynamics. Based on this literature review, the chapter outlines a theoretical framework for the book and presents clear hypotheses about the anticipated effects of the GFC on social spending across advanced welfare states.

The chapter then continues to provide a quantitative analysis of the effects of the GFC on the political dynamics that shape social spending in advanced welfare states. It uses panel data for twenty-eight OECD countries during the precrisis (1990–2007) and postcrisis (2008–2013) periods to test the extent to which EU and domestic variables affect social spending. The findings indicate notable differences in the influence of EU membership on social spending before and after the crisis. They also show the emergence of political partisan effects on social spending postcrisis. Additional analysis of party manifestos for fifty-nine national elections across twenty-seven EU member states from 2008 to 2017 confirms the emergence of left-right party divisions over social welfare since the start of the crisis. This finding is significant, as political partisan effects were absent in the decades preceding the crisis. These results suggest that a significant shift has taken place in the politics of social spending across advanced welfare states in the wake of the Great Recession.

Chapter 3

This chapter analyzes the expansion of EU authority over social and economic policy areas and its effects on member state social spending. It begins by examining how EU economic policies may have spillover effects on domestic social policies. It also explores how the EU has incorporated social objectives into its agenda. This overview reveals how complementarities and tensions between EU economic and social policies have affected member states. The chapter identifies the ideas that influenced EU policymaking before the crisis and how the GFC disrupted the predominant consensus. This analysis provides insight into the findings of EU-level effects from chapter 2. For instance, how and why the influence of EU membership and policies have been altered after the GFC. Finally, the chapter provides an in-depth analysis of the polarization and partisan conflict that has arisen postcrisis over EU social and economic policies. This conflict has taken place between member states and EU institutions and in the form of heated interstate disputes. This highlights the fact that ideologically infused partisan politics, which place advocates and opponents of austerity in contention with one another, have become significant in influencing EU social and economic policymaking postcrisis.

Chapters 4–8

Chapters 4 through 8 cover five in-depth case studies that provide detailed accounts of how the politics of social spending was altered after the GFC. These chapters analyze EU member states representative of different worlds of welfare state capitalism: Germany, the UK, Sweden, Spain, and the Czech Republic. By observing welfare state dynamics before and after the GFC, these chapters help to identify the causal mechanisms that influence social spending in each country. These case studies confirm that a profound shift has taken place in the postcrisis era in which political parties once again matter for social spending. This is in contrast to the preceding decades, where partisan effects on welfare spending were absent. These chapters also identify how different welfare state types have mediated political divisions. Although partisan effects were present in all countries postcrisis, the degree of polarization was affected by aspects of the welfare state, such as the size and generosity of automatic stabilizers.

Chapter 9

Chapter 9 provides a final analysis of the politics of social spending in advanced welfare states before and after the GFC. It reviews trends in the quantitative data and case-study-specific findings to provide a comprehensive overview of the effects of the crisis. Although all states were negatively affected by the Great Recession, there was considerable variation in government social spending responses to this event. This indicates that while the pressures that welfare states faced were similar, political and institutional differences resulted in considerable social spending variation. The partisan composition of government, EU membership and policies, and welfare state institutions each played key roles in shaping policymaking decisions, whether to expand or reduce social spending. Ultimately, this book concludes that a striking realignment has occurred in the politics of social spending. Whereas the precrisis period was characterized by a widespread consensus over neoliberal welfare reforms, postcrisis there has been a repoliticization of the welfare state and the re-emergence of partisan influences on social spending across advanced capitalist economies. This new dynamic is critical to understanding contemporary welfare state politics.

CHAPTER 2

Crisis and the Politics of Social Spending

The 2008 global financial crisis (GFC) dramatically altered the political dynamics that shape social expenditures in Europe. While the influence of political differences was largely absent in the decades before the crisis, the postcrisis period saw the emergence of partisan effects on social spending. Left-right divisions over welfare have not only significantly shaped European social spending but are more prevalent in party platforms after the crisis. Whereas EU membership was negatively correlated with social spending precrisis, it was not significant afterward. But the European Fiscal Compact, which includes strict debt and deficit requirements for signatories, was negatively correlated with social spending.

Social spending is an important measure of government responsiveness to macro-economic changes (Iversen and Soskice 2010). Welfare spending is important after economic crises as it offers a buffer against the negative distributional effects of market downturns. In the EU, social spending is influenced by domestic politics and EU institutions and policies. Research on the influence of these variables on social spending after the GFC, however, has been inconclusive and requires further examination. While the EU may help to coordinate welfare responses, the spillover effects of EU economic policies, such as budgetary restrictions, may lower social spending (Crespy and Menz 2015; Ferrera 2005; Hassenteufel and Palier 2015; Kvist and Sari 2007; Schmitt and Starke 2011; Trubek and Trubek 2005). Findings on partisan effects are similarly uncertain. While some research suggests that partisan effects are weaker after crises (Armingeon 2012; Lipsmeyer 2011), others verify the significance of partisanship on social spending (Cusack, Iversen, and Rehm 2008; Herwartz and Theilen 2014; McCarty 2012; Starke, Kaasch, and van Hooren 2014).

This chapter identifies the variables that influence social spending in Europe and analyzes how these relationships have been altered in the wake of one of the worst economic shocks in decades. While EU membership and domestic politics are theorized to affect social spending, their influence is likely to be altered by the GFC. The crisis resulted in worse social and economic conditions, challenged existing social policy approaches, and resulted in higher political polarization (Algan et al. 2017; Funke, Schularick, and Trebesch 2015; Mian, Sufi, and Trebbi 2014). As a result, the precrisis welfare consensus was seriously undermined. We should expect the policies and ideas that guided European welfare development, therefore, to be re-evaluated postcrisis at the EU and domestic levels. The lower the ideological consensus between left and right parties over welfare, the more likely we are to see partisanship influence social spending. Given the polarized postcrisis political environment and the increased salience of socioeconomic issues, we should expect social policy differences between left and right parties to increase (Finseraas and Vernby 2011) and partisan effects to be significant.

This chapter will begin by exploring literature on the effects of EU membership and domestic partisanship on social spending. It will explore the intermediary role that welfare states play in shaping political conflict and social spending. This section will also highlight theoretical expectations for why economic crises might alter these relationships. The next section will provide a statistical analysis of twenty-eight OECD countries precrisis (1990–2007) and postcrisis (2008–2013). This model will test whether social spending is affected by EU and domestic variables. It will also analyze how social spending dynamics have been altered after the GFC. The third section will offer an overview of EU social spending trends before and after the crisis to provide context and an explanation of the statistical findings. The final section concludes.

Multilevel Governance and EU Effects

Theoretical accounts have long acknowledged the effects of EU authority on government decision making (Haas 1968; Schmitter 1969; Sandholz, and Sweet 1998; Sandholtz, Sweet, and Fligstein 2001). Within the EU, policymaking in areas such as the economy is no longer the sole purview of national governments but occurs within a multilevel European governance structure (Hooghe and Marks 2001; Bache and Flinders 2004; Leuffen, Rittberger, and Schimmelfennig 2012). EU authority over areas such as economic governance thus may have spillover effects on other policies. Even though EU rules may apply to a narrow policy area, member states may find that regulatory compliance affects other policies, even those outside EU jurisdiction (Schmitter 2002). For instance, Maastricht Treaty debt and deficit requirements for Eurozone members affect national budgets, which have consequences for other policies. Research indicates that social spending has been shaped by EU-level rules (Crespy and Menz 2015; Ferrera 2005; Hassenteufel and Palier 2015; Kvist and Sari 2007; Scharpf 2002; Trubek and Trubek 2005). For example, there is evidence that EU membership influences social spending across welfare regimes (Schmitt and Starke 2011). In the case of France, EU institutions were found to affect social spending, especially unemployment, healthcare, and pension policies (Hassenteufel and Palier, 2015). Along with spillover effects, when EU policy decisions have distributional effects, we should see increased political conflict that reflects left-right party differences (Hooghe and Marks 2006).

Domestic Political Partisan Effects

Along with EU-level effects, domestic partisan politics are identified as influential for welfare spending (Allan and Scruggs 2004; Bradley et al. 2003; Huber, Ragin, and Stephens 1993; Finseraas and Vernby 2011; Iversen and Soskice 2006, 2010; Starke 2006; Starke, Kaasch, and van Hooren 2014). This is due to different coalitions represented by left and right parties. Conservative parties are traditionally representative of middle- and upper-class interests and tend to be less supportive of redistribution (Bradley et al. 2003; Iversen and Soskice 2006, 2010). Right-leaning governments often favor balanced budgets and a smaller welfare state (Boix 2000; Iversen and Soskice 2006, 2010). Left-leaning parties, by contrast, represent middle- and lower-class interests and tend to favor higher social spending that benefits their core constituents (Allan and Scruggs 2004; Bradley et al. 2003; Garrett 1998; Hicks and Swank 1992; Huber and Stephens 2000; Korpi 1983, 1989; Korpi and Palme 2003). Social spending is, therefore, hypothesized to be influenced by left-right partisanship (Iversen and Soskice 2010; Starke 2006; Starke, Kaasch, and van Hooren 2014).

In addition to party preferences on specific issues, it is important to evaluate issue salience within party platforms. This allows for a more nuanced analysis of not only how a party positions itself on issues, such as redistribution and welfare, but also the attention they give to specific policies. Parties as strategic actors are perceived to be responsive to voters and emphasize the issues seen as important to their constituents (Bremer 2018). As voters' issue preferences change over time, it is expected that the attention that parties attribute to these issues will shift in response (Bélanger and Meguid 2008; Petrocik 1996; Petrocik, Benoit, and Hansen 2003). That said, given issue ownership considerations, parties should be expected to selectively emphasize policies they have perceived competence in and downplay those they are seen as weaker on compared to other parties (Petrocik 1996). In the wake of an economic crisis, for example, centrist parties might be expected to increase the salience of economic issues as material concerns become more important to voters (Margalit 2013; Singer 2011; Traber, Giger, and Häusermann 2018). Parties, however, may pursue divergent responses as their "ownership" of issues differ (Green and Hobolt 2008; Wagner and Meyer 2014). Center-left parties, like Social Democrats, who traditionally supported strong welfare states, in this case, might be expected to increase the salience of socioeconomic issues and favor higher social spending. By comparison, center-right parties might also increase the salience of socioeconomic issues but instead focus on fiscal discipline rather than higher social spending (Bremer 2018). In this case, as the salience of socioeconomic issues increases, left-right partisan divisions become more pronounced.

Partisan theories have been challenged by the "New Politics" literature, which argues that political differences have little effect on social spending (Pierson 1994, 1996, 2001; see Starke 2006). Due to the unpopularity of welfare cuts, both left- and right-wing parties are conditioned to see retrenchment as less desirable (Boeri, Boersch-Supan, and Tabellini 2001; Herwartz and Theilen 2014; Starke, Kaasch, and van Hooren 2012, 2014; Taylor-Gooby 2001). Welfare expansion also created well-organized interest groups, such as pensioner lobbies, ready to mobilize to resist benefit reductions (Pierson 1994). Finally, welfare states create path dependencies that ensure new measures, and spending efforts tend to reflect those in place (Bonoli and Palier 2000; Scharpf and Schmidt 2000).

Two-Dimensional Party Politics

More recent literature has sought to conceptualize party politics along two dimensions, the traditional left-right dimension centered around issues of redistribution and a second nationalist-international dimension (Häuser-mann, Picot, and Geering 2013; Kriesi et al. 2008, 2012; Manow, Palier, and Schwander 2018). These two dimensions can also be thought of as repre-senting socioeconomic and sociocultural axes. Applying this framework, party competition and positioning on various policies can be mapped along both dimensions with some more closely fitting to one axis or another while others reflect an interaction of these two axes. While welfare state politics has traditionally operated along the socioeconomic left-right dimension, there are questions about whether sociocultural national-international concerns have come into play in recent years. This has been a more pressing question with the rise of populist radical right (PRR) party support across Europe as these parties tend to frame welfare in more nationalist terms.

Of particular importance is whether mainstream centrist parties' wel-fare positions change in response to the presence of new challenger parties. In other words, does the presence of new niche parties transform party competition and shift politics from a single left-right dimension toward a multidimensional dynamic (Häusermann, Picot, and Geering 2013). This question has gained particular attention with the rise of PRR parties across much of Europe in the mid-2010s. Kriesi et al., for example, focus on how PRR parties have mobilized new social conflicts around the sociocultural national-international dimension of party politics (2008, 2012). Green par-ties may similarly be seen to mobilize politics around issues of the environ-ment and globalization. For the purposes of this discussion, the focus is not on explaining the emergence of these niche parties, but how their presence might affect mainstream party positions on key issues, notably welfare.

Some literature suggests that mainstream parties do in fact respond to the emergence of niche rival parties by shifting their emphasis or position on certain issues (Abou-Chadi 2016; Spoon, Hobolt, and de Vries 2014; van de Wardt 2015). Wagner, however, finds that niche parties primarily com-pete by emphasizing select noneconomic issues, such as immigration, rather than a broader range of policy areas (2012). This may be because mainstream parties have already staked strong ownership claims over issues such as welfare, which provide fewer strategic opportunities for niche par-ties to gain support. PRR parties, for example, have little perceived compe-tence in socioeconomic areas and therefore focus mainly on sociocultural issues such as immigration (Mudde 2007). Polk and Rovny, for example, found that after the Great Recession, while PRR parties tended to stress sociocultural issues, center-left and center-right parties de-emphasized these issues, focusing instead on socioeconomic ones (2018). Similarly, rather than trying to compete on new issue dimensions perceived to be "owned" by rival niche parties, mainstream parties after the Great Recession responded by returning to their ideological roots and increasing competition along the left-right dimension (Abou-Chadi 2016; Savage, 2019a)

When PRR parties do embrace social policies, it is often along welfare chauvinist lines, which reflects a sociocultural national-international dimension. While framed as a prowelfare position, the focus tends to be on restricting access and benefits to migrants and other perceived "outsiders" rather than welfare expansion. Research on the impact of PRR parties on healthcare, for example, indicates that while it is clear that PRR parties emphasize exclusionary policies, it is less evident that they increase funding or improve healthcare services for the "native" populations that they claim to support (Falkenbach and Greer 2018; Greer 2017). There are also arguments that welfare chauvinist policies that seek to restrict immigrant access to social benefits is part of a broader neoliberal agenda aimed at welfare retrenchment (Guentner et al. 2016; Keskinen, Norocel, and Jørgensen 2016). In this case, the "prowelfare" position of PRR parties that is often envisioned along nationalist lines is reframed along a more traditional left-right dimension. Some research suggests that mainstream parties do respond strategically to PRR parties on welfare state issues, but this reaction is along the left-right political dimension rather than the national-international dimension, with center-left parties shifting further to the left in support of welfare than their center-right counterparts (Krause and Giebler 2019). This indicates that even after accounting for the influence of PRR party competition, we should expect center-left parties to adopt higher social spending than center-right parties.

The extent to which party conflict has become two-dimensional remains an open question. Kriesi et al. and others have suggested that we need a new framework for European politics that incorporates a national-international dimension. In evaluating this claim, some scholars have found that there is no evidence for this new political conflict line and that with the exception of European integration, party positions on policy issues are structured solely by left-right conflict (van der Brug and van Spanje 2009). Despite the emergence of new conflicts within the electorate, Stoll argues that party-level conflict over policies continues to be along a left-right dimension (2010). Similarly, Green-Pedersen argues that while new cleavages may have formed among electorates around certain issues, from a top-down perspective elite party actors continue to pursue policies along more traditional left-right divides (2019). The question is not whether new social conflicts have emerged along multidimensional lines, but whether this shifting dynamic shapes party behavior and competition and how it applies to specific policy areas (Green-Pedersen 2019).

This book is focused on the politics of social spending rather than the reshaping of European party politics more broadly. To understand party competition over welfare and how parties position themselves on social spending, it is vital to understand the dimension along which this conflict takes place. While key issues such as EU integration, immigration, and the environment have risen in importance in recent years, the political dynamics shaping these policies may be distinct from those shaping welfare policies. Whereas issues such as immigration may fall more prominently along a national-international political dimension, welfare policies still fit more closely with the traditional left-right axis (Green-Pedersen 2019; Krause and Giebler 2019). Even with the rise of PRR parties that frame social policy in more nationalist welfare chauvinist terms, there does not appear to be an electoral realignment around welfare, which continues to be predominantly defined by a traditional left-right divide. Analyzing World Values Survey data, Dalton, Farrell, and McAllister find that attitudes about income inequality and the role of the state in providing welfare are correlated almost exclusively with a left-right political dimension (2011). By comparison, other issues such as support for democracy and tolerance of outsiders are more closely aligned with the sociocultural national-international dimension than with left-right conflict (Dalton, Farrell, and McAllister 2011). It also appears that there was an increase of political conflict over social spending post-crisis along the left-right dimension (Savage 2019a). In other words, welfare state politics became more strongly defined by the left-right dimension post-crisis rather than increasingly two-dimensional.

Worlds of Welfare Capitalism

There is a rich literature on the significance of welfare states in explaining variations in social spending (Esping-Andersen 1999; Häusermann and Palier 2008; Pierson 1996, 2001). First, the distinct historical and institutional characteristics of welfare states are argued to shape the kinds of strategies governments adopt in response to socioeconomic changes (Scharpf and Schmidt 2000). Second, these institutions play an important role in structuring the political debates and policy choices of actors within states regarding social spending (Bonoli and Palier 2000). Third, these institutions affect the position and influence of various stakeholders involved in the policymaking process. Different welfare systems, therefore, mediate the patterns of political conflict over social spending (Palier and Thelen, 2010).

The comparative welfare state literature, building upon the influential work of Gøsta Esping-Andersen, identifies several distinct welfare regimes in Europe: Nordic, Continental European, Southern European, Eastern European, and Liberal.[1] One advantage of this typology is that focusing on the institutional aspects of the welfare state provides a framework for identifying cross-national differences (Palme et al. 2009). While the institutional complexity that exists across countries makes any attempt to categorize different models of social protection a process of simplification, such typologies offer a useful starting point for social policy analysis (Palme et al. 2009). Empirical data and policy analysis provide some confirmation of the existence of distinct social protection systems in advanced capitalist states that conform to these five types. Research finds that government responses to income and employment shocks cluster in accordance with the welfare state types described above (Dolls, Fuest, and Piechl 2009, 2010). Additional research suggests that countries can be placed into distinct groups based on social policies that correspond with Nordic, Liberal, Continental, Southern, and Eastern welfare state types (Castles and Obinger 2008).[2] It is useful to briefly examine each welfare state type to understand how they are structured and how they differ from one another. This comparison will help to explain how welfare state types mediate political conflicts over social spending.

---

1. In *Three Worlds of Welfare Capitalism*, Esping-Andersen uses the categories Liberal, Corporatist-Statist, and Social Democratic to differentiate welfare types. Additional typologies have been added for southern and eastern European welfare systems that constitute separate distinct categories. It is important to note that no welfare system corresponds with the ideal type, but rather represents a complex mix of policy goals and institutional arrangements. These welfare types, however, serve as a useful heuristic to conceptualize differences across advanced states.

2. For further studies on comparative welfare system clustering see (Esping-Andersen 1990; Castles and Mitchell 1992; Starke, Obinger, and Castles 2008)

Nordic Welfare States

Nordic welfare states are distinguished by their generous and universal welfare benefits and by high levels of taxation to fund costly social expenditures. These regimes are notable for their low levels of poverty, income disparity, and gender inequality. Nordic welfare states have high employment rates, in part due to large public sectors and activation policies (Häusermann and Palier 2008). The scope of social policy is also quite comprehensive, with the state exercising a large role in welfare provision (Kvist 1999). Nordic welfare states have strong automatic stabilizers that increase social spending during times of economic downturn (Starke, Kaasch, and van Hooren 2012). Since these countercyclical welfare responses are automatic and do not require political action, they can circumvent some of the contentious political debates that can arise over proposed increases in discretionary social spending (Starke, Kaasch, and van Hooren 2012). The financial strain of social spending increases is likely to be more pronounced in Nordic states, even compared with other large welfare states, such as those in continental Europe. This is because the social spending is primarily publicly financed rather than funded through individual contributions (Palme et al. 2009).

Liberal Welfare States

Liberal welfare states are notable for lower levels of government social spending, relying instead on market-based benefits. Means-tested programs targeted toward at-risk populations, such as low-income citizens, are common in these regimes, rather than universal benefits. Traditional political conflict within these systems has been characterized as a struggle between left-wing welfare supporters and right-wing free-market advocates. Since social transfers are granted to low-income citizens, rather than provided through earned benefits, there tends to be lower levels of public support for increased social spending within these states. Lower-income welfare recipients are generally less well-represented within the political process and, therefore, less capable of advocating for the expansion of welfare benefits (Häusermann and Palier 2008; Taylor-Gooby 2001). In other words, the working poor, low-skilled laborers, and the unemployed not only face higher levels of income inequality and poverty, making them more reliant on welfare services, but they are politically marginalized and less able to advocate for themselves. But whereas rising income inequality remains a significant problem in Liberal welfare states, a high degree of labor market flexibility enables them to avoid some of the insider-outsider divisions found in other social protection systems (Iversen and Soskice 2010).

Continental European Welfare States

Continental European welfare states favor wage equality and employment protection over full employment strategies (Iversen and Wren 1998). These welfare states typically offer high levels of protection and wage coordination for standard employment, while at the same time penalizing nonstandard work. Employment protection for core workers limits labor market access to outsiders, especially low-skilled workers, who face more precarious employment, poorer wages, and lower levels of social protection (Iversen and Soskice, 2010). This creates a significant divide between labor market insiders, who are provided with adequate social insurance, and outsiders, who do not have access to the same welfare provisions. This has created a significant problem for many states as social security benefits are typically provided through insurance schemes funded by payroll taxes (Häusermann and Palier 2008). This insider-outsider divide is central to the politics of social spending in these welfare states (Rueda 2007).

Southern and Eastern European Welfare States

While constituting distinct welfare types, southern and eastern European welfare states are founded on a similar institutional model as that found in continental European welfare states.[3] Consequently, these welfare states face similar difficulties with labor market dualization and lower social solidarity. Regular workers benefit from strong employment protection and generous social benefits, while outsiders have limited access to welfare. Compared to continental European welfare states, social protection in southern and eastern European countries is more limited, offering fewer welfare benefits and lower levels of social spending (see figure 5). Whereas

---

3. The modern continental welfare state owes much of its origins to the policies and institutions implemented by German chancellor Otto von Bismarck during the nineteenth century. The legacy of this type of welfare system is still prominent in the politics and policies of many states across Europe, including those in eastern and southern Europe.

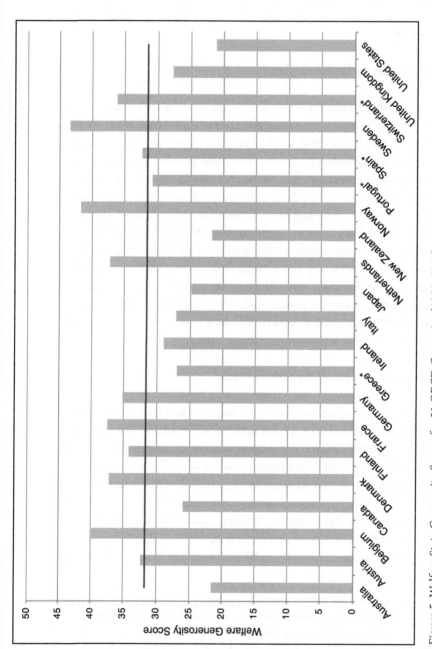

Figure 5. Welfare State Generosity Scores for 21 OECD Countries (1980–2007)

* Greece data missing for the year 1980; Portugal data only available for years 1996 through 2007; Spain data only available for years 1983 through 2007; Switzerland data only available for years 1983 through 2007.

Source: Comparative Welfare Entitlements Dataset (Scruggs, Detlef, and Kuitto 2014)

many continental European welfare states have substantial automatic stabi-lizers that increase social spending during economic downturns, smaller welfare states in southern and eastern Europe lack such strong automatic counter-cyclical responses (Dolls, Fuest, and Piechl 2010). As a result, social spending decisions are subject to more intense political debates and parti-san divisions (Starke, Kaasch, and van Hooren 2012).

Although they share similarities, there are important distinctions that separate southern and eastern European welfare state types. Southern Euro-pean welfare states are notable for low levels of social assistance and a strong reliance on the family as an informal source of welfare support (Palme et al. 2009). The family in southern European welfare states acts as both a source of social protection, through the provision of care and support, as well as a source of production, through the establishment of family businesses (Karamessini 2007). The core workforce predicated on a male breadwinner model enjoys high employment protection and job stability, while labor market outsiders, for example youth and women, face high unemployment rates and receive low levels of social protection (Karamessini 2007). As a result, dualization is more pronounced in these systems than in continental Europe. The quality of social protection is also lower in southern Europe. Unemployment benefits, health, job training, minimum wage benefits, and other types of social assistance are often underfunded or absent in these regimes (Palme et al. 2009). Old age benefits, however, are fairly well-developed and early retirement policies are frequently used as a way to address issues of unemployment (Palme et al. 2009).

Eastern European welfare systems have distinct social protection arrangements characteristic of the region's history and development. These regimes have a strong corporatist tradition, similar to those found in conti-nental European welfare states. This system was present in many countries prior to communist rule and continues to exercise an important influence in present-day welfare policies, including pension systems, unemployment benefits, and labor market rules (Deacon 1997; Golinowska, Hengstenberg, and Żukowski 2009; Offe 1993; Potůček 2009). The importance of the con-tinental model is evident in the postcommunist goals of these welfare states. The prevailing logic of these welfare states since independence has been to protect individual employment and wages, rather than reduce income inequalities (Palme et al. 2009). Institutional structures to address issues related to unemployment were essentially nonexistent in these regimes dur-ing the communist era, and new institutions and policies had to be adopted to address these concerns as states adjusted to new market-based economies (Elster, Offe, and Preuss 1998). Unlike continental European regimes, however, eastern European welfare states exhibit more universalistic tendencies reflecting the high degree of coverage that existed under the communist system (Aidukaite 2011; Potůček 2009).

Another important feature of the eastern European welfare model is the liberalization of social and economic policies beginning in the early 1990s. After the collapse of the Soviet Union, eastern European states began to transition toward democracy and market-based economies. During this time, considerable efforts were made to liberalize various aspects of the eastern European welfare state. These changes coincided with broader economic restructuring. These neoliberal reforms, however, did not constitute a wholesale dismantling of the welfare state or the convergence toward a liberal welfare state model (Aidukaite 2011; Potůček 2001, 2009; Saxonberg and Sirovátka, 2009). By the start of the GFC, eastern European welfare states were much smaller, offering fewer social benefits and less protection, particularly in the areas of healthcare and unemployment, than their counterparts in western and northern Europe (Eurostat 2015; Palme et al. 2009).

In sum, welfare states play an important role in mediating domestic political conflict. For example, in well-funded welfare states in western and northern Europe, sizeable automatic stabilizers allow for social spending to increase in response to economic decline without the need for political debate over discretionary budgets (Cohen and Follette 2000; Dolls, Fuest, and Piechl 2010). In other words, political questions about social spending expansion versus retrenchment may not even enter the agenda, or at least to a lesser extent in wealthier welfare states, and partisan conflict may be more muted (Starke, Kaasch, and van Hooren 2012). By contrast, less well-funded welfare states with weaker automatic stabilizers must rely more on discretionary social spending to offset the negative effects of economic downturns. As a result, there is a greater likelihood that social spending will be subject to partisan struggles in these welfare states (Starke, Kaasch, and van Hooren 2012). Examples of these highly polarized political debates over social spending can be found in a number of countries in southern Europe after the GFC, such as Italy, Spain, and Greece. Ultimately, welfare states play an important role in mediating political conflict over social spending. To understand the significance of these institutions, welfare state type is used as a control variable in the statistical models. The case study chapters of this book will also explore the politics of social spending before and after the GFC in five countries representative of each distinct welfare state type.

EU and Domestic Effects After Crisis

Despite the significance attributed to EU membership and domestic politics, there are several theoretical reasons why a crisis might alter social spending dynamics. Crises raise social concerns to the forefront of the policymaking agenda, thus acting as a catalyst for welfare state and EU action (Kingdon 1995; Kuipers 2006; Singer 2011; Vis, Van Kersbergen, and Hylands 2011; Vis and van Kersbergen 2007). Crises can also act as critical junctures which challenge prevailing ideas and policies (Blyth 2002; Capoccia 2015). Events like the Great Recession can act as "shocks" to party systems and result in major shifts in political dynamics and conflict over various issues (Hooghe and Marks 2018). The GFC, for example, raised serious questions about the neoliberal consensus that had formed across parties precrisis (De Grauwe 2008; Obstfeld and Rogoff 2009; Palley 2010). Theoretically, partisan conflicts over market regulation, redistribution, and the role of the state and EU in providing social protection should increase after a crisis (Hemerijck 2013; Starke, Kaasch, and van Hooren 2014; Vis, Van Kersbergen, and Hylands 2011).

Crises may alter EU social policy goals and practices as existing policies are challenged, resulting in different social spending patterns. The influence of EU membership is, therefore, likely to be different after a crisis. Partisan effects on social spending may also change after a crisis as polarization rises. Several studies suggest that political polarization increases after an economic crisis (Algan et al. 2017; Funke, Schularick, and Trebesch 2015; Mian, Sufi, and Trebbi 2014). As social conditions worsen, ideological polarization in society and in the political arena increases (Akdede 2012; Pontusson and Rueda 2008). As ideological polarization between parties grows, we should expect partisan differences to be more influential for social spending (Finseraas and Vernby 2011).

As social and economic concerns become more important for voters after a crisis, political parties are incentivized to respond to the material needs of their constituents. Under these conditions, left-wing parties are likely to favor social spending increases that benefit their core low- and middle-income constituents, while right-wing parties, who represent higher-income voters, prefer welfare retrenchment and fiscal discipline (Ahrend, Arnold, and Moeser 2011; Bremer 2018; Starke, Kaasch, and van Hooren 2014). Thus, the GFC provided a window of opportunity for left-wing parties to embrace social spending and distance themselves from neoliberal policies seen as a major cause of the crisis (Bremer 2018).

Along with creating political opportunities, crises also establish conditions for ideological shifts (Blyth 2002). Left-leaning parties are likely to blame "the market" for the crisis and look to governments for solutions. By contrast, right-wing parties are likely to identify government regulations or the size of the state as problematic (Starke, Kaasch, and van Hooren 2014). Polarization over welfare should increase after the GFC as left-leaning parties renew support for the welfare state, in line with their traditional values, while conservative parties, informed by promarket ideology, are unlikely to shift their positions in favor of a more generous welfare state (Bremer 2018). In fact, there is evidence that conservative governments have used worsening economic conditions as an excuse to pursue social spending cuts (Amable, Gatti, and Schumacher 2006; Korpi and Palme 2003). Informed by these theoretical expectations, two main hypotheses are tested:

Hypothesis 1 (H1): Crisis as Critical Juncture

In line with theoretical accounts of crises as critical junctures that generate significant and long-lasting shifts in political competition and policies (Blyth 2002; Capoccia 2015; Capoccia and Kelemen 2007; Hernández and Kriesi 2016; Hooghe and Marks 2018; Kingdon 1995; Kuipers 2006; Vis, Van Kersbergen, and Hylands 2011), this book analyzes whether the dynamics that influence social spending across advanced welfare states were substantially different before and after the GFC. The GFC should act as a critical juncture that challenged the precrisis welfare consensus that existed between political parties and at the EU level, thereby disrupting social spending dynamics. Not only should social spending levels be different before and after the crisis, but the significance and effects of independent variables at the domestic and EU levels should be altered.

Hypothesis 2 (H2): Political Polarization over Welfare

The second hypothesis is that after the GFC, we should expect greater partisan divisions over welfare, with left-leaning parties adopting more generous social spending than conservative parties. There are several reasons why this should be the case. First, by challenging the neoliberal welfare consensus that existed between left and right parties, the crisis created the possibility for greater partisan conflict over social spending. Second, the crisis brought welfare concerns to the forefront of the policy agenda. This made social spending a more salient issue and created a window of opportunity for parties to distance themselves from their political opponents over welfare. In these conditions, the influence of parties on social spending is likely to become more significant (Finseraas and Vernby 2011). Third, left-leaning parties are more likely to adopt generous postcrisis social spending that benefits their core constituents, made up of lower- and middle-income voters (Ahrend, Arnold, and Moeser 2011; Bremer 2018; Starke, Kaasch, and van Hooren 2014). Finally, as the neoliberal welfare consensus was challenged, the potential for a shift in social policy positions was more likely on the left than the right (Blyth 2002; Bremer 2018). Given the promarket ideology that is central to right-leaning parties, an embrace of government intervention and generous social spending is highly unlikely postcrisis. By comparison, left-leaning parties are more likely to renew their support for the welfare state, in line with their traditional values and the demands of their core voters (Bremer 2018).

Model

To measure the effects of domestic and EU-level factors on social spending before and after the GFC, the analysis employs fixed and random effects panel data models. The dataset for these models includes information for twenty-eight OECD countries (N=28) for the period 1990–2013 (T=24). Although social spending has several dimensions, including unemployment, family, and old-age policies, total social spending as a percentage of GDP (gvt_ss_total) is used as a dependent variable, as it is an important measure of overall government response to economic changes (Iversen and Soskice 2010). These models analyze whether social spending is affected by EU membership and partisan control of government. They also test the hypothesis (H1) that the GFC altered social spending dynamics. To do so, interaction variables are included for each independent variable to determine their effects on social spending precrisis (1990–2007) and postcrisis (2008–2013). This provides statistical evidence of the influence of the GFC on social spending relationships and tests whether the same independent variables are significant in each period, and if so, the strength and direction of these effects.

The first model is a fixed-effects panel data model that tests the effects of EU membership and political parties on social spending across countries and over time. Several demographic and economic control variables are included to ensure that the effects of these factors are held constant. The second model builds upon the first and includes the effects of EU policies, specifically the Europe 2020 Strategy and the European Fiscal Compact, which are hypothesized to affect member state social spending. The third and final model includes all the independent variables from the previous models but uses random effects panel data to include the influence of welfare state types. Since welfare state institutions are time-invariant, a random-effects model is needed to account for the influence of these systems on social spending. In other words, the third model allows us to see how welfare state types affect social spending and hold these effects constant.

EU Membership and Policies

To analyze the effects of EU membership versus nonmembership on social spending, dummy variables have been introduced in each model for the precrisis period (eu_pre-crisis) and an interaction variable for the postcrisis period (eu_post-crisis). In the second and third models, variables have been included for the adoption of two specific EU policies, the EU 2020 strategy, and the European Fiscal Compact, which are hypothesized to affect domestic social spending. With its emphasis on the goals of increased social protection and inclusion throughout Europe, the EU 2020 strategy is expected to have a positive effect on member state social spending. Conversely, the debt and deficit requirements in the European Fiscal Compact impose significant budgetary constraints on national governments, which may result in lower social spending.

Domestic Politics

To examine the relationship between political parties and social spending, the model includes variables for conservative, center, and left[4] party control

---

4. Coding for conservative, center, and liberal parties are based on the 2013 World Bank Database of Political Institutions.

of government precrisis (center_pre-crisis, left_pre-crisis) and postcrisis (center_post-crisis, left_post-crisis). The conservative party is the reference category. The expectation is that relative to conservative parties, left-leaning parties will be correlated with higher postcrisis social spending (H2).

Control Variables

The following control variables have also been included in the model:

1. *Postcrisis*: tests for a structural break associated with the GFC.
2. *Welfare state type*: tests for the effects that different worlds of welfare capitalism have on social spending. A variable with categories for Nordic, Liberal, Continental European, Eastern European, and Southern European welfare states is included in the third model.[5] The Liberal welfare state type is used as the reference category.
3. *GDP per capita (gdp_per)*: tests whether demand for social spending is income elastic (Wagner's law) (Iversen and Soskice 2010; Lamartina and Zaghini 2011). It also controls for automatic stabilizers tied to changes in income levels.
4. *Economic openness (econ_open)*: tests whether exposure to global markets increases social spending demands (Garrett 1998; Rodrik 1999).
5. *Unemployment rate (unemp_pop)*: controls for social spending increases associated with rising unemployment levels, including automatic stabilizers (Iversen and Soskice 2010).
6. *Population under 15 (pop_under_15)*: controls for the effects that the size of the nonworking population under fifteen years of age has on social spending.
7. *Population over 65 (pop_over_65)*: controls for the effects that the size of a pension-age population over sixty-five years of age has on social spending.
8. *Voter turnout (vturn)*: tests whether high voter turnout is correlated with greater social spending (Kenworthy and Pontusson 2005).

---

5. While the effects of these welfare state types are accounted for in the first two fixed effects models, due to the time-invariant nature of these institutions, their specific effect cannot be measured directly. Therefore a random-effects model (model 3) is needed to identify the influence of individual welfare state types on social spending.

Results

Table 1 presents the regression analysis results. The models show that EU membership precrisis was negatively correlated with social spending. The magnitude of this effect is sizable, with social spending 1.8 to 2.1 percent lower in EU members than nonmembers. This corresponds with welfare liberalization and social spending retrenchment that was widely adopted across the EU at this time. Precrisis EU welfare reforms were informed by neoliberal ideas that emphasized competitive, efficient, and smaller welfare states. Social spending cuts were more pronounced among EU members than nonmembers precrisis, as neoliberal pressure to reduce the size of generous European welfare states was stronger. Postcrisis, however, EU membership is positively correlated but not significant in the first two models, indicating that social spending differences between EU members and nonmembers were not substantial. In model three, EU membership is positively correlated, with a 1 percent increase in social spending relative to nonmembers. This indicates that a significant change has occurred from the precrisis period when EU membership was negative compared with nonmembers. As neoliberal policies and ideas were undermined by the GFC, pressure for EU members to cut welfare was reduced. EU policies, such as the European Economic Recovery Plan, encouraged social spending stimulus at the start of the crisis, reflecting this lessening of pressure to cut welfare. In fact, both EU members and nonmembers adopted social spending increases immediately after the GFC.

Although EU membership was not negatively correlated with social spending postcrisis, the European Fiscal Compact was associated with a 0.9 percent decrease in social spending. This indicates that EU measures aimed at encouraging fiscal discipline as the crisis continued resulted in lower social spending. This corresponds with expectations that EU-imposed austerity negatively affects welfare spending as governments face pressure to reduce budgets (Crespy and Menz 2015; Hassenteufel and Palier 2015; Kvist and Sari 2007; Schmitt and Starke 2011).

The models show that left-leaning parties postcrisis (left_post-crisis) are correlated with a 1.1 to 1.2 percent increase in social spending compared with conservative parties (see table 1). Whereas left parties held no relationship with social spending precrisis, they became significant postcrisis. This indicates greater partisan influence on social spending after the GFC (Cusack, Iversen, and Rehm; Herwartz and Theilen 2014; McCarty

2012; McManus 2018, 2019; Starke, Kaasch, and van Hooren 2014). The lack of significance of parties precrisis may be accounted for by the fact that during this period, political differences narrowed as parties on the left and right adopted similar neoliberal social policies (Häusermann and Palier 2008; Hendrik, Schäfer, and Manow 2004; Leschke and Jepsen 2012). Further empirical evidence supports the lack of influence that partisanship had on social spending in the precrisis period (Huber and Stephens 2000; Kittel and Obinger 2003; Kwon and Pontusson 2010; Potrafke 2009). It is important to note that the narrowing of left-right party differences does not suggest that intraparty differences disappeared altogether. Debates between parties over social policy may have persisted in some cases, but support for promarket welfare reforms dominated party platforms on the left and the right at this time. Critical juncture theories suggest that such consensus is more likely during times of stability and will persist until challenged by a crisis event (Blyth 2002; Capoccia 2015).

Model three highlights the effects of welfare state types on social spending.[6] As expected, Continental European (7.9 percent) and Nordic welfare states (7.2 percent) were associated with higher social spending than were Liberal welfare states. While lower than their generous Western European neighbors, Eastern European welfare states (3.6 percent) had higher social spending than their Liberal counterparts. Southern European welfare states were not statistically significant, indicating that social spending in these regimes was similar to that of Liberal welfare states. These models offer important and surprising findings, as they not only confirm the effects of EU and domestic variables on social spending, but also that the GFC has substantially altered the relationship between these variables (H1).

Further context can be given to these findings by examining social spending patterns in the EU over time. Figure 6 presents total EU social spending before and after the GFC. It shows that during the 1990s, social spending declined across the EU. For EU-15, social spending on average fell by more than 1.5 percent of GDP between 1995 and 2000. Although social spending increased slightly in the early 2000s, for EU-15 it returned to its

---

6. While not measured directly in the fixed effects models 1 and 2, the influence of welfare state type, along with other time-invariant variables not explicitly included, are accounted for in the error term. This ensures that the effects of these unobserved variable effects are accounted for when calculating the effects of independent and control variables.

Table 1. Regression Analysis
(Total Government Social Spending as a % of GDP)

Variables	I gvt_ss_total	II gvt_ss_total	III gvt_ss_total
gdp_per	2.70E-05	2.92E-05	3.24E-05
	(−2.86E-05)	(−2.87E-05)	(−2.77E-05)
econ_open	−0.0163	−0.0151	−0.0149*
	(−0.00966)	(−0.00946)	(−0.00764)
unemp_pop	0.305***	0.317***	0.326***
	(−0.0657)	(−0.0619)	(−0.0621)
pop_under_15	0.00724	0.0231	0.0797
	(−0.179)	(−0.178)	(−0.163)
pop_over_65	0.775***	0.795***	0.853***
	(−0.159)	(−0.162)	(−0.165)
vturn	0.00272	0.00186	0.00269
	(−0.0307)	(−0.0301)	(−0.0249)
post_crisis	−0.0834	−0.103	−0.164
	(−0.444)	(−0.432)	(−0.424)
eu_pre-crisis	−2.118*	−2.140*	−1.772*
	(−0.841)	(−0.835)	(−0.79)
eu_post-crisis	0.773	0.986	1.022*
	(−0.564)	(−0.554)	(−0.545)
center_pre-crisis	−0.533	−0.549	−0.38
	(−0.666)	(−0.638)	(−0.611)
left_pre-crisis	−0.0892	−0.0976	−0.0858
	(−0.254)	(−0.254)	(−0.246)
center_post-crisis	1.38	1.266	1.17
	(−1.099)	(−1.085)	(−1.068)
left_post-crisis	1.206*	1.150*	1.098*
	(−0.466)	(−0.48)	(−0.493)
eu_2020		0.0747	0.019
		(−0.246)	(−0.255)
eu_fiscal_compact		−0.923**	−0.945**
		(−0.297)	(−0.305)
continental			7.900***
			(−1.538)
nordic			7.181***
			(−2.193)
eastern			3.546*
			(−1.398)
southern			1.531
			(−1.33)
Constant	8.899	8.161	1.989
	−4.943	(−4.917)	(−4.752)
Observations	672	672	672
Number of country_id	28	28	28
R-sq: within =	0.5843	0.5900	0.5881
between =	0.1799	0.1897	0.7026
overall =	0.2406	0.2499	0.6850

* p < 0.05, ** p < 0.01, *** p < 0.001

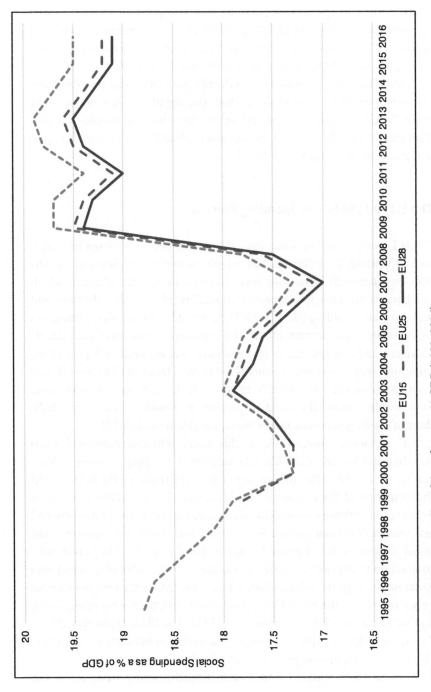

Figure 6. EU Total Government Social Spending as a % GDP (1990–2016)
Source: Eurostat 2018

lowest point (17.3 percent of GDP) by 2007 just prior to the GFC. Social spending for EU-25 and EU-28 declined even further and by 2007 had reached its lowest levels of the period. Social spending increased considerably at the start of the crisis and by 2008 was 2.4 percent higher than its 2007 low. This sharp increase reflects the effects of automatic stabilizers and stimulus measures put in place to offset the negative effects of the crisis. Since the GFC began, social spending has fluctuated but remained higher than precrisis levels. The next section will analyze EU social spending pre- and postcrisis to explain these trends.

The EU and the Social Spending Precrisis

While European welfare states have historically been associated with high social spending, the 1990s marked notable welfare reductions across countries (see figure 6). This shift was informed by neoliberal ideas, which emphasized fiscal discipline, privatization, deregulation, liberalization, and reduced state spending (Rodrik 2011). Inspired by this ideology, European welfare states were, in part, blamed for persistent problems of high unemployment and low growth, as it was argued that generous job protection, minimum wages, and social benefits led to high labor market costs (European Commission 1997; OECD 1994, 1997). Long-term unemployment, for example, remained around 10 percent in Germany, France, and Italy, three of the largest economies in the region (Hemerijck 2013).

EU economic integration, at this time, reflected neoliberal ideas (Leschke and Jepsen 2012). The introduction of the Single European Market Act in the late 1980s, the signing of the Maastricht Treaty in 1992, and the formation of the Economic and Monetary Union in 1999 all signaled growing EU authority over regional economic matters. Integration created asymmetries between economic policies, which were Europeanized, and social policies, which remained at the national level. EU integration constrained domestic decision making and limited the ability of governments to define social goals (Scharpf 2002). This is evident in the neoliberal social policy reforms of the 1990s that led to benefit cuts, tightening of eligibility, and welfare retrenchment across the EU (Thelen 2014; Hemerijck 2013). This trend helps to explain the negative correlation between EU membership and social spending precrisis (see table 1).

Welfare retrenchment led to greater inequality and poverty across the

EU even among more egalitarian welfare states in northern and western Europe (Kenworthy 2008; Hemerijck 2013). By the 2000s, pressure grew for more focus on social concerns at the EU level (Scharpf 2002; Hemerijck 2013). Corresponding with these concerns, EU welfare spending increased in the early 2000s (see figure 6). In 2000, the EU introduced the "Lisbon Strategy," which emphasized the complementarities between markets and welfare states (Hemerijck 2013). While the Lisbon Strategy was an unprecedented attempt to incorporate social issues into the EU agenda, mechanisms to ensure positive feedback between social and economic goals were not clearly established or remained absent altogether (Armstrong, Begg, and Zeitlin 2008). For instance, 2006 European Commission guidelines for Lisbon Strategy implementation failed to reference social objectives in its criteria for member states (Armstrong, Begg, and Zeitlin 2008). Additionally, few Lisbon Strategy funds went toward social objectives, being used instead toward job creation and other economic goals (Armstrong, Begg, and Zeitlin 2008). The prevailing philosophy seemed to suggest that social goals would be inherently advanced by promoting economic success (Dieckhoff and Gallie 2007; Armstrong, Begg, and Zeitlin 2008). Consequently, welfare reforms continued to represent a neoliberal approach (Leschke and Jepsen 2012). In the mid-2000s, EU social spending declined once again (see figure 6).

The promarket principles that guided precrisis EU social spending were met with little political resistance, as many parties on the left and right embraced neoliberal reforms (Hendrik, Schäfer, A. and Manow 2004; Swank 2000; Taylor-Gooby 2001 2004; Leschke and Jepsen 2012; Häusermann and Palier 2008). Danish flexicurity,[7] Third Way policies in the UK,[8] and activation policies in Sweden all reflected a common shift toward market-based welfare state preferences. The acceptance of neoliberal reforms across parties helps to explain the lack of significance that partisan-

---

7. Flexicurity refers to a welfare state approach, first introduced in Denmark in the 1990s, that combines labor market flexibility with generous and proactive social security measures.

8. Third Way policies, which were adopted by the New Labour government, attempted to achieve positive social and economic outcomes through promarket reforms. The belief was that neoliberal reforms, such as privatization and investment in human capital, would lead to higher economic gains that would translate into improved social conditions. This approach emphasized the responsibility of the individual to take care of one's economic and social well-being over government intervention.

ship had precrisis as left-right political differences over social expenditures narrowed (see table 1).

The EU and the Social Spending Postcrisis

The GFC marked a turning point, as automatic stabilizers and stimulus measures resulted in higher EU social spending. Not only did social spending change after the crisis, but so too did the effects of EU and domestic variables on such expenditures (H1). Postcrisis, EU membership no longer affected social spending (see table 1). Rather than creating pressure for welfare cuts, EU institutions immediately after the GFC advocated for members to increase social spending, for example, through the European Economic Recovery Plan (European Commission 2008). Between 2007 and 2009, EU social spending on average increased by 3.5 percent of GDP (Eurostat 2011). This was higher than the OECD average and helps to explain the lack of significance of EU membership, as EU members and nonmembers implemented similar social spending responses to the crisis. The European Fiscal Compact, however, was negatively correlated with social spending. This suggests that the fiscal constraints in the compact reduced social spending among signatories. This provides some confirmation that EU policies may have spillover effects on social spending.

The Politicization of Postcrisis Social Spending

After the GFC, partisanship significantly affected social spending (H2). This reflects the politicization of welfare and growing left-right divisions over social expenditures. Whereas conservative parties have tended to favor fiscal discipline and welfare cuts, left-leaning parties have questioned neoliberal orthodoxy and emphasized the need for more social spending. The statistical model provides evidence of these postcrisis partisan effects on social spending (see table 1). While the focus of this analysis is on total social spending as a percentage of GDP, there is evidence that partisanship has affected different welfare categories after the GFC. Dalton, Farrell, and McAllister, for example, find that the partisan composition of government has had a significant effect on different social spending categories including education, health, and social security, with center-left governments dedicating a larger portion of their budgets to these welfare programs than center-right ones (2011). Savage finds similar partisan effects on disaggregated social expenditure categories postcrisis, with center-left governments spending more on old age, unemployment, childcare, and disability benefits than center-right governments (2019b).

Analysis of party manifestos for fifty-nine national elections across twenty-seven EU countries since the crisis started (2008–2017) also shows that there is a correlation between left-right party position and support for welfare expansion versus retrenchment (see figure 7).[9] "Left-right party position" is measured using the right-left ideological index (RILE) from the Manifesto Project dataset, which places parties on a scale from –100 left to +100 right. "Welfare expansion support" is calculated as the sum of the welfare expansion (per504) minus the welfare limitation (per505) variables from the dataset. The result is a variable that measures the net mentions in a manifesto of the need to maintain or expand welfare spending minus the need to cut social expenditures. As figure 7 shows, postcrisis, left-leaning parties emphasize welfare expansion in their manifestos, whereas right-leaning parties favor welfare cuts (H2). Tables for precrisis elections are not shown as no relationship between left-right party position and welfare preferences existed during this time. These findings are in line with an analysis of European social democratic party platforms, which shows a convergence with right-leaning parties in favor of neoliberal welfare reforms precrisis and a strong shift to the left in defense of the welfare state postcrisis (Bremer 2018).

Two points should be made regarding manifestos. First, parties may not always pursue the policies outlined in their manifestos. Second, as left-leaning parties have been primarily in opposition postcrisis, it may be easier for them to advocate for more social spending and ignore the fiscal constraints that ruling governments face. In either case, this analysis demonstrates that welfare spending has become a partisan issue that left

---

9. This analysis includes data for the following national elections: 2008—Austria, Italy, Lithuania, Romania, Slovenia, Spain; 2009—Bulgaria, Germany, Greece, Luxembourg, Portugal; 2010—Belgium, Czech Republic, Hungary, Latvia, Netherlands, Slovakia, Sweden, UK; 2011—Cyprus, Denmark, Estonia, Finland, Ireland, Latvia, Poland, Portugal, Slovenia, Spain; 2012—France, Greece, Lithuania, Netherlands, Romania, Slovakia; 2013—Bulgaria, Czech Republic, Germany, Italy, Luxembourg, Hungary, Latvia; 2014—Bulgaria, Hungary, Latvia, Sweden; 2015—Croatia, Estonia, Greece, Spain, UK; 2016—Croatia, Cyprus, Ireland, Spain; 2017—Bulgaria, France, Germany, Netherlands.

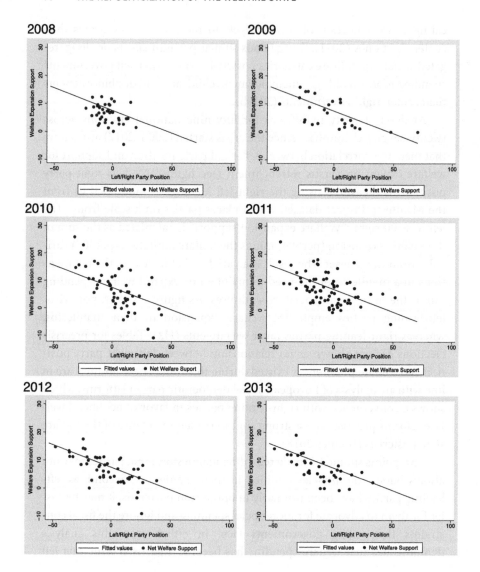

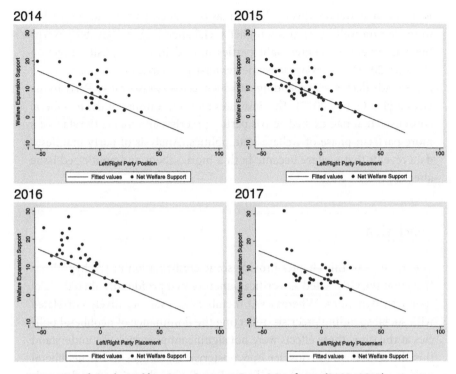

Figure 7: Left-Right Welfare State Support: Party Manifestos (2008–2017)
Source: Manifesto Project 2018

and right parties have portrayed differently in their platforms. Precrisis, such left-right divisions over social spending were absent from party manifestos. Findings from the panel data analysis also indicate that in line with manifesto policy positions, left-leaning parties adopted higher social spending than their conservative counterparts postcrisis (see table 1).

It is valuable to look at how the GFC affected the extent to which different parties focused on socioeconomic issues. Party attention to the fiscal and welfare concerns should increase after a crisis as social and economic conditions deteriorate and voters focus more on these topics. Tavits and Potter, for example, find that parties pay more attention to redistribution as inequality worsens and voters demand government action (2015). In the fallout of the GFC, economic security and material well-being did become leading concerns among voters (Margalit 2013; Traber, Giger, and Häusermann 2018). In response, the salience of socioeconomic issues increased for both center-left and center-right parties after the Great Recession (Bremer 2018; Polk and Rovney 2018). But the position that parties took on issues such as welfare diverged. Whereas center-left parties moved further to the left on welfare, favoring higher social spending and greater government intervention, center-right parties moved in the opposite direction (Bremer 2018). For example, some center-right parties in response to the crisis made deep social spending cuts such as the Conservative Party in the UK (Taylor-Gooby 2012). This indicates an undermining of the neoliberal consensus that had existed across parties precrisis and marks the start of a more partisan phase of welfare state politics. Analysis of party manifesto data reveals that welfare became both a more salient and politicized issue after the GFC.

Conclusion

The findings in this chapter provide some confirmation of the hypothesis (H1) that the GFC acted as a critical juncture that profoundly altered social spending dynamics. Whereas EU membership was negatively correlated with social spending precrisis, reflecting the dominance of neoliberal policies at the time, these effects were not significant postcrisis. To understand this shift, we have to consider how postcrisis challenges to the neoliberal welfare consensus affected social spending. Before the crisis, social spending cuts were higher among EU members than nonmembers, as prevailing neoliberal ideas emphasized the need for European governments to reduce the size of their generous welfare states. The crisis not only challenged neoliberal ideas and policies but created demands for more social spending, which reduced pressure on EU members to cut welfare. As a result, the postcrisis social spending of EU members did not differ significantly from non, as most states adopted strong social spending responses at the beginning of the GFC. The European Fiscal Compact, however, was negatively correlated with social spending, suggesting that fiscal constraints imposed by the EU on signatories resulted in lower social spending.

The effect of partisanship on social spending was significant postcrisis (H2). This is notable as the influence of political differences was absent before the GFC. Left-right divisions not only affected social spending but were more prevalent in party manifestos post-crisis. This suggests that welfare spending has become a more salient and contentious political issue. Pressure to cut social spending has had distributional effects and has led to increased polarization. This discontent is evident, most visibly in southern

Europe, in antiausterity protests and rising support for populist parties opposed to welfare retrenchment.

These results suggest, that not only did the GFC alter social spending dynamics (H1), but that it did so in a way in which partisan effects on social spending became significant (H2). What is noteworthy about the politicization of welfare postcrisis is that the effects of partisanship were present across all countries, even those less affected by the recession, for example, Sweden and Germany. Partisan divisions over social spending have also continued even as the crisis subsided and growth has returned to Europe. This indicates that these debates are not a temporary response to the crisis but reflect a lasting shift in political dynamics. Partisan politics will likely continue to influence European social spending in the years to come. Rather than creating a more unified EU politically, socially, and economically, contentious debates over social spending may lead to a divergence between member state welfare preferences.

The upcoming chapters in this book will analyze in greater detail this repoliticization of the welfare state after the GFC. Chapters 4 through 8 will examine the politics of social spending in Germany, the UK, Sweden, Spain, and the Czech Republic, each representative of a distinct welfare state type. Before delving into specific country case studies, however, the next chapter will look more closely at the influence of EU institutions and policies on social expenditures before and after the GFC. In doing so, it will help to explain the rising influence of partisanship on social spending in postcrisis Europe.

CHAPTER 3

The European Union

> "Our Union has always been a social project at heart. It is more
> than just a single market, more than money, more than the euro.
> It is about our values and the way we want to live,"
> —Jean-Claude Juncker, European Commission President (2014–2019)

The above statement, made by European Commission President Juncker at the 2017 European Social Summit, defines the EU as not purely an economic project, but also fundamentally a social one. The effects of European integration on member states have been shaped by complementarities and tensions that exist between EU economic and social policies and goals. For much of its history, the evolution of the EU was driven by a desire for ever deeper economic integration, with social policy objectives remaining secondary to economic goals. Over time, however, a greater emphasis has been placed on the importance of including a social dimension in the EU agenda. In recent years, efforts such as the poverty and social exclusion reduction targets outlined in the Europe 2020 Strategy and the adoption of the European Pillar of Social Rights have been made to expand the role of the EU in social policy. Although a greater commitment has been made by the EU to address social issues, it remains uncertain whether social goals will remain secondary to economic objectives and, if so, how this continued asymmetry might affect the well-being of citizens throughout Europe.

This chapter analyzes the evolution of EU authority over social and economic policy areas and its effects on the social spending of member states. This includes an examination of how the EU has incorporated social goals into its agenda and the spillover effects of EU economic policies on domestic social policy. This historical overview will help to identify the growing significance that EU membership and policies have had on member state social spending. Finally, it explores the prevailing ideas that influenced EU social and economic decision making over time. In doing so, it will analyze how the GFC disrupted the prevailing policy consensus and how ideologically infused partisan politics has influenced the social and economic policymaking process.

In the decades leading up to the crisis, neoliberal policies gained widespread support across member states and at the EU level. As a result, political conflict over social spending was relatively muted at this time, as demonstrated by the lack of statistical significance of partisanship precrisis (see chapter 2, table 1). Reflecting the influence of neoliberal ideas at this time, EU institutions advocated for welfare state liberalization and social spending cuts. The severity of the GFC, however, not only raised social concerns to the forefront of the EU policy agenda, generating demand for higher social spending, but also raised serious questions about the efficacy of neoliberal ideas and policies. In the immediate aftermath of the GFC, EU institutions encouraged members to adopt higher social spending to limit the negative distributional consequences of the crisis. This marked a reversal of precrisis EU recommendations for members to reduce social spending (European Commission 2008, 2009b). By 2010, however, the EU once again began to promote neoliberal policy recommendations, primarily in the form of austerity measures such as fiscal limits and budgetary constraints. Thus, despite EU membership no longer being negatively correlated with social spending (see chapter 2, table 1), specific EU policies, such as the European Fiscal Compact, put pressure on members to lower public spending and introduce welfare state cuts. The postcrisis environment, however, has given rise to sharp political divisions over social spending that have played out in domestic and EU policymaking. The next section will provide an overview of the influence of the EU on social spending before and after the GFC.

The EU and the Welfare State Precrisis

European Economic Integration and Liberalization (1990s)

Although European welfare states have traditionally been associated with generous social spending, neoliberal welfare reforms were introduced across EU member states beginning in the 1990s. An emphasis on economic competition began to challenge the scope and capacity of welfare states (Begg, Draxler, and Mortensen 2008; Scharpf and Schmidt 2000). Neoliberal ideas and policies promoted by international organizations, such as the IMF and World Bank, became ascendant as government leaders and policymakers began to subscribe to "Washington Consensus" notions of how best to promote investment, competitiveness, and growth. These policies emphasized price stabilization, fiscal discipline, privatization, deregulation, the liberalization of trade and capital markets, and lowered state spending (Rodrik 2011).

According to neoliberal arguments, European welfare states were hindrances to economic growth and competition and were blamed in part for persistent problems of high unemployment and low economic growth in the region (European Commission 1997; OECD 1994, 1997). Long-term unemployment at this time, for instance, remained around 10 percent in Germany, France, and Italy, three of the largest economies in the EU (Hemerijck 2013). Strong job protection, high minimum wages, and generous social benefits were cited as a source of this problem, as they increased labor market costs. The implication was that well-funded and comprehensive European welfare states undermined the efficiency of the market, generating high levels of unemployment and low levels of growth. In response, neoliberal welfare reforms and social spending reductions would need to be implemented to allow the welfare state to take on a stronger market supporting role.

European integration and economic harmonization during this time reflected neoliberal ideas as the European Commission and other EU institutions worked to promote cross-border investment and trade with the aim of strengthening the European Economic Governance structure (Leschke and Jepsen 2012). Responding to concerns of "Eurosclerosis," EU economic integration began to expand greatly with the adoption of the Single European Market Act in the late 1980s (Hemerijck 2013; Scharpf 2002). EU authority over economic matters continued to increase throughout the decade, culminating with the signing of the Maastricht Treaty in 1992 and the formation of the Economic Monetary Union (EMU) in 1999 (Hemerijck 2013; Scharpf 2002). Maastricht Treaty criteria for joining the EMU—requiring states to maintain government deficits below 3 percent of GDP, keep debt levels below 60 percent of GDP, sustain low inflation, and ensure stable interest rates—were founded on neoliberal recommendations (Hemerijck 2013). EU economic integration at this time, therefore, represented a clear move toward promarket policies and the expansion of EU authority to intervene in the domestic markets of member states. This economic integration had spillover effects on welfare states, as it not only reduced the capacity of member states to define their own economic policies, but it limited the ability of governments to determine their own social goals (Scharpf 2002).

The process of European integration created asymmetries between economic policies, which were gradually Europeanized, and social policies, which remained at the national level (Scharpf 2002). This bifurcation allowed neoliberal economic discourse to frame the EU agenda almost exclusively in terms of market efficiency, integration, and liberalization (Scharpf 2002), which led to the introduction of social policy and labor market reforms across member states focused on competition, labor market liberalization, and reduced government expenditures. With the aim of removing barriers to workforce participation and improving labor market efficiency, these policies were accompanied by benefit cuts, tightening of eligibility requirements, and overall welfare state retrenchment (Hemerijck 2013). Due to the comparative generosity of European welfare states, pressure to reduce social spending was more pronounced in Europe than in other OECD countries. It is unsurprising then to see that social spending reductions were higher in EU members than nonmembers before the crisis (see chapter 2, table 1).

Although neoliberal policies helped to improve monetary stability, budgetary restraint, labor market flexibility, and workforce activation in the EU, welfare state retrenchment led to higher levels of inequality and poverty throughout the region (Hemerijck, 2013). This trend was true even among the more egalitarian and well-funded welfare states in Scandinavia and continental Europe (Kenworthy 2008; Hemerijck, 2013). While neoliberal welfare reforms did not result in a regional convergence toward a Liberal welfare state model, there was a significant reduction of social spending across EU member states (Thelen 2012). By the end of the decade, disenchantment with welfare retrenchment and worsening social conditions led to calls in some quarters for more focus on social issues at the EU level (Hemerijck 2013; Scharpf 2002).

Social Investment Strategies (2000s)

During the 2000s, a new social investment approach that argued that social policy can foster increased productivity and economic growth while better protecting individual well-being became a central tenet of the EU's agenda (Hemerijck 2013). Social investment policies adopted by both left- and right-wing parties at this time were based on the neoliberal idea that social policy should primarily play a market-supporting role. The social investment approach attempted to reconcile the need for strong social protection with widely accepted neoliberal beliefs about the importance of market efficiency and competition. In the 2000s, the EU raised its social policy ambitions by adopting new social objectives. Titled the "Lisbon Strategy," this agenda was influenced by social investment ideas that emphasized the positive complementarities between markets and an active and dynamic welfare state (European Council 2000).

While the Lisbon Strategy represented an unprecedented attempt to incorporate social issues into the EU agenda, asymmetries persisted between social and economic goals at the EU level and neoliberal ideas remained influential in EU policymaking. In essence, the Lisbon Strategy made clear that the social agenda was subordinate to the economic one. The prevailing philosophy seemed to be that social objectives would be inherently advanced by promoting economic success, so priority should be given to growth and job creation (Dieckhoff and Gallie 2007; Zeitlin 2008). Welfare reforms during the precrisis period, therefore, continued to be informed by neoliberal recommendations such as the individualization, decentralization, and privatization of social services (Leschke and Jepsen 2012).

In sum, the decades preceding the Great Recession saw the widespread liberalization of social policies across the EU. During the 1990s, neoliberal reforms aimed at reducing welfare spending as a means to stimulate economic growth and address high levels of unemployment gained support throughout the region. By the early 2000s, concerns over growing inequality, poverty, and social exclusion led to a greater focus on social issues at the EU level. This was coupled with a social investment approach that emphasized the beneficial role that welfare states could play in promoting economic growth and competition. Economic goals, however, remained the top priority, and EU pressure for members to liberalize their welfare states and reduce social spending continued. This pressure was met with relatively little political resistance as many political parties on the left and right embraced these neoliberal welfare reforms (Hendrik, Schäfer, and Manow 2004).

The EU and the Welfare State Postcrisis

Crisis-Management Stimulus Measures (2008–2010)

The GFC marks a significant turning point in EU social spending, as governments adopted stimulus measures to offset the negative effects of the crisis. Not only did the social spending patterns of EU member states change, but so too did the relationship between the EU and welfare states. In the postcrisis period, EU membership is no longer negatively correlated with social spending (see chapter 2, table 1). This indicates that the social spending of EU members was similar to that of nonmembers after the crisis. Rather than creating top-down pressure for social spending cuts, EU institutions immediately after the crisis advocated for members to increase welfare spending (European Commission 2008). As the crisis continued, however, specific EU policies, such as the European Fiscal Compact, once again began to put pressure on member states to reduce social spending (De la Porte and Heins 2016).

Due to the increased need for social protection, such as unemployment and family benefits, a higher percentage of state revenue was absorbed by the welfare state after the GFC. Social spending on average across member states increased from 26.1 percent of GDP in 2007 to 29.6 percent in 2009 and stabilized afterward (Eurostat 2011). The trend is similar for Economic and Monetary Union (EMU) members, where social spending increased from 26.8 percent in 2007 to 30.4 percent in 2009 (Eurostat 2011). Despite recent decades of liberalization and welfare retrenchment, social spending in EU member states increased significantly after the GFC and has been higher than the OECD average. Across the OECD, social spending as a percentage of GDP rose from around 19 percent of GDP in 2007 to 22 percent by 2009, remaining around this level since (OECD 2012).

By early 2008, it became clear that EU institutions and member states needed to take strong and rapid actions to address the unfolding crisis. Recognizing the need for a coherent regional response, the European Commission in 2008 introduced the European Economic Recovery Plan, which offered a comprehensive framework for coordinated action at the national and EU levels (European Commission 2008). The recovery plan included economic and social dimensions that sought to restore market confidence, stimulate investment in EU economies, create jobs, and offer social support and training to unemployed workers (European Commission 2008). The recovery plan provided an authoritative plan for member states to coordinate stimulus packages (European Commission 2009b). Additionally, the EU dedicated €200 billion (US$294 billion) in structural funds, representing around 1.5 percent of EU GDP, toward regional recovery efforts (European Commission 2009b). The EU, therefore, provided resources and recommendations in support of national stimulus efforts to revitalize domestic economies, address unemployment, and protect socially vulnerable groups. This had the effect of reducing pressure on member states to cut social spending, as investment in the welfare state was seen as vital at the start of the GFC.

Structural Reforms and Austerity Measures (2010–Present)

At the same time that the EU encouraged member states to adopt stimulus spending to protect citizens and bolster domestic economies, considerable efforts were undertaken to reinforce and strengthen EU economic governance in an attempt to restore market confidence, create buffers against further financial market contagion, and limit the potential of future crises. Efforts such as the expansion of the ECB's mandate to act as a lender of last resort and the establishment of European Supervisory Authorities to regulate EU financial markets constituted a major expansion of EU authority over economic activities in the region. As the crisis wore on, additional measures were adopted to create closer fiscal integration across the EU, particularly among EMU members. In 2011, the EU adopted legislation known as the "six-pack," which committed all twenty-eight EU members to strict government deficit and debt limits (European Commission 2012a). Member states, for example, are now required to submit financial and budgetary compliance reports to the European Commission and Council of Ministers for scrutiny (European Commission 2012a). An additional set of measures, the "two-pack," was introduced in 2011 for EMU members requiring increased surveillance of national budgets (European Commission 2012a).

A 2012 European Council report outlined the need to strengthen the Eurozone architecture to integrate financial, budgetary, and economic frameworks (European Council 2012). Since domestic policies do not operate in isolation from one another and may affect other member states, the report called for establishing common rules to coordinate state behavior (European Council 2012). A major legislative piece of this initiative was the

European Fiscal Compact, which established binding rules for all signatories to lower their structural deficits not to exceed 0.5 percent of GDP and to meet strict budgetary requirements (European Commission 2012a). The fiscal compact also required governments to adopt balanced budget rules that had to be incorporated into national legal systems, ideally at the constitutional level (European Commission 2012b). As a result of this legislation, the EU gained more control and oversight of the economic activities of member states, which represented a further loss of sovereignty for national governments.

Further EU economic integration led to a shift away from early stimulus spending to a strategy of fiscal austerity and the reintroduction of neoliberal policies (De la Porte and Heins 2016). In addition to new EU austerity rules, several EU member states faced with severe debt crises required bailout funds from the EU, ECB, and IMF. These bailouts were conditional on the adoption of austerity measures and structural reforms. By 2010, it was clear that several countries were struggling with mounting sovereign debt and deficit problems. Greece, Ireland, Portugal, Spain, and Cyprus each received emergency bailout loans from the EU and IMF. As part of these bailout agreements, each state introduced extraordinary fiscal adjustment programs to limit government spending. Between 2009 and 2014 Greece cut its deficits from 13.6 percent to 3 percent of GDP; Ireland cut its deficit from 12.2 percent of GDP to 3 percent of GDP by 2015; Portugal cut its deficit from 9.1 percent to 3 percent of GDP by 2013 (European Commission 2014). Spain, Italy, France, and Iceland made similar reductions to their budget deficits at this time. Adjustment packages and fiscal reductions were also encouraged by the EU and IMF for Hungary, Latvia, and Romania (European Commission 2014).

EU-imposed austerity measures aimed to improve fiscal discipline, particularly in the Eurozone, and establish greater economic stability throughout the region. But these policies also had a profound effect on European welfare states. Fiscal consolidation put constraints on social spending as governments were required to lower public spending. This has been problematic, as balanced budgets and other economic concerns have often been given priority over social issues. These austerity measures, which constitute a clear return of neoliberal ideas and policies, highlight the conflict that persists at the EU level between economic and social objectives. In the aftermath of the GFC, this has led to increased polarization and intense partisan conflict over EU social and economic policies. This has placed advocates of austerity against a growing opposition, who have called into question the social and economic costs of these measures. It has also led to wider divergence in social outcomes, with citizens in southern Europe facing worse social and economic conditions than many of their counterparts in northern Europe, calling into question the meaning and viability of a common European social model (Leschke and Jepsen 2012).

Austerity has been promoted at the EU level by conservative actors in both EU institutions and member states as an effective means to address debt and deficit problems and restore market confidence. These policies, however, have received greater scrutiny in recent years. According to critics, rather than having a net benefit, austerity may stifle growth and generate worse social and economic problems. In fact, critics argue that austerity itself has been the primary cause for slow growth and high unemployment in the region (ECFR 2012; European Parliament 2013). Opponents of austerity argue that public cuts in education, research and development, and social benefits have had long-term negative effects on economic growth. Controversy has also arisen over the uneven manner in which austerity has been imposed on member states. Fiscal reductions for the Eurozone amounted to around 1.5 percent of GDP in 2012 and another 1 percent of GDP in 2013 (ECFR 2012). Yet such reductions have been extremely uneven across countries. For instance, while Spain introduced large budget cuts worth nearly 3 percent of GDP in a single year, other countries, including Germany, only made negligible cuts (ECFR 2012). The result has been a reduction in social benefits in some states and maintaining generous welfare support in others.

This has led to considerable variations in social risks across countries. For example, while youth unemployment was 16.4 percent for the Eurozone, it was considerably higher in Greece at 38.8 percent and in Spain at 32.7 percent (Vanhercke, Sabato, and Bouget 2017). By comparison, youth unemployment in 2016 was only 5.6 percent in Germany (Vanhercke, Sabato, and Bouget 2017). Whereas the population at risk of poverty or social exclusion in 2015 was 41.3 percent in Bulgaria and 37.4 percent in Romania, it was only 16 percent in Sweden (Vanhercke, Sabato, and Bouget 2017). Similarly, the working population at risk of poverty in 2015 ranged from 18.8 percent in Romania to 3.5 percent in Finland (Vanhercke, Sabato, and Bouget 2017). Due to marked differences in levels of social protection, conditions have differed greatly among EU member states. This has created disunity within the EU as some citizens have faced higher social and economic burdens than others as a consequence of fiscal consolidation and welfare cuts.

Postcrisis Social and Economic Policymaking

The GFC challenged the neoliberal welfare consensus and led to a wider debate in the EU over whether austerity results in positive economic and social outcomes. Proponents of austerity, such as former German finance minister Wolfgang Schäuble and former UK chancellor of the exchequer George Osborne, argued that fiscal discipline was vital to reducing excessive debt and restoring market confidence throughout the EU. Support for austerity measures, for example, has been a cornerstone of Angela Merkel's conservative governments' platform both domestically and in negotiations at the EU level. Left-wing parties, on the other hand, have shifted further to the left since the crisis began and have called into question the efficacy of these measures. Far-left parties have also gained support in states such as Greece and Spain running on antiausterity platforms that favor greater public investment in the welfare state. By undermining neoliberal ideas and policies, the GFC has created a window of opportunity for greater political contestation over EU social and economic policies. This has led to a shift in the political landscape across Europe. Questions remain, however, about what drove EU crisis-management response, notably debates over austerity, with scholars identifying structures, ideas, and political competition as important explanatory factors.

The Influence of Structures, Ideas, and Politics in EU Crisis Response

One of the key theoretical frameworks to explain EU-level conflict over austerity is that structural imbalances between distinct capitalist growth models resulted in divisions between core and peripheral states within the EU. Notably, the structure of the EMU is a better fit for the export-led economic models dominant in northern Europe and ill-suited to the demand-led models more common in the periphery (Hall 2014; Iversen et al. 2016; Regan 2017). Asymmetries in the political economies of member states, reflecting different national varieties of capitalism, shaped the crisis-management responses pursued by governments (Boltho and Carlin 2012). State self-interest among northern export-oriented economies led these states to insist on monetary and fiscal discipline. The relative economic strength of northern states lent credence to the idea that sovereign debt was the core problem requiring fiscal discipline. Rather than viewing the crisis as a common existential challenge for the EU requiring structural reforms to the financial system, northern governments were able to claim that the Eurozone crisis stemmed from the fecklessness of peripheral states (Hall 2014). The logic of national growth models is also seen as important within domestic politics, as electorates in northern lender countries, such as Germany, were perceived as unwilling to bail out southern member states without strict conditionality (Newman 2015). Austerity, at least at the EU level, from this perspective has largely been depoliticized as government positions reflect a domestically unified response based on varieties of capitalism. Institutional asymmetries between national political economies, in other words, are the main drivers behind the proausterity agenda in Europe, not political and ideological divisions.

Colin Hay challenges the varieties of capitalism framework, however, arguing that while capitalist institutional diversity exists, it is less clear that national economies can be categorized into distinct and discrete types (2019). Instead, this theoretical approach to comparative political economy is based on ideal types that do not reflect the actual configurations of capitalism within countries and may distort real-world analysis (Hay 2019). This raises questions about whether EU member states can be grouped into two distinct types of national growth models or whether there is more variation within and across these clusters of countries. Consequently, the formation of government positions vis-à-vis austerity may not fall along a simple north-south growth model divide but may vary more widely. Lehner and Wasserfallen, for example, find that political contestation over EU crisis responses fell along a one-dimensional line between advocates of fiscal transfer versus fiscal discipline (2019). Rather than a clear divide between northern creditor and southern debtor states based on their respective economic models, some scholars claim that ideational factors played an important role in determining states' positions (Brunnermeier, James, and Landau 2016; Lehner and Wasserfallen, 2019). France, for example, was the country that held the most extreme pro-fiscal-transfer position. Belgium also fell into the pro-fiscal-transfer camp. Neither position can be explained by each country's national capitalist model, as both are northern export-oriented economies (Lehner and Wasserfallen 2019).

Whereas the comparative political economy literature focuses on national institutional incentives and the role they played in shaping the post-crisis EU social and economic agenda, other literature emphasizes the role of ideas as drivers of policy outcomes. Despite blame for the GFC being largely attributed to neoliberalism, it has remained a remarkably resilient ideology in the postcrisis period (Blyth 2013; Crouch 2011; Schmidt and Thatcher 2013). Ideational scholars argue that ideas provide interpretive frameworks for actors to identify preferences and take political action (Béland and Cox 2011; Parsons 2007; Schmidt 2002). Kinderman finds that in Germany and Sweden, conservative firms and think tanks used discourse as a power resource to advocate for aggressive neoliberal reforms including welfare state liberalization and labor market flexibilization and deregulation (2017). This argument suggests that neoliberal ideas and discourse are the drivers of policy preferences, not the varieties of capitalism present within each country (Kinderman 2017). After a crisis, ideas help to define the event and identify the "acceptable" solutions to resolve the problem (Blyth 2001). Cox, for example, argues that there is a "path-shaping power of ideas" that has a "powerful legitimizing impact" on proposed policies (2001, 485). In this case, the proausterity agenda in the EU was shaped by hegemonic neoliberal ideas that remained prevalent across Europe and was promoted by key actors even after the crisis. Rather than viewing the Eurozone crisis as a conflict between the distinct political economies in core and peripheral states, some scholars argue that there is a prevailing neoliberal agenda that has been advanced by elites across countries in both the core and periphery as well as EU institutions aimed at promoting free-market social and economic reforms (De la Porte and Heins 2016; Pureza and Mortágua 2016).

Unlike the comparative political economy approach, where national positions on austerity are predominantly shaped by capitalist growth models irrespective of government partisan composition, ideational approaches view actors such as EU officials, economists, and political parties as key norm entrepreneurs who play an active role in shaping postcrisis policies. In this case, ideological divisions within and across states continue to matter. The dominant analysis of the crisis as a problem of fiscal irresponsibility of indebted peripheral states requiring austerity from this perspective was shaped by conservative academics, think tanks, and private- and public-sector actors whose ideas reinforced neoliberal responses to the Eurozone crisis (Matthijs and McNamara 2015). In other words, ideas and normative actors play an important role in establishing the divisions of EU level conflict over austerity (Carstensen and Schmidt 2018).

These ideological divisions over EU crisis responses may reflect established modes of political polarization and party competition structured along left-right lines even in northern member states such as Austria, France, Germany, and the UK (Wendler, 2014a, 2014b; Wonka, 2016). As ideological polarization increases between parties, as was the case after the GFC, the left-right partisan composition of government will have a stronger influence on social and economic policy preferences (Finseraas and Vernby 2011). These partisan preferences are expected to influence national positions in EU policymaking (De Wilde, Leupold, and Schmidtke 2016). Kriesi et al., for example, find that EU issues such as fiscal and monetary policy have become increasingly affected by political party competition (2008, 2012). Maatsch finds that the left-right economic position of parties influenced parliamentary positions on crisis responses (2014). Whether a country was a recipient of bailout funds, however, also played an important role, with parliaments in debtor states tending to favor anticrisis stimulus measures (Maatsch 2014). Public support for fiscal transfers in the EU, rather than reflecting a unified national position based on economic growth models, was found to be correlated with left-right preferences (Kleider and Stoeckel 2019).

Although the comparative political economy approach provides a valuable lens, ideas and the domestic politics of governments are also argued to play important roles in shaping EU economic and social policy. Schulze-Cleven and Weishaupt, for example, find that partisan political actors have autonomy and strategic agency over policymaking decisions, contradicting arguments that government positions are the result of particular economic models (2015). While institutions have important explanatory value, they argue that normative legacies and political parties play a key role in the co-constitution of government interests and should be given greater acknowledgment in the study of political economy (Schulze-Cleven and Weishaupt 2015). Responses to the crisis can, therefore, be understood as the result of interactions between institutions, actors, and ideas (Schirm 2020). In this case, while economic structures and welfare state types matter for crisis responses, they are not deterministic, and ideas and politics still shape policy preferences. According to ideational scholars the prevalence of neoliberal reactions to the Eurozone crisis reflects the relative coercive and ideational power that conservative actors held in the policymaking process (Carstensen and Schmidt 2018).

Left-Right Divisions and EU Crisis Responses

The electoral dominance of center-right parties across the EU in the wake of the GFC, in countries such as in Germany and the UK, coupled with support from the ECB and European Commission helped to legitimize a pro-austerity agenda (De Grauwe 2011; EUCE 2013; Regan 2012). This ideological position was strengthened by conservative epistemic communities, which established networks and personal links among conservative actors within and across countries and at the EU level. The strength of the connections across think tank networks were found to be stronger among center-right actors than center-left ones, signaling that these networks may have had an advantage in advancing their normative preferences (Plehwe, Neujeffski, and Krämer 2018). The ability of conservative organizations to operate across national borders and facilitate interactions between domestic and EU-level actors helps to explain the prominence and diffusion of the pro-austerity agenda and policies postcrisis (Plehwe, Neujeffski, and Krämer 2018). In the case of Ireland, for example, Dukelow argues that the austerity measures imposed by the EU and IMF were met with support by domestic conservative political elites and business representatives, which reinforced the neoliberal paradigm that had underpinned social and economic policymaking in Ireland for decades (2016).

But whereas conservative governments and actors dominated the EU policymaking process throughout most of the crisis and neoliberal ideas remained resilient, over time a left-wing response began to question the orthodoxy of neoliberal-inspired austerity and social spending cuts. For example, Sweden's conservative-led government, under the leadership of Prime Minister Fredrik Reinfeldt, was an important ally in supporting austerity in the EU. The electoral success of Sweden's Social Democrats in 2014, however, led the country to alter its position and to call for the EU to grant more flexibility on its austerity requirements and to focus more on social problems. By contrast, the German government has remained insistent on the need for EU member states to remain committed to budgetary discipline (*Spiegel* 2014). Critics of German-backed austerity argue that it is not international markets that are preventing countries from borrowing sensibly to fund stimulus efforts, but officials in Berlin and Brussels who are limiting the policy options of members (*Foreign Policy* 2015). This political conflict has taken on wider significance, with member states and EU institutions falling into opposing camps over austerity.

Further fuel was given to this debate in 2015 when Greece's coalition government, led by the far-left Syriza party, came into power by riding a wave of widespread public discontent over the austerity measures that were part of the country's bailout agreements. After the adoption of these measures, the Greek economy sank further into recession, unemployment soared, and, due to social benefits cuts, vulnerable populations were put further at risk (*Independent* 2015a). Prime Minister Alexis Tsipras, the Syriza leader, vowed to renegotiate his country's economic bailout terms but faced significant resistance from other EU members, including Germany, Finland, and the Netherlands, who expressed reluctance to grant further debt write-offs to Greece (BBC 2015a). The position of the Greek government also placed the country in conflict with the "troika" of the EU, ECB, and IMF, who provided bailout funds and established the conditions for Greek reforms. Prime Minister Tsipras stated that his government would no longer work with the troika or accept new bailouts, which raised questions of how the state would pay off its debt burdens (BBC 2015b).

The drama in Greece led to concerns that Syriza's stance would embolden antiausterity movements in other Eurozone countries, such as Italy and Spain, which would further destabilize European markets. For example, inspired by the recent success of Syriza in Greece, the radical left Podemos party in Spain made significant gains in national politics. As part of its platform, the party vowed to renegotiate the terms of the country's bailouts and secure write-offs of Spanish debt (BBC 2015c). Running on a populist antiausterity platform, Podemos organized mass rallies of tens of thousands of citizens in Madrid and exercised a strong influence on the national government. The populist Five Star Movement in Italy has also run on a similar antiausterity platform, arguing that the Italian national debt needs to be renegotiated (*Wall Street Journal*, 2015a).

Social and economic policymaking has become highly politicized post-crisis, with support weakening for mainstream center-left and center-right parties who have dominated EU politics for decades. This polarization of European politics has had important effects at the EU level. The 2014 European Parliamentary elections saw a challenge to the status quo as anti-establishment parties on the far left and far right made significant gains at the expense of traditional centrist parties. The anti-EU UK Independence Party (UKIP) won 27.5 percent of the vote in this election, receiving more support than either the center-right Conservative or center-left Labor parties (BBC 2014a). The far-right National Front Party finished first in the election with nearly 25 percent of the vote and almost one-third of France's seats in the legislative body (France-Politique 2014). Spain's Podemos party garnered nearly 8 percent of the vote in the European Parliamentary election and earned five seats in the body, displacing several mainstream parties (BBC 2014b). Not only did these results come as a shock to the European establishment, but they also represented the first time that anti-EU parties had gained seats in the European Parliament (Reuters 2014a).

Political Partisanship at the EU Level

At the heart of this political sea change has been a re-evaluation of neoliberal orthodoxy that has led to fierce partisan arguments over austerity. While there was nearly universal support for neoliberal policies before the GFC, these policies have come under intense scrutiny after this event. Within this contentious political environment, social spending has been subject to heightened partisan conflict, even at the EU level. Party manifesto data for the 2014 European Parliamentary elections, for example, exhibits left-right divisions over welfare expansion versus retrenchment. This is a similar pattern as that seen in national elections postcrisis, with left-leaning parties more favorable to social spending increases than their conservative counterparts (see figure 8). This partisan divide over welfare was present in both northern and southern European countries, suggesting that political differences were present even in states with different economic growth models. This evidence suggests that social spending has become a salient issue at the EU level, and one influenced by left-right ideological partisan divisions.

Deteriorating social and economic conditions left many Europeans disillusioned with EU institutions and mainstream political parties. This has led to political conflict over EU social and economic policies and a questioning of neoliberal ideas. In response, the EU and IMF have re-evaluated their positions vis-à-vis austerity to some extent, with each acknowledging failure to account for the negative social and economic consequences of fiscal restraint on struggling member states (*Bloomberg* 2013a; IMF 2013; *Washington Post* 2013). EU institutions have played an important role in this political conflict over social and economic policies. On the one hand, the EU has served as the originator and enforcer of much of the region's austerity policies, yet on several occasions it has broken with fiscal policy conservative hardliners. For example, in 2012, then European Commission

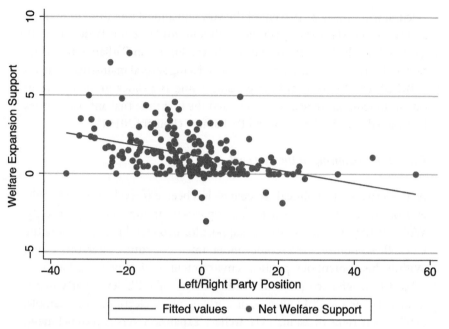

Figure 8. Left-Right Welfare State Support: Party Manifestos European Parliament Election 2014
Source: Euromanifesto Project 2016

president José Manuel Barroso made quite a stir when he announced that while he believed austerity policies were "fundamentally right," that this approach had "reached its limits" (*Spiegel* 2013a). Citing a lack of "political and social support" for austerity, he suggested that in the short-term fiscal constraints should be relaxed and "a stronger emphasis on growth" would be needed (*Spiegel* 2013a). Unsurprisingly, this statement elicited immediate backlash from German officials, such as Foreign Minister Guido Westerwelle, who warned that "growth cannot be purchased with new debts," and from Herbert Reul, leader of the German conservatives in the European Parliament, who stated that "the Commission president is putting the euro rescue in question" (*Spiegel* 2013a). In addition to inciting further conflict over austerity, the commissioner's statement reflected the EU's shifting position regarding austerity.

Jean-Claude Juncker, Barroso's successor as European commissioner, took a similar position as his predecessor. While acknowledging the importance of budgetary discipline, Mr. Juncker argued that austerity on its own would not bring about economic growth or job creation (RTE 2014). This softening of the position of the European Commission on austerity has led to conflict between Brussels and conservative-led governments. The ECB's decision to implement a program of Eurozone government bond purchasing in 2015, for example, represented a clear break with many conservative-led governments, who held the deeply entrenched belief that central banks should not undertake quantitative easing measures to buy public debt (*Wall Street Journal* 2015b).

Despite some softening of their positions, the EU and IMF continued to support austerity as a long-term solution to the EU's economic woes. The move by the European Commission to grant governments additional time to reduce their budget deficits stems largely from political reality and the fact that many of these targets were largely unattainable (Reuters 2013). Critics on the left claim that the EU's acknowledgment of the harm caused by austerity has largely been symbolic and has not been met with substantial policy change (Reuters 2013). According to many observers, EU policies after the crisis have been too focused on addressing economic issues, such as debt and deficit concerns, while ignoring important social problems. This strategy, referred to as "balanced budget fundamentalism" (De Grauwe 2011) or "austeritarianism" (Hyman 2015), has put a greater burden on member states to lower social spending as a means to restore economic growth. This strategy, however, perpetuates imbalances between social and economic objectives at the EU level, which has the potential to not only exacerbate social problems but to undermine growth.

Balancing welfare protection needs against fiscal concerns remains a major issue in the EU. Although austerity measures have put welfare states under further strain, there have been some attempts at the EU level to pay greater attention to social issues. The European Social Pillar, for example, represents a progressive albeit incomplete "socialization" of the European Semester (Zeitlin and Vanhercke 2017). The adoption of the Social Pillar has allowed for more consultation between EU officials, social partners, and the public (Vanhercke, Sabato, and Bouget 2017). As a result, social issues have gained more prominence in the EU agenda as evidenced by the high number of country-specific recommendations that focus on social welfare generally (Bekker 2015) and poverty and social inclusion in particular (Urquijo 2017). Although some important social policy initiatives have been adopted by the EU, there has been a failure to rebalance social and economic dimensions of EU governance, with economic objectives continuing to hold more weight than social concerns (Vanhercke, Sabato, and Bouget2017). Achieving a balanced policy approach will require compromise and consensus among different political actors. The polarization of EU social and economic policymaking postcrisis, however, may undermine the formation of a new consensus, as ideological standoffs are likely to continue.

Conclusion

Ideologically infused politics have become increasingly important in postcrisis EU social and economic policymaking. If the precrisis period was defined by a political consensus over neoliberal policies, with promarket welfare reforms being implemented across EU member states, these policies and their ideological underpinnings have been subject to far more scrutiny and debate postcrisis. While EU membership was correlated with social spending cuts precrisis, this relationship no longer holds true in the postcrisis period. In large part, this change is due to member state stimulus spending, which was encouraged by EU institutions during the early stages of the crisis to offset the negative social and economic costs. As the crisis continued, however, EU economic policies had negative spillover effects on member state social spending. The European Fiscal Compact, for example, put pressure on signatories to reduce government debt and deficits, which was often achieved through welfare cuts.

At the start of the GFC, member states and EU institutions agreed on the need for stimulus spending and greater European financial market oversight and economic regulation. As the crisis wore on, however, considerable partisan differences emerged over the best long-term solutions to restore growth and stability to the region. The dividing line in this struggle has been between advocates and opponents of austerity. This political conflict highlights the continued asymmetries between economic and social policy goals at the EU level. Although social concerns continue to be identified as a key element of EU policy objectives, critics argue that the main focus remains on economic goals. According to opponents, the EU's continued emphasis on austerity threatens to undermine the European social model and may lead to increased social and political instability (*Foreign Policy* 2015). While some economic reforms aimed at better market governance and fiscal discipline may be necessary, critics say that these policies must be coupled with welfare state investments to address social issues, such as rising inequality and poverty.

Political conflict over social and economic policies has taken place between member states and EU institutions in the form of interstate disagreements and has manifested itself in domestic politics. The next chapters will provide an in-depth analysis of country case studies, representing five distinct welfare state types, to identify how partisanship has influenced social spending across countries since the start of the GFC. These cases will also examine the important ways in which the unique social protection systems present in different countries mediate these political debates. Ultimately, these cases will provide empirical evidence that the GFC has created a realignment of welfare state politics.

CHAPTER 4

Germany

Continental European Welfare State

> "If Europe today accounts for just over 7 per cent of the world's population, produces around 25 per cent of global GDP and has to finance 50 per cent of global social spending, then it's obvious that it will have to work very hard to maintain its prosperity and way of life."
>
> —Angela Merkel, German Chancellor (2005–2021)

German chancellor Angela Merkel made the above statement in an interview with the *Financial Times* in 2012. The quote, however, has been repeated often since as a warning of the costs of European welfare states (*Financial Times* 2012a). The underlying message is that Europe spends far too much on social policies, which threatens its global competitiveness (Begg 2015). This leaves little choice but for national governments to cut back their welfare states and focus instead on fiscal discipline. Ms. Merkel's statement should come as no surprise, as austerity has been a key component of her conservative Christian Democratic Party's (CDU) platform after the GFC, both at home and in negotiations with the EU and other member states over the formulation of European-wide social and economic policies. This proausterity position reflects prevailing neoliberal beliefs and highlights the importance of ideology and politics in influencing social spending in Germany and across the EU postcrisis.

At the same time that Germany has been a stalwart supporter of fiscal austerity and welfare state retrenchment, political divisions over social spending have grown domestically. Parties on the left, who once supported neoliberal welfare and labor market reforms, have begun to question the efficacy of these policies and to call for more, rather than less, social spending. As a result, the influence of political divisions over welfare state spending have increased. What is perhaps most surprising about this repoliticization of the German welfare state is that by most measures, Germany was largely unaffected by the GFC. Unemployment remained low and economic growth was stable throughout the crisis, indicating that postcrisis social spending has been driven by politics rather than the severity of the economic crisis itself (Farnsworth and Irving 2011).

Germany is an important case study for several reasons. First, Germany is representative of a Continental European welfare state and is often identified in the literature as a classic example of this ideal regime type (Esping-Andersen 1990, 1999; Pierson 1996, 2001; Häusermann and Palier 2008). Second, Germany is a major economic and political power within the EU and is highly influential in shaping economic and social policies throughout the region. This chapter will begin by investigating German welfare policies and social spending in the decades building up to the GFC. The chapter will then examine the stimulus response undertaken by the German government in the immediate aftermath of the GFC. This section will highlight how the welfare state shaped the content of the stimulus measures. It will identify the important break that these policies represent from precrisis social spending patterns. Finally, the chapter will analyze the key role that partisanship has played in influencing long-term social spending in Germany. Partisanship has not only been instrumental in shaping social spending domestically but has been influential in defining the policy positions Germany has taken in deliberations with EU institutions and other member states. Changing political dynamics have played a key role in defining Germany's position in postcrisis EU social and economic policy debates, setting advocates and opponents of austerity against one another.

German Welfare State Precrisis (1990–2007)

Welfare State Liberalization

Historically, German welfare state policies have reflected continental European traditions, in which the core workforce is well-protected and receives generous social benefits. Several neoliberal labor market and welfare reforms, however, were introduced prior to the GFC. Most notably, between 2002 and 2004 the German government implemented the Hartz IV reforms, which lowered unemployment and social benefits for core workers and introduced new activation policies to encourage labor market access for outsiders (Seeleib-Kaiser and Fleckenstein 2007). The government lowered unemployment insurance, for example, from three years to one year, representing a significant reduction in benefits for regular workers (Dribbusch 2004). The government, however, also implemented additional social benefits for families to encourage female workforce participation and a move away from the traditional male breadwinner model (Lewis et al. 2008).

While some groups, who saw these new measures as an attack on the traditional social protection measures enjoyed by labor market insiders, resisted these changes, the policies were largely introduced with minimal political conflict (Trampusch 2005; Thelen 2009). This is because these neoliberal reforms did not constitute a wholesale overhaul of the welfare system, and considerable protection and benefits for the core workforce remained intact (Thelen 2009). Skilled workers in core industries, such as manufacturing and those working in large firms, continued to benefit from strong employment protection, wage guarantees, and social benefits (Thelen 2009). In fact, the main focus of economic policy debates immediately preceding the GFC concerned a shortage of skilled workers in firms (Möller 2010). This signaled that although the Hartz reforms lowered unemployment benefits, skilled workers would largely be unaffected by these changes as it was unlikely that they would remain unemployed for more than a year. Instead, the most obvious losers under the new legislation were low-skilled laborers and the long-term unemployed, indicating the continuance of labor market dualization (Thelen 2009). As a result, while there was an initial nationwide outcry against the neoliberal-inspired Hartz IV reforms, this opposition grew weaker over time and concentrated within certain regions as the legislation came into force (Dribbusch 2004).

There are two important lessons to draw from the Hartz IV reforms. First, these legislative proposals represented a neoliberal reform of the German welfare state and labor market that coincided with more widespread promarket reforms throughout the EU. The prevailing logic of neoliberalism dominated the political debate over social policy and labor market reforms at this time, promulgated at the international level by organizations such as the IMF, OECD, and the EU. The 1994 *OECD Jobs Study* and the *1997 European Employment Strategy*, for example, provided authoritative guidelines for the types of neoliberal reforms that states should implement (OECD 1994; European Commission 1997). This neoliberal agenda was widely accepted across political parties in Germany who supported the necessity of these reforms given the high unemployment and slow economic growth that persisted in the country. It is important to recognize, however, that these social reforms did not constitute a convergence of the German welfare state toward a Liberal model, but rather incremental neoliberal reforms intended to promote competition, efficiency, and growth.

Second, these liberalization policies were largely depoliticized as they achieved widespread support across political parties. The Hartz IV reforms built upon earlier neoliberal reforms introduced by a center-right coalition government consisting of the Christian Democratic Union (CDU) and the Free Democratic Party (FDP) (Zohlnhöfer and Herweg 2012). The Hartz IV reforms themselves were introduced by a left-leaning Social Democratic Party (SDP) and Green Party coalition government, led by SPD chancellor Gerhard Schröder (CEPS 2014). Subsequent neoliberal reforms were introduced in 2006, which lowered the maximum period for claiming unemployment further, under a new coalition government led by the CDU and SPD (CEPS 2014).

Overall, there was widespread acceptance of neoliberal-inspired welfare reforms across all major political parties in Germany precrisis. Using statistical analysis to identify the effects of party ideology on social spending in Germany before the GFC, Niklas Potrafke finds that politics had little influence (Potrafke 2012). Potrafke indicates that the welfare policies and social spending adopted by left- and right-wing governments were quite similar (Potrafke 2012). This suggests that precrisis social spending in Germany was not as politically controversial as it became after the GFC. Additional research supports the finding that social spending was less influenced by partisanship in Germany before the crisis (Seeleib-Kaiser, Van Dyk, and Roggenkamp 2008; van Kersbergen, 1995; Zohlnhöfer and Herweg, 2012). The decades before the GFC, therefore, saw the introduction of neoliberal welfare reforms and social spending cuts in Germany, which were widely supported across political parties.

German Welfare State Postcrisis

Crisis-Management Stimulus Measures (2008–2010)

In contrast to the precrisis period, which saw welfare liberalization and retrenchment, social spending increased in Germany in the wake of the GFC. The government's response was also more in line with traditional continental European welfare policies rather than liberal welfare policies. This last point is important as it appears that the German welfare state model was influential in shaping the initial crisis response. Whereas nearly all OECD countries adopted some form of social spending stimulus early in the crisis, these countercyclical responses varied considerably across countries and did not reflect a common neoliberal policy approach. This is surprising given the overwhelming trend among OECD states toward welfare liberalization precrisis and the similar problems faced by governments at the onset of the crisis. Specific social policy responses adopted in various countries were highly influenced by existing welfare state types. The stimulus response of the German government confirms the importance of welfare state institutional legacies.

At the start of the GFC, the German government undertook a series of stimulus measures designed to ensure continued employment for labor market insiders and the preservation of skilled labor in the workforce. As discussed earlier, both strategies are key elements of the Continental European welfare state approach to protecting citizens during times of economic downturn. This strategy, which relied on active state intervention in the labor market, was in contrast to Liberal welfare states, such as the UK, which pursued more market-based approaches, such as offering subsidies and other incentives for firms to hire workers (Chung and Thewissen 2011). The German welfare response instead reflected a corporatist strategy in which tripartite negotiations between the government, labor unions, and employers allowed workers to agree to wage restraints and reduced work hours in exchange for guaranteed job security. This social partnership between the government and the main actors in the economy was integral to reducing unemployment after the crisis. This approach is a prominent example of the German government's reliance on existing nonmarket coordinating mechanisms rather than market-based strategies. The initial response of the German government, therefore, represented a break from the neoliberal policies adopted precrisis and a return to more traditional Continental European social protection strategies.

In 2009, the German government introduced two stimulus packages with a combined value of more than €80 billion ($112 billion). The first package, titled "Securing Jobs by Strengthening Growth," provided €31 billion ($43 billion) to support domestic financial markets and the hard-hit manufacturing sector (Chung and Thewissen 2011). The second stimulus package, titled the "Pact for Employment and Stability in Germany," provided around €50 billion ($69.5 billion) to reduce tax burdens, bolster consumer demand, and encourage investment (Chung and Thewissen 2011). Included in these stimulus packages were commitments that the federal government would provide funds to supplement employment costs in return for a pledge by Germany's largest firms to avoid mass job cuts (Jackson 2009). To protect the core workforce, the federal government worked with labor unions and firm representatives to modify an existing tripartite agreement that would extend benefits and provide additional funds for short-time work schemes (ILO 2009). The agreement allowed employers to lower labor costs by reducing the number of work hours and wages of employees as demand worsened, without the need for layoffs. The government provided funds to offset these reductions in working hours and labor costs through the form of partial unemployment benefits, that ensured that workers did not see a significant decrease in their wages. These measures enabled employers to retain their skilled workers in return for guaranteeing job safety and training for employees. From 2008 to 2009, the eligibility period for these short-time work schemes was temporarily extended from six to twenty-four months, during which time more than 3 percent of the entire workforce was enrolled in these programs (EIRO 2009a, 2009b, 2009c, 2009d; OECD 2010a).

Short-time work schemes were an important alternative to layoffs as the German labor market coped with a decline in international demand for goods and services. These schemes promoted temporary reductions in working time by providing wage replacement benefits for employees who worked less than their normal hours. The extensive use of short-time work schemes is largely credited for the low postcrisis unemployment rates in Germany, despite an overall decrease of demand in the international market and slower economic growth (Chung and Thewissen 2011). According to research by Joachim Möller, the number of jobs saved by short-time work schemes was equivalent to approximately 360,000 employees (2010).

A second important feature of the renegotiated tripartite agreement was the allowance of greater flexibility in the management of the working-hours account model. The working-hours account model allowed employers to decrease staff costs without having to make job cuts by reducing the working hours of employees and limiting the need for overtime. This working-hours account model allowed for a shock absorption equivalent to approximately 529,000 employees (Möller 2010). This represents a large number of jobs retained through nonmarket coordination of employment. Combined, flexible working accounts, short-time work schemes, overtime reductions, and other work-time policies accounted for a reduction in working hours equivalent to 1.39 million full-time employees (Möller 2010). These measures principally helped to protect core labor market positions, particularly jobs within the male-dominated manufacturing industry (Eichhorst, Feil, and Marx 2010; EIRO 2010).

Another measure included in both stimulus packages that ensured employment protection for labor market insiders was the expansion of an early retirement scheme for older employees (European Commission 2009a). These policies were designed to help workers over fifty-five years of age gradually transition into retirement, which would allow for the opening up of new jobs. If an employee above fifty-five years of age agreed to reduce their working time by half, the employer would pay only 70 percent of the employee's reduced wage and pension and the federal government agreed to pay the additional costs (EIRO 2009e). This ensured that pensions of the older workforce could be safeguarded while more positions could be filled by younger workers. The stimulus packages also introduced activation policies intended to increase skill levels within the workforce through investments in on-the-job training and job placement programs (Chung and Thewissen 2011). To encourage female workforce participation, the stimulus packages included family support policies, including a 4.3 percent expansion of child benefits and a tax-free child allowance (European Commission 2009a).

In sum, at the start of the crisis, the German government adopted a series of stimulus measures designed to stabilize financial markets, bolster economic growth, and provide social protection for its highly skilled core workforce. These stimulus measures were in line with traditional Continental European welfare state policies focused on the employment and wage protection of core workers. These measures reflect a shift away from neoliberal welfare policies that had been highly influential in Germany in the two decades preceding the GFC.

While generous welfare spending increases offered a stronger safety net for core workers, labor market outsiders continued to receive low levels of social protection. Short-time working schemes, for instance, were targeted at permanent core workers at the expense of their temporary counterparts (Cho and Newhouse 2013; Lim 2000). Collectively agreed-upon provisions to bolster social protections were also more likely to cover employees with standard contracts or those working in large firms (Glassner and Keune

2012). Some means-tested benefits targeting labor market outsiders were introduced, such as increased family benefits and active labor market policies, that helped to alleviate the rising poverty among the nontraditional workforce (Mahoney and Thelen 2010; Streeck and Thelen 2005; Thelen 2009). But these measures did little to address the problem of dualization, as core workers were the main beneficiaries of social spending increases and workforce protection policies. For instance, out of 1.4 million short-time workers registered in Germany in June 2009, 78 percent were men while only 22 percent were women (German Federal Employment Agency 2009).

In addition to the discretionary social spending increases adopted by the government, several automatic stabilizing mechanisms exist as part of the German welfare state. These automatic stabilizers helped to ensure that no matter what measures the government agreed upon in the immediate wake of the GFC, social spending would increase to meet the needs of citizens as economic and social conditions worsened. According to research by Dolls, Fuest, and Piechl, automatic stabilizers in Germany absorbed 48 percent of the income shock and 62 percent of the unemployment shock generated by the economic crisis, well above the EU average (2012). These generous automatic social spending increases played a key role in stabilizing disposable incomes and household demand. As a result, although Germany was affected by the economic downturn after the GFC, the country remained on relatively good social, economic, and financial footing.

Unlike states such as the United States and the United Kingdom, who rely heavily on financial market services, the German economy was not as hard hit by the earliest wave of the GFC. As the crisis continued, however, reduced demand for exports began to have negative effects on German economic growth. Although slower growth led to significant workforce layoffs in many states, due to high levels of employment protection, strong automatic stabilizers, and generous stimulus measures, unemployment remained considerably lower in Germany than in the rest of the OECD. In fact, not only did the German labor market fare far better than most of its EU counterparts, there was lower unemployment throughout the crisis than in the two preceding decades. The unemployment rate in Germany from 1990 until the start of the crisis in 2007 was 8.73 percent, with a high of 11.3 percent in 2005 (OECD 2015a). In the aftermath of the GFC, however, the unemployment rate in Germany was 6.2 percent, reaching 5 percent in 2014, its lowest level since national reunification (OECD 2015a).

This positive labor market performance has been important because, while problems of dualization persist, low levels of postcrisis unemployment have minimized political conflict between labor market insiders and outsiders. Low unemployment has also ensured that employee contributions to social programs have remained high. This allowed the conservative government to introduce gradual welfare reductions, rather than making drastic cuts to social programs due to budgetary constraints. As we will see, this latter scenario has been a problem in southern Europe and eastern Europe that has resulted in social dislocation and intensified political conflict in these countries.

The size and scope of the German welfare state helped to limit domestic political conflict and reduce social and economic hardship, even among less protected outsider groups. As a result, Germany did not have a high degree of political volatility and turnover postcrisis. In fact, not only did Angela Merkel's CDU party remain in power since the start of the GFC, but in the 2013 national elections the CDU and its sister party the Christian Social Union (CSU) won an overwhelming majority with 41.5 percent of the vote (Parties and Elections 2015). The chancellor not only secured a historic third-term victory but came just five seats short of an absolute parliamentary majority (*Guardian* 2013a). According to many analysts this strong margin of victory signified a prominent sentiment among German citizens that they were well-protected from the crisis under the CDU's leadership (*Guardian* 2013a). This election result is in stark contrast to political trends throughout the rest of the Eurozone, where ruling parties were voted out of office in twelve of the seventeen member states (*Guardian* 2013a). By 2012, the ruling governments in more than half of the EU's twenty-eight member states had been forced to end their terms prematurely or had been voted out of office (Deutsche Welle 2012; Deutsche Bank 2012; Regan 2012). In most cases, deteriorating social and economic conditions combined with negative public perceptions of the government's ability to adequately protect its citizens were the driving forces behind these political changes (Deutsche Bank 2012; Regan 2012).

The Politics of Austerity (2010–Present)

While Germany has not been faced with the high degree of political instability seen in some EU member states, political partisanship has been extremely important in driving postcrisis social spending. Although the initial crisis-management response of the government took the form of fiscal stimulus, as the crisis wore on the German government made reductions to social spending and introduced a series of austerity measures. In the early stages of the crisis, stimulus measures were seen as necessary to support financial sectors, restore market confidence, bolster employment, stimulate domestic demand, and provide social protection. As the crisis continued, budgetary constraints and debt and deficit concerns became a primary focus of the conservative-led government. Informed by neoliberal ideas, the ruling center-right CDU party has taken the position that fiscal discipline offers the best approach to lowering the national debt and restoring confidence in the economy (EUCE 2013). Due to its relatively stable economic footing, German austerity measures have been more gradual and minor than in other EU member states. This has resulted in less political conflict and social instability than in other harder-hit countries, for example southern European member states. These austerity measures, however, do signal a return by the German government to neoliberal economic principles and a shift from short-term expansionary social spending to longer-term welfare liberalization and retrenchment.

Government spending reductions have been a key element of the CDU party platform and have played a key role in defining the German policy position domestically and in a wider EU context. As the GFC progressed, conservative parties in Germany embraced austerity and welfare retrenchment. By 2011, the center-right coalition of the CDU and FDP introduced a budget that aimed to reduce government spending by nearly €72 billion ($100 billion) between 2011 and 2015 (EUCE 2013). Included in the budget were measures to eliminate more than ten thousand public-sector jobs, reduce government payrolls, lower child services payments, and scale back unemployment benefits (Market Watch 2010; EUCE 2013). In the buildup to the 2013 national elections, Angela Merkel and her CDU party announced additional cuts to government spending worth up to €6.3 billion ($8 billion), with the goal of balancing the budget (CNBC 2013). In the 2013 report "Medium-Term Budget Goals of the Federal Government," the Federal Ministry of Finance, led by Wolfgang Schäuble, advocated for further social spending cuts, including almost €8.6 billion ($11 billion) in cuts to the national health fund, cuts to pension payments for early retirement, and a €1.6 billion ($2 billion) cut in government contributions to the pension system (*Spiegel* 2012a, 2012b). Following the same trend, the 2014 federal budget, presented by Mr. Schäuble, included an additional €4 billion ($5.4

billion) in spending cuts, including cuts of several hundred million euros to the Federal Employment Agency budget and caps for parental leave programs (*Financial Times* 2013). The overall goal of these reductions was to establish a balanced budget by 2016 and for Germany to serve as a leading example for other EU member states to follow (*Spiegel* 2012b).

This embrace of austerity and corresponding social spending cuts is in keeping with expectations of conservative political parties found in the welfare state literature. Namely, that in response to economic shocks, governments led by conservative parties will be less supportive of redistribution and social spending compared with states governed by left-leaning parties (Ahrend, Arnold, and Moeser 2011; Bremer 2018; McManus 2019; Starke, Kaasch, and van Hooren 2014). The policies of the conservative CDU-led government seem to confirm these theoretical expectations and offer some evidence of the importance of partisanship in influencing postcrisis social spending. As mentioned earlier, due to its relatively positive economic performance and low unemployment levels after the GFC, Germany has not seen the same degree of social and political instability found in other EU members, most notably in southern Europe, nor has it witnessed the same degree of political polarization. But while political divisions are less pronounced in Germany than in some other EU countries, left-right divisions have grown among political parties over social spending.

Postcrisis Political Divisions

Within Germany, there is clear support for fiscal discipline and welfare retrenchment among the conservative CDU ruling party. This position has also been widely supported by the FDP, a conservative political party that has long favored neoliberal policies (ECFR 2012). But whereas the leading Social Democratic opposition party (SPD) supported neoliberal policies precrisis, most notably passing the Hartz IV reforms while in power in the mid-2000s,[1] the party shifted further left after the crisis and called for greater government intervention and higher social spending (ECFR 2012).

Similarly, although the SPD largely refrained from using fiscal policy to stimulate growth while in power precrisis, it was a leading architect of the

---

1. Although by the late 2000s tensions had grown within the SPD over the perceived negative effects of the Hartz IV reforms, this opposition did not substantially alter the party's position.

stimulus packages adopted by the CDU/SPD grand coalition after the GFC, claiming many of the policies as its own (ECFR 2012). After the 2009 general elections, the SPD abandoned the grand coalition with the CDU, moving politically and ideologically further to the left. While recognizing the need for a certain degree of fiscal discipline, the SPD has been far more in favor of social spending increases and a higher top tax rate to pay for welfare programs (ECFR 2012). The SPD has also been critical of the effects that austerity may have on economic growth domestically and throughout the EU (ECFR 2012). A visible change in the SPD's position, since the start of the crisis, has been its shift over the official retirement age. While a member of the grand coalition with the CDU/CSU from 2005 until 2009, the SPD had been in favor of establishing the age of retirement at sixty-seven years (Potrafke 2012). In 2010, however, the SPD came out against this policy and sought to lower the age of retirement, indicating a move toward more generous social policies (Potrafke 2012). Since the onset of the crisis, the two other major political parties in Germany, the Green Party and Liberal Party, have also favored more social spending (Armingeon and Baccaro 2015; ECFR 2012; Hübner 2013).

Welfare was a major point of contestation in the 2017 national elections. Although the CDU won nearly 33 percent of the vote, making it the largest party in the Bundestag, it was unable to form a ruling coalition for over four months after the election (*Guardian* 2017a). To resolve this stalemate, the CDU entered into negotiations with the SPD to form another grand coalition. Although these efforts were eventually successful, the talks highlighted key differences over welfare. Reeling from their worst postwar election results and seeking to reassure their constituents of their commitment to social democratic values, the SPD made generous social spending and expanded welfare programs key demands as they entered into negotiations. Signaling their shift further to the left on welfare, the SPD called for major reforms to German healthcare that would replace the existing dual public-private healthcare system with a universal insurance system (Reuters 2018a). The SPD also made demands for higher tax rates on wealthy individuals and corporations to fund social spending in areas such as pensions and family care. While the CDU was able to deny a number of the SPD's welfare demands, including rejecting the call for a universal healthcare system and higher taxes, they agreed to invest over €2 billion ($2.3 billion) in social housing by 2021 and €33 billion ($37.3 billion) for a variety of social programs including childcare (Reuters 2018a). The SPD was also able to negotiate additional government investments in education, elder care, and student loans (*Bloomberg* 2018). The deal ultimately led to a compromise between the CDU and SPD, but these negotiations highlighted party divisions over social spending.

Overall, while dissent and political conflict over social spending has not been as pronounced in Germany as in some other EU member states, it has grown since the start of the GFC. While supportive of neoliberal welfare state and labor market reforms in the 1990s and 2000s, since the crisis the SPD has moved further to the left and has favored greater government intervention and higher levels of social spending. Although social spending decisions were largely depoliticized in Germany before the crisis, with all the major parties favoring some form of liberalization (Potrafke 2012), welfare has become subject to more partisan debate after the crisis.

The Effects of Partisanship at the EU Level

As one of the leading proausterity voices in Europe, Germany provides an interesting case to analyze how national politics shaped government preferences regarding EU crisis responses. Domestic partisanship was influential in the German government's position in its negotiations with other member states and EU institutions over how best to address the Eurozone crisis. Conservative party leadership in Germany was influential in promoting austerity measures for all Eurozone members. From the perspective of the CDU, the primary causes of the sovereign debt crisis that wreaked havoc throughout the Eurozone stemmed from a lack of fiscal discipline among profligate member states (Armingeon and Baccaro 2015; ECFR 2012). This belief was echoed by both the CSU and FDP, who share a similar conservative view of the causes of the debt crisis. By framing the Eurozone crisis as a problem of fiscal discipline and irresponsible borrowing on behalf of specific member states, the CDU and its conservative allies discounted claims that its causes were related to structural problems and imbalances within the currency union (Armingeon and Baccaro 2015). As a result, policies aimed at addressing these structural issues were downplayed by the CDU, which called instead for debt and deficit limits and domestic reforms. The argument was that budget consolidation would reduce the risk of insolvency and would bolster market confidence, thus allowing states to borrow more easily and invest in long-term growth. From this perspective, austerity, rather than prolonging the economic downturn and undermining social safety nets, as opponents claimed, was seen as the key to ensuring growth and well-being in Europe by conservative actors in Germany (ECFR 2012).

The CDU-led German government has been a leading advocate for austerity in the EU. The emphasis on fiscal discipline and structural reforms, which were prominent features of the EU's response to the Eurozone crisis, reflected German policy preferences. For example, constitutional limits on national budget deficits, which are a requirement of the European Fiscal Compact, are based on the Schuldenbremse, or "debt brake" mechanism, found in the German constitution (Armingeon and Baccaro 2015; ECFR 2012; *Economist* 2011). Structural reform conditionality for members requiring bailouts to manage their domestic debt problems was also supported by Germany and its conservative allies (EUCE 2013). The German government also opposed debt mutualization proposals and the purchasing of government debt in the form of bond-buying schemes. The CDU, for example, was opposed to Eurobonds, citing the so-called "no bailout" clause in the Maastricht Treaty, which specifies that states should not be liable for, nor assume, the commitments or debts of other member states (CFR 2010; ECFR 2012). In a speech to the German Parliament in 2012, Angela Merkel went so far as to announce that there would be no EU debt sharing or the establishment of Eurobonds "as long as I live" (*Spiegel* 2012c). CDU officials were worried that such measures would create a moral hazard, establishing disincentives for debt-stricken countries to undertake necessary reforms. From this standpoint, these policies would require German citizens to foot the bill for the poor economic decisions of other EMU members

Identifying similar concerns of moral hazard, the CDU-led German government came out against the ECB's bond-buying schemes (ECFR 2012). When in 2012 Mario Draghi, head of the ECB, announced that the central bank would initiate a program of purchasing the government bonds of struggling Eurozone members to lower their borrowing costs and offer a degree of debt relief, it had the effect of calming international financial markets but was met with strong opposition by many conservative German government officials (Bulmer 2014; *Spiegel* 2012d). Jens Weidmann, the head of the Bundesbank, Germany's central bank, and a prominent member of the ECB Governing Council, for instance, repeatedly opposed the ECB's bond-buying plan, considering the program not only a threat to EU recovery but arguing that the policy was anathematic to the founding principles of the Bundesbank (*Financial Times* 2012b; *Wall Street Journal*

2012b). Prominent CDU members, including the deputy parliamentary floor leader Michael Fuchs, came out against the ECB's bond-purchasing scheme, arguing that the central bank should encourage struggling Eurozone members to continue reform efforts, rather than providing cheap money that might discourage such restructuring (Reuters 2015a). Despite German opposition, the ECB went ahead with its program to purchase sovereign debt, which from March 2015 through September 2016 introduced €60 billion ($68 billion) a month into the EU economy and provided more than €1 trillion ($1.1 trillion) in total (Reuters 2015b, 2015c). Although they were unable to halt the bond-buying program, German pressure led the ECB to adopt certain requirements, for example, only allowing members who agreed to austerity conditions to be able to apply for bailout funds (*Spiegel* 2012e).

The fact that many key EU economic policies have been predicated on the necessity of austerity speaks to the power and influence of neoliberal ideas pushed by conservative-led governments such as in Germany. In no small part, Germany's influence in EU policymaking and its ability to advocate for fiscal conditions on other member states is because it is an engine of growth in the EU and the largest contributor to the Eurozone bailout funds (Bulmer 2014). It also speaks to the powerful role that partisanship has played in EU social and economic policymaking. Though the German government has been one of the leading advocates of austerity, it had support from other center-right governments in the Eurozone, including the Netherlands and Finland. Together these countries supported a proausterity agenda that put pressure on indebted peripheral member states, including Greece, Italy, Ireland, Portugal, and Spain, to introduce budget cuts resulting in social spending reductions (EUCE 2013).

To underscore the importance that the CDU and its coalition of center-right governments have played in defining EU social and economic policies, it is useful to examine the alternative positions of other German political parties. The SPD, for instance, favored a different approach to addressing the Eurozone crisis. Whereas the CDU, CSU, and FDP all emphasized austerity, the SPD was more receptive to the need to couple fiscal discipline with better social protection. For example, in 2013, Martin Schulz, president of European Parliament and leading SPD official, appealed to Chancellor Merkel to change her position on EU austerity, arguing that more consideration should be given to the social and economic hardships faced by citizens in struggling peripheral states (*Spiegel* 2013b). The appeal was an attempt to convince the CDU to eschew its hardline emphasis on austerity and acknowledge that more needs to be done to address social issues, such as high youth unemployment and growing wage disparities within EU countries, particularly in hard-hit southern Europe (*Spiegel* 2013b).

While the SPD supported some fiscal constraints, for example backing the European Fiscal Compact, they have also been more critical of austerity (Armingeon and Baccaro 2015; Hübner 2013). The SPD, for instance, supported the ECB's bond-buying quantitative easing program, a position favored by the left-leaning Greens and Left Party as well (Armingeon and Baccaro, 2015; Hübner, 2013). There was also support on behalf of some SPD members for mutualized debt mechanisms, such as Eurobonds. As president of the European Parliament and later leader of the SPD, Martin Schulz, for example, came out against austerity and in favor of Eurobonds, arguing that a more lenient approach was needed toward southern Europe (Adler-Nissen and Kropp, 2016). Similarly, leading SPD officials such as finance minister Peer Steinbrück and parliamentary leader Frank-Walter Steinmeier have spoken in favor of Eurobonds (Dullien and Guérot 2012). Despite this, however, the SPD has not formally embraced Eurobonds as part of its party platform and has taken the position that while a progrowth agenda is needed, debt reduction and structural reforms are also necessary in Europe's periphery. This may be due to negative public reactions to pooled debt proposals (ECFR 2012; EU Observer 2014; Policy Network 2015).

Although the SPD gave up on ambitions for a common Eurobond, the party was less supportive of strict austerity and continued to favor some form of debt mutualization. For example, the SPD along with the Greens and the German Council of Economic Experts proposed the introduction of a European Redemption Fund that would create a joint debt vehicle for EMU members, but unlike Eurobonds would be temporary (Bofinger et al. 2011; Bruegel 2012; Doluca et al. 2012).

While support for stricter fiscal rules might continue under an alternative governing coalition led by the SPD, greater credence would likely be given to policies that favor closer economic policy coordination at the EU level and the need for a growth strategy for indebted member states to offset the consequences of austerity. Dullien and Guérot, for example, use an index to map German party positions regarding Eurocrisis responses along a neoliberal versus neo-Keynesian scale (2012). This data shows a clear partisan divide between right-leaning parties (CDU/CSU and FDP), who favor a neoliberal position, and left-leaning parties (SPD, Die Linke, and the

Greens), who have embraced a more neo-Keynesian approach. Given this partisan division, it is reasonable to expect that the German negotiating position in EU social and economic policymaking would likely be different if a change in domestic political leadership were to occur (ECFR 2012). While this may be unlikely given the continued support that Angela Merkel's government has received, this idea highlights the influence that conservative party leadership has had in defining Germany's social and economic policy positions domestically and in negotiations with the EU. The fiscal discipline the CDU has encouraged has shaped EU recovery efforts and has been a defining feature of contentious political debates in Europe.

Overall, while many actors in Germany favored proausterity positions, policymaking was far from unified and depoliticized. European measures to address the financial crisis were a major point of partisan conflict within the German parliament (Wonka 2016). These contentious parliamentary debates fell along the established left-right dimensions as EU policymaking was tied to redistributive concerns (Wendler 2014a). This suggests that while the political economy of Germany may have been influential in shaping national preferences regarding Eurozone crisis responses there was still room for political agency and competition. In other words, ideological conflicts and partisan politics played an important role in shaping German preferences regarding the EU crisis response.

Conclusion

The initial shock of the GFC triggered immediate social spending increases in Germany in the form of automatic stabilizers and government stimulus measures. This increase represented a shift away from neoliberal-inspired welfare reductions that had been introduced in previous decades. As the crisis continued, however, the conservative CDU government turned away from stimulus and toward austerity and social spending cuts. Although such neoliberal policies were widely supported across parties in Germany before the GFC, after this event partisan divisions over these policies have grown. Although Germany has not seen the same degree of political upheaval as some other EU member states, with the center-right CDU remaining in power, differences have grown between parties on the left and right. Most notably, the SPD has moved further to the left and has embraced higher social spending as an alternative to the austerity measures and welfare cuts favored by the conservative-led government. Divisions over welfare were present in the negotiations between the CDU and SPD to form a grand coalition after the 2017 general elections. The SPD's demands in these talks, such as the implementation of a universal healthcare system and higher top tax rates to fund more social spending, underlines the party's recommitment to its traditional left-wing social democratic values and policies.

Partisanship has not only affected social spending in Germany but has been influential in the interstate negotiations between Germany and highly indebted EU peripheral states over austerity. Before the crisis, neoliberal reforms were introduced to welfare states and labor markets across the EU with widespread political support. In the wake of the GFC, policies advocating further welfare retrenchment have been met with greater political resistance. These challenges to the neoliberal welfare consensus have placed Germany's conservative CDU government, and its proausterity center-right allies, in direct conflict with other EU member states, particularly those in southern and eastern Europe, who have faced the burden of these policies. At times, this political divide has also put the German government in conflict with EU institutions that have raised some concerns about the negative effects of austerity. In sum, the GFC challenged the neoliberal welfare consensus that existed across parties in Germany before the crisis and powerfully altered political dynamics. After this critical juncture, social spending has become a much more visible political issue and one that is highly influenced by party control of government. This partisanship has had profound effects on social and economic policies within Germany and across the EU.

CHAPTER 5

United Kingdom

Liberal Welfare State

> "We need to move from a low wage, high tax, high welfare society
> to a higher wage, lower tax, lower welfare society."
> —David Cameron, UK Prime Minister (2010–2016)

The Conservative Party in the UK placed neoliberal policies at the center of its postcrisis social and economic platform. The above quote, given in a 2012 press conference by then prime minister David Cameron to defend his government's plan to cut welfare spending by an additional £12 billion ($19 billion), highlights the influence of neoliberal ideas in the UK postcrisis. Since returning to power in 2010, the Conservative Party introduced more than £61 billion ($40 billion) in social benefit cuts and abandoned earlier welfare commitments, such as the goal of substantially reducing child poverty levels by 2020 (*New York Times* 2018a). This austerity platform resulted in the largest cuts to the UK welfare state since World War II (*New York Times* 2010a; Lupton et al. 2013). But whereas the left-wing Labour Party had embraced neoliberal welfare reforms before the GFC, it has since called for limits to austerity and expanded social protection. Under the former leadership of Jeremy Corbyn, who rose to power within the party on a strong antiausterity platform, the Labour Party moved even further to the left, ideologically abandoning its former neoliberal-inspired Third Way policies. Disagreements between the Conservative Party and Labour Party over austerity and welfare reductions indicate heightened ideological divisions on the left and the right and the rising influence of partisanship on social spending. This chapter will explore the evolution of this political conflict and how partisanship has shaped social spending in the UK after the GFC.

The UK is often cited as a classic example of a Liberal welfare state, which relies on limited means-tested social programs targeted toward at-risk populations (Esping-Andersen 1990; Pierson 1996, 2001; Häusermann and Palier 2008). The UK is also a significant global economic actor with a large financial market and banking sector, which was heavily affected by the GFC. In the aftermath of this event, the UK government was a front-runner in pursuing fiscal consolidation and welfare retrenchment in the EU. The UK is therefore an important case study for analysis to understand how the GFC has reshaped the politics of social spending. This chapter will explore social spending trends in the UK before and after the crisis, paying close attention to the role political partisanship has played in influencing these patterns. The chapter will begin by examining UK social spending in the two decades prior to the GFC, which were notable for the widespread acceptance of neoliberal welfare reforms across political lines. The next section will examine the stimulus measures adopted by the government in response to the crisis. In particular, this section will identify how the stimulus measures adopted by the government represented an important break from earlier social spending patterns. Finally, this chapter will analyze the increasingly important role that partisan politics has played in defining long-term postcrisis social spending in the UK. This chapter will demonstrate that not only has partisanship been a key driver of social spending, but that since the onset of the GFC these divisions have taken on increased importance in defining UK welfare policies and the country's position in EU social and economic policy debates.

UK Welfare State Precrisis (1990–2007)

Welfare State Liberalization

In the two decades before the GFC, the UK government oversaw the transition of the welfare state from a model of passive social assistance to one emphasizing workforce activation and personal responsibility. These neoliberal welfare reforms encouraged individuals to support themselves through participation in market activities rather than relying on government support. This introduction of promarket policies into the social sphere was done with widespread support across political parties. Historically, political divisions in the UK have existed between parties on the left, who favored a strong welfare state and high levels of social spending, and parties on the right, who favored a smaller and more efficient welfare state (Allan and Scruggs 2004; Boix 2000; Huber and Stephens 2001; Korpi and Palme 2003; Taylor-Gooby 2001). In the decades preceding the GFC, however, these political divisions were largely muted as an ascendant neoliberal policy agenda was embraced by parties on both ends of the political spectrum (Taylor-Gooby 2001, 2004). As political differences narrowed, the influence that parties had on social spending became less significant. The result was widespread political support for welfare state liberalization in the UK.

During the 1990s and 2000s, there was considerable convergence of the policy positions of UK political parties in support of neoliberal reforms (Taylor-Gooby 2001, 2004). After a considerable electoral defeat in 1992, many members of the Labour Party began to rethink their historical commitments to a large public sector, high tax rates, and generous social spending, viewing these policies as no longer financially sustainable or electorally viable (Taylor-Gooby 2001). By the 1997 general election, the Labour Party's position vis-à-vis the welfare state was far more in line with the Conservative Party's view that social policies should support economic competitiveness rather than promote social equality. This new neoliberal position was prominent in the Labour Party's 1994 Commission on Social Justice report as well as its 1997 general election manifesto (Labour Party 1994, 1997).

By the mid-1990s, the New Labour[1] party, under the leadership of Tony Blair, became strong advocates of Third Way policies that emphasized social investment strategies to reconcile social welfare with a liberal market approach. Third Way advocates argued that social and economic policies can be mutually reinforcing and that policies such as workforce activation programs could encourage increased productivity and economic growth (Hemerijck 2013). In short, New Labour wanted to transform the welfare state from a passive benefit provider to an active labor market promoter. From this perspective, social welfare was best achieved not through direct government interventions and expenditures, but rather by activating individuals through policies such as workforce skill development and job placement programs. This social investment approach would then be coupled

---

1. New Labour refers to a period from 1994 to 2010 in which the British Labour Party was led by Tony Blair and then by Gordon Brown. This period is notable for the shift in the social and economic policy position of the party in favor of social investment Third Way strategies, which emphasized workforce activation and the need to adopt a promarket welfare system.

with careful means-tested social programs and justified by individual contributions to economic competitiveness (DSS 1998).

Once in office, beginning in 1997, New Labour pursued social policies similar to those of the previous Conservative-led government, including fiscal restraint, welfare retrenchment, and the introduction of market-based social policies, including the partial privatization of the pension system (Hodson and Mabbett 2009; Taylor-Gooby 2001). Under the leadership of New Labour, the UK welfare state was largely reoriented to replace passive social benefits with workforce activation policies (Häusermann and Palier 2008). This labor market activation strategy was widely supported by parties on the left and right as the best means to promote competitiveness. As a result, during the 1990s and 2000s, political differences between the left-leaning Labour and right-leaning Conservative parties were fairly minor. While disagreements persisted over issues, such as minimum wage levels and the extent of means-tested government interventions, these differences were largely a matter of degree rather than based upon deeper ideological differences (Taylor-Gooby 2001).

Overall, during the 1990s and 2000s, there was a notable shift in the UK toward welfare state retrenchment and the introduction of neoliberal policies into the social sphere (Hemerijck, Knapen, and van Doorne 2009). Political parties on the left and the right began to pursue policies that emphasized the importance of a market-oriented welfare state that would encourage workforce participation, skill development, individual responsibility, and competition while disavowing the passive social benefits of the past (Lee and McBride 2007; Swank 2002). Due to the convergence of welfare positions across parties precrisis, debates over social spending became less contentious (Stoesz 1996, 2002; Swank 2002; Taylor-Gooby 2001). The widespread acceptance of neoliberal ideas and policies across political parties goes a long way to explain the lack of statistical significance that partisanship had on social spending during this period.

UK Welfare State Postcrisis

Crisis-Management Stimulus Measures (2008–2010)

While precrisis political parties on both the left and right encouraged less state involvement in the social arena, the severity of the GFC necessitated significant government intervention to stabilize domestic markets and minimize social costs for citizens. As a major international economic actor, the UK was severely affected by the global financial collapse in 2008 (Chung and Thewissen 2011; Hodson and Mabbett 2009). By the end of 2006, of the top thirty largest banks globally, four were located in the UK, accounting for 12 percent of the total stock market value of the group (Laeven and Valencia 2010). The UK economy, therefore, represented one of the largest international banking sectors in the world at the start of the crisis, second only to the United States (Laeven and Valencia 2010). Due to their dominance in international banking and finance, the bank failures that occurred in the wake of the GFC were particularly damaging to the UK economy. By 2009, the top thirty banks globally had lost more than 52 percent of their stock market value, representing a significant loss (Laeven and Valencia 2010). The collapse of international financial markets and banking resulted in a sharp drop in GDP, rising unemployment, and lower demand for goods and services in the UK. In response to this rapid economic decline, the government introduced stimulus measures, which included social spending increases, to offset the negative effects of the crisis.

In reaction to the crisis, the ruling Labour government decided to move forward with its 2007 social spending plans, based on the assumption of steady growth, fearing that cuts would prolong the recession and deepen its effects (Hills 2011; Lupton et al. 2013). While GDP declined, social spending rose to more than 30 percent of GDP from 2008 through 2010, the highest it had been in nearly thirty years (Lupton et al. 2013). An important aspect of the "fiscal stimulus" response of the Labour government is that much of the countercyclical welfare support came through the continuation of previously planned real increases in social spending, rather than the adoption of special additional legislative measures (Lupton et al. 2013). Therefore, it is important to analyze overall social spending, rather than just stimulus measures, to understand the full scope of the government's response to the recession. By increasing social spending in real terms, as well as other areas of public spending, the Labour government allowed deficits to rise, an issue that would come to the forefront as the crisis wore on (MacLeavy 2011).

It is important to note that while this government intervention was in contrast to the limited state intervention strategies that were dominant pre-crisis, the types of policies adopted were very much in line with traditional Liberal welfare state practices. For example, although the British government actively supported financial and banking sectors, providing a bailout

package of £500 billion ($785 billion) to ensure liquidity, granting govern-
ment guarantees of bank debts, and purchasing toxic assets, it adopted a
more hands-off approach to welfare post-crisis (Chung and Thewissen
2011). UK stimulus measures continued to encourage a market-based strategy to address social and economic issues. For example, the government's
policies relied on demand-led labor market policies, rather than through
direct state intervention, to promote workforce activation and reduce
unemployment. Around 10.5 percent of UK stimulus spending was dedicated to active labor market measures aimed at encouraging workforce participation (ILO 2011). In contrast to Continental European welfare states,
such as Germany, which relied on corporatist strategies of active state intervention in the labor market and direct negotiations with companies and
employee associations, the UK employed market-based strategies to reduce
unemployment, such as offering tax incentives and subsidies for firms to
hire employees (Chung and Thewissen 2011). Beginning in January 2009,
for example, employers received a subsidy of £2,500 ($3,900) for the hiring
of any person who had been unemployed for more than six months (HM
Treasury 2009). In 2009, the government also allocated more than £3 billion ($4.72 billion) to fund programs designed to get the unemployed back
to work, including job search initiatives and workforce training programs
(Chung and Thewissen 2011; EIRO 2009f; HM Government 2009).

   Although stimulus measures primarily focused on active labor market
policies, some small increases were made to certain welfare programs, such
as a slight increase in the maximum unemployment benefits for middle-
and high-income earners (HM Treasury 2009). A small temporary bonus
for pensioners and for families with children was also introduced at this
time (Chung and Thewissen 2011). In composition, the welfare response of
the UK government to the crisis can largely be characterized as a liberal
one. For example, while the focus of some stimulus policies, like those of
Germany, was to guarantee employment protection, the UK adopted
market-based incentives to address rising unemployment, such as corporate tax breaks for firms to hire workers. In sum, the early crisis responses
of the UK government relied on market-oriented welfare policies and limited targeted social benefits. This response affirms the importance of welfare state institutional legacies in shaping social policies.

   In keeping with the lower levels of social spending associated with Liberal welfare states, UK stimulus measures were less generous than many of
the packages implemented by their European counterparts. While marking

a shift toward expansionary social spending, the stimulus measures implemented in the UK between 2008 and 2010 were equivalent to 1.4 percent of
GDP, far lower than many other OECD countries (ILO 2011; OECD 2009).
The duration of this stimulus spending was also considerably shorter in the
UK than in other countries. Beginning in 2010, there was a sharp drop-off
in public spending and the introduction of significant welfare cuts, corresponding with the Conservative Party's ascension to power in that year's
general election (*Economist* 2013; ILO 2011; OECD 2009).

On the one hand, the policies adopted by the UK government in the
immediate aftermath of the GFC represented an important change from the
precrisis period. The initial response to the crisis was marked by greater
government intervention and social spending increases than in the previous two decades. On the other hand, UK stimulus measures still largely
reflected a liberal approach to social and economic policymaking, favoring
market-based approaches to restoring growth, reducing unemployment,
and protecting vulnerable citizens. The influence of liberal ideas is evident
in the size, timing, and content of the UK's stimulus package.

In addition to the discretionary social spending increases adopted by
the government at the start of the crisis, automatic stabilizers provided an
important source of social protection in the UK. Automatic stabilizers in
the UK absorbed 35 percent of the income shock, just below the EU average
of 38 percent (Dolls et al., 2012). Automatic stabilizers also absorbed 42%
of the unemployment shock in the UK, compared with an EU average of
47% (Dolls, Fuest, and Piechl 2012). These automatic stabilizers provided
an immediate buffer against the effects of the GFC. Although the income
and unemployment shock absorption of these automatic stabilizers was
below the EU average, which is characteristic of the lower levels of social
protection offered by Liberal welfare states, the response was far stronger
than in southern and eastern Europe, reflecting the maturity and wealth of
the welfare system in the UK (Dolls, Fuest, and Piechl 2012).

Whereas weak automatic stabilizer responses have resulted in greater
political conflict over discretionary social spending in southern and eastern
Europe, such contestation has been less pronounced in the UK. This is due,
in part, to the UK's centralized government system, where the ruling party
has considerable influence over legislation. In other words, along with an
automatic stabilizer response that was stronger than that in southern and
eastern Europe, the structure of the UK government helped reduce political
conflict over social spending. For instance, whereas decisions to enact bud-

getary cuts nationwide are made in London, local governments are tasked with implementing these reductions (*New York Times* 2018b). Thus much of the ire that has grown over these austerity measures has been directed more at local politicians and less at the national government (*New York Times* 2018b). But although the UK has not witnessed the same degree of volatility in national politics as in peripheral EU member states, political turnover did occur after the GFC, as the ruling Labour Party was voted out of office in 2010 in favor of the Conservative Party. Whereas the left-leaning Labour Party favored stimulus and increased social spending, the electoral victory of the Conservative Party marked a clear shift in government policies in favor of austerity and welfare state retrenchment.

The Politics of Austerity (2010–Present)

The Conservative Party's success in the 2010 UK general election, which resulted in the formation of a coalition government with the Liberal Democrats,[2] led to a noteworthy shift in government policy, as stimulus was abandoned in favor of austerity measures intended to address debt and deficit concerns. This electoral change had a considerable impact on the welfare state, as social spending became a major target of budget cuts. A primary objective of the Conservative legislative agenda was to introduce some of the most significant cuts to the UK welfare system since the start of the postwar period (Lupton et al. 2013; *New York Times* 2010a). The Conservative chancellor of the exchequer, at this time, George Osborne, emphasized the centrality of social spending cuts to lowering the deficit, describing welfare reductions as "a key component of successful fiscal consolidation" (HM Treasury 2010, 6). Nearly two-thirds of the cuts adopted by the Conservative-led coalition government were directed at social spending (van Kersbergen, Vis, and Hemerijck 2014). Reductions in social assistance for vulnerable groups, such as women, children, the poor, and the unemployed, were particularly severe (Taylor-Gooby 2013; van Kersbergen, Vis, and Hemerijck 2014). Social spending accounted for nearly one-third of Britain's annual budget, and the Cameron administration aimed to reduce it by about £20 billion (US$30 billion) from 2010 to 2014, representing approximately 10

---

2. Although working in a coalition government with the Liberal Democrats, the Conservative Party made the decision to implement extensive social spending reductions (Ellison 2016).

percent of government outlays (*New York Times* 2010a). In October 2010, Chancellor Osborne unveiled a series of major welfare cuts, including a £7 billion (US$11 billion) reduction in social spending (Gardiner et al. 2010). This was in addition to £11 billion (US$17 billion) in social spending cuts that were made in an emergency budget earlier that June as part of a welfare reform package (Gardiner, Bromund, and Foster 2010). While agreeing to reductions in 2010, many Liberal Democrats opposed the size of these cuts (Ellison 2016). This highlights the fact that the coalition government's pro-austerity agenda was driven by Conservative Party leadership. Conservative policies resulted in benefit reductions, eligibility restrictions, and the elimination of some social programs altogether (Lupton et al. 2015).

While all three of the main political parties in the UK (Conservative, Labour, and Liberal Democrat) agreed on the need to lower the budget deficit in their 2010 election platforms, the Conservative Party's position was striking in terms of the timing, scale, and scope of their proposed cuts. The Labour Party and the Liberal Democrats argued that if implemented too early, social spending reductions could harm economic recovery, whereas the Conservatives argued for immediate cuts (Ellison 2016; UK Women's Budget Group 2010). The 2010 Conservative budget proposed a ratio of spending cuts to tax increases of 4 to 1 (UK Women's Budget Group 2010; Lupton et al. 2015). By comparison, the Liberal Democrats proposed a ratio of spending cuts to tax increases of 2.5 to 1 and the Labour Party proposed a 2 to 1 ratio (UK Women's Budget Group 2010). These differences in party platforms highlight the extent to which Conservatives prioritized spending cuts compared to the more modest positions of the Liberal Democrats and Labour Party (Ellison 2016). The exceptional scale and speed of welfare cuts and the composition of reforms, such as the 2012 Welfare Reform Act[3] introduced by the Conservative-led government, were largely ideological, reflecting a neoliberal vision of a smaller welfare state and greater individual responsibility (Taylor-Gooby 2012; Lupton et al. 2015). Favoring neoliberal policies, Conservatives identified Labour's social spending initiatives, such as those aimed at tackling child poverty and improving social

---

3. The Welfare Reform Act, introduced by the Conservative-led government in 2012, replaced several means-tested benefits with a universal credit and the introduction of maximums on the amount of social benefits a recipient can receive (Van Kersbergen, Vis, and Hemerijck 2014). The act also increased work incentives and allowed for a greater role for the private sector in welfare provisions (Taylor-Gooby 2013).

mobility, as costly and wasteful (Ellison 2016). This highlights a growing divide between parties in the UK over social spending (Taylor-Gooby 2013). The adoption of sharp social spending reductions in 2010 reflects this division, as Conservative plans for welfare cuts went far beyond the proposals made by the Liberal Democrats or Labour to address the deficit. Interestingly, the welfare cuts introduced by the Conservative Party were not accompanied by tax increases, which would have helped address the budget deficit but would have negatively impacted the Conservative Party's middle- and higher-income core constituents. This suggests that the Conservative platform reflected the ideological position and strategic interests of the party.

Social spending cuts continued throughout Prime Minister Cameron's tenure in office as his administration remained committed to welfare retrenchment after winning the 2015 election. With its return to power, the Conservative Party moved forward with its plans to impose £12 billion (US$19 billion) in additional cuts to the UK welfare budget by 2018 (Conservative Party 2015; *Guardian* 2015a; Osborne 2014). These policies included across-the-board cuts to most working-age benefits, reductions in universal credit allowances, and further cuts to housing, child, and disability benefits (ESRC 2015). The household welfare benefit cap, for example, was lowered in 2015 from £26,000 (US$41,000) to £23,000 (US$36,000) (*Guardian* 2015b; *Mirror* 2015b). To achieve this target, Conservatives significantly increased the pace of welfare cuts, indicating further social spending decreases over time, rather than a slowdown of retrenchment (*Guardian* 2015b). Reflecting neoliberal ideas of limited state intervention, the Conservative-led government also supported a "Big Society" initiative that emphasized the role that individuals, communities, and charitable organizations, rather than the government, should play in providing social support (BBC 2010; Cameron, 2010).

Although David Cameron stepped down as prime minister in 2016 in the wake of the Brexit referendum, the Conservative-led government, under the new leadership of Theresa May, continued the austerity program and welfare state cuts of her predecessor. Philip Hammond, the successor to George Osborne as chancellor of the exchequer, for example, maintained the Conservative government's aim of maintaining balanced budgets. In his 2017 budget, Hammond kept benefit freezes in place, meaning that, due to inflation, individuals claiming Jobseeker's Allowance, Employment and Support Allowance, income support, housing benefits, Universal Credit, child tax credits, working tax credits, and child benefits would receive less support (*New Statesman* 2017). Analysis of the 2017 budget by the Office of Budget Responsibility indicated that after rollout, the universal credit program, introduced in the 2012 Welfare Reform Act, was less generous on average than the benefits and tax credits it replaced (Office of Budgetary Responsibility 2017).

Overall, the House Commons Library estimates that by 2021 working-age social security benefits will be £37 billion ($46 billion) less than in 2010, when the Conservative Party first took office (*Guardian* 2018). According to data collected by Frank Field, the chair of the Work and Pensions Select Committee, after nearly a decade of austerity, social spending on benefits for the UK's poorest families has been cut by nearly 25 percent (*Guardian* 2018). Disability benefits, including personal independence payments and employment and support allowance (ESA), have declined by almost 10 percent (*Guardian* 2018). There have been considerable reductions in many other welfare programs as well, including £4.6 billion ($5.7 billion) less for tax credits, £3.6 billion ($4.5 billion) less for universal credit, £3.4 billion ($4.2 billion) less for child benefits, £2.8 billion ($3.5 billion) less for disability benefits, £2 billion ($2.5 billion) less for ESA and incapacity benefits, and £2.3 billion ($2.8 billion) less for housing benefits (*Guardian* 2018). In addition to benefit cuts, the government put forward planned spending cuts from 2017 to 2020 for several public agencies. The Department for Work and Pensions, for example, had experienced funding cuts of around 40 percent in real terms by 2020 (*Guardian* 2017b).

Postcrisis Political Divisions

While postcrisis social spending has been largely defined by the ruling Conservative Party, the political consensus over welfare, which was widespread precrisis, has fragmented after the GFC. The Labour Party, for instance, blamed Conservative austerity measures for the slowest economic recovery in over a hundred years, a failure to address the deficit, and cuts that would return public spending in Britain to 1930s levels (Labour Party 2015a). The Labour Party, as well as the Liberal Democrats and Green Party, were critical of the Conservatives' 2012 plan to enact £12 billion (US$19 billion) in welfare cuts, arguing that these reductions would negatively impact the average UK citizen. Ed Milliband, former head of the Labour Party, attacked Conservative social spending cuts, arguing that they were harmful to welfare recipients, such as individuals and families receiving child benefits (*Financial Times* 2015).

As the leading opposition party, Labour Party leaders have argued that Conservatives have been more interested in cutting welfare than reforming it to facilitate workforce participation (Labour Party 2015b). This increased political conflict over social spending, indicates that ideological differences have grown between parties over welfare since the start of the GFC. For example, whereas the Conservative Party called for massive cuts in working-age benefits, the Labour Party supports maintaining existing benefit levels (*Independent* 2015b). The Liberal Democrats have proposed plans to increase working-age benefits by 1 percent (*Independent* 2015b). The Greens have gone even further to suggest that the current benefits system should be scrapped and replaced with a more comprehensive and generous guaranteed universal basic income for all citizens (*Independent* 2015b). In the 2015 elections, Labour proposed an increase in the minimum wage to £8 (US$12) per hour by 2019 and a reduction in university tuition fees from £9,000 (US$13,845) to £6,000 (US$9,230) (*Independent* 2015b). The Greens' election manifesto also favored increasing the minimum wage to £10 (US$15) an hour by 2020 and a green investment program, which they argue will create more than a million new jobs (*Independent* 2015b).

Following their loss to the Conservative Party in the 2015 general election, the Labour Party moved noticeably further to the left under the leadership of Jeremy Corbyn, a self-identified democratic socialist. Labour's return to its traditional left-wing values and policies can be seen in its 2017 national election manifesto. Citing concerns over rising income inequality and poverty, Labour's manifesto proposes increased taxes on wealthy individuals and corporations to fund higher public spending, including a £30 billion ($37 billion) increase to the NHS budget and additional funds for free student tuition, expanded childcare, the reinstatement of housing benefits, and a minimum wage increase to £10 per hour by 2020 (Labour Manifesto 2017). The manifesto rejects proposals to raise the pension age further. It also plans to put an end to zero-hour contracts that do not guarantee a minimum number of work hours. Building upon this manifesto, John McDonnell, Labour's shadow chancellor of the exchequer, prepared an "antiausterity" budget in 2018 as an alternative to the Conservative government's budget. Labour's alternative budget proposed a higher top tax rate to fund more public services and higher social spending (Labour Party 2018). The foundation of Labour's new platform is to increase taxes and reverse many of the cuts the Conservative-led government made to the welfare state. These policies represent an ideological shift within the Labour Party, which has become more critical of neoliberal capitalism. Reflecting this new position, Jeremy Corbyn promised to put an end to "greed is good" capitalism and to expand the state's role in the economy through the provision of more public services and higher welfare spending (*New York Times* 2018c).

Along with generating larger partisan divisions between political parties on the center-left and center-right, worsening social and economic conditions in the UK have led to the rise of the populist radical right (PRR) anti-EU United Kingdom Independence Party (UKIP). UKIP leveraged public disillusionment with the EU and mainstream political parties to achieve greater electoral success. In the 2015 general election, UKIP received a 12.6 percent share of the vote, representing a 9.5 percent increase since the 2010 elections (BBC 2015d). The party advocated for the exit of Britain (Brexit) from the EU and for more protectionist policies. UKIP has also advocated for stricter immigration policies, including greater limitations on access to welfare (McManus 2021). UKIP, for example, pledged in its 2017 and 2019 manifestos to limit access to the National Health Service (NHS) and other social services for immigrants until they have made five years of tax contributions (UKIP 2017, 2019). Similarly, UKIP wants to limit access to child benefits solely to permanent residents (*Telegraph* 2015). In line with the party's more conservative approach to the issue of immigration, UKIP also favors the liberalization and privatization of healthcare. In particular, UKIP has proposed privatizing key health services such as hospitals and surgeries (*Guardian* 2013b). It has also argued for the creation of a voucher system that would allow citizens to opt out of the National Health Service altogether (*Guardian* 2013b).

Beyond its Euroskeptic message, UKIP and other PRR actors embraced anti-immigration and welfare chauvinist positions. In some ways, this might be seen as an attempt to reframe left-right redistributive issues, in which PRR parties have little perceived competence (Mudde 2007), in nationalist terms. Advocates of the UK's departure from the EU, for example, not only railed against EU elites but connected the referendum to issues such as immigration and healthcare. One of the most infamous examples of this was the false claim made by the official Vote Leave campaign that the UK sent roughly £350 million per week to the EU, funds that could be used by the NHS. In addition to arguing that the EU posed a direct threat to NHS funding, UKIP argued that EU membership encouraged higher levels of immigration into the UK, which placed a greater burden on the healthcare system.

Under the leadership of populist prime minister Boris Johnson, the Conservative Party has proposed further healthcare restrictions on immigrants be put in place post-Brexit. Indicating the influence of PRR ideas and policies, the current Conservative-led government has adopted the position that foreigners need to reside in the UK and pay taxes for five years before gaining access to healthcare and other welfare benefits (Conservatives 2019). This represents a clear take-up of UKIP's 2015 election manifesto proposal. This populist strategy aims to incite fear of "outsiders" to help justify discriminatory health policies, particularly against marginalized groups (Speed and Mannion 2017).

But while welfare chauvinism and exclusionary policies have gained traction in the UK, it is unclear that the politics of social spending has been recast along a more sociocultural dimension. For example, while the Conservative Party took a stronger stance on immigrants, representing a co-option of UKIP's position, the party continued to support austerity and social spending cuts. This is in line with literature that suggests that even after accounting for PRR influence, welfare politics continues to be structured along the left-right political dimension (Guentner et al. 2016; Keskinen, Norocel, and Jørgensen 2016; Krause and Giebler 2019).

In addition to its success domestically, UKIP won a decisive victory in the 2014 elections for the European Parliament, receiving 26.8 percent of the vote (European Parliament 2014). Not only did this represent an incredible 10.7 percent increase from its previous results in the 2009 European Parliamentary elections, but UKIP was able to beat out both mainstream political parties, the center-left Labour Party and the center-right Conservatives (European Parliament 2014). UKIP's success rests on a growing populist movement that has gained momentum as more and more voters have felt the negative social and economic effects of austerity policies and have become disheartened with traditional political parties and the broader EU project.

The Effects of Partisanship at the EU Level

According to research by Thiemo Fetzer, both UKIP's electoral success and the decision of UK voters to support Brexit can be attributed to the austerity measures and social spending cuts implemented by the Conservative-led government beginning in 2010 (Fetzer 2018). This analysis suggests that individuals and regions of the UK that were more negatively impacted by austerity, including deeper welfare cuts, were more likely to support UKIP and Brexit (Fetzer 2018). This research goes on to suggest that had austerity-induced welfare reforms not been introduced, the Leave campaign would have been unsuccessful (Fetzer 2018). If this is the case, the Conservative Party's proausterity agenda not only profoundly affected social spending, but powerfully altered the future of the EU as the UK's decision to leave marks an end to seventy years of ever-greater political and economic European integration.

In addition to being a potentially key factor in explaining Brexit, the proausterity position of the Conservative Party also influenced EU social and economic policies in the wake of the GFC. Along with the German chancellor Angela Merkel, UK prime minister David Cameron was an advocate for austerity and fiscal discipline as the best strategies to address the Eurozone crisis. Representing a clear contrast between left and right party positions over how to handle the economic crisis, in 2010 Democratic US president Barack Obama wrote to Prime Minister Cameron and other EU leaders warning that premature cuts in government spending and social welfare could create further economic instability and potentially lead to a double-dip global recession (*New York Times* 2010b). Indicating his contrasting perspective, Prime Minister Cameron in a speech to world leaders at the 2011 World Economic Forum meeting in Davos, Switzerland, stated that "Those who argue that dealing with our deficit and promoting growth are somehow alternatives are wrong. You cannot put off the first in order to promote the second" (Cameron 2011). Cameron remained insistent on the need for austerity to resolve the economic crisis in Europe and continued to see high levels of public spending, on areas including welfare, as barriers to achieving this objective (*Economist* 2010a; EUCE 2013).

By contrast, the Labour Party, particularly under the leadership of Jeremy Corbyn, has been vocally opposed to EU austerity measures. In a 2018 meeting of center-left European parties, Mr. Corbyn argued against the "failed neoliberal policies" adopted in recent decades and emphasized his party's commitment to building a "socialist Europe" (*Independent* 2018). He also praised the success of the center-left government in Portugal, which reversed austerity policies, adopted higher social spending, and was able to achieve positive economic results (*Independent* 2018). The opposition of the Labour Party to EU austerity highlights the ideological differences that have emerged between parties on the left and right in the UK. In light of these divisions, political party control of government has become more significant in shaping the UK's position in EU social and economic policy negotiations.

Conclusion

Although political partisanship did not influence social spending in the UK prior to the GFC, as there was considerable support across parties for welfare liberalization, the crisis was a critical juncture that generated a clear shift in government policies and reshaped the politics of social spending. In the immediate wake of the GFC, the ruling Labour government adopted stimulus measures that included social spending increases. These measures represented an important break from precrisis policies, which emphasized social spending cuts and limited government intervention. The victory of the Conservative Party in the 2010 general election, however, marked the beginning of considerable welfare state retrenchment (EUCE 2013). Over the course of nearly a decade, the Conservative-led government has introduced the largest cuts to the UK welfare state since the end of the Second World War (Lupton et al. 2013; *New York Times* 2010a). These cuts reflect the Conservative Party's continued support for neoliberal ideas and policies. Although supportive of neoliberal welfare reforms before the crisis, the Labour Party has opposed social spending cuts postcrisis as the orthodoxy of these policies has come under greater scrutiny. Labour's opposition to welfare cuts only became stronger under the leadership of Jeremy Corbyn, who came to power on an antiausterity platform. Labour's resistance to Conservative policies goes beyond mere political opportunism and reflects a broader ideological shift, as the party, in recent years, has moved further to the left on issues such as welfare and economic governance, re-embracing its traditional left-wing values and policies. This includes commitments to higher taxes to fund more generous social spending. In sum, since the start of the GFC, political differences have increased between parties over austerity and welfare in the UK, and partisanship has become a key factor in shaping social spending (McManus 2018).

Conservative Party control of government has not only set the course of domestic policies in favor of austerity and social spending cuts after the GFC, but it has also influenced the UK's position in the EU. Under Conservative Party leadership, the UK has been a leading voice for austerity in EU policymaking, along with other conservative governments. David Cameron was a strong proponent of fiscal discipline and public spending reductions as the best means to address the Eurozone crisis. There is also evidence to suggest that the austerity and social spending introduced by the Conservative-led government may have been an important factor in explaining public support for Brexit (Fetzer 2018). If so, the Conservative Party's decision to cut social spending has profoundly affected the future of the EU. Ultimately, the UK provides compelling evidence for the influence that conservative party control of government has had on social spending after the GFC and the consequences of these policies domestically and across the EU.

CHAPTER 6

Sweden

Nordic Welfare State

"Like many societies, we went too far in our welfare-state ambitions."
—Anders Borg, Swedish Minister of Finance (2006–2014)

The statement by former conservative Swedish minister of finance Anders Borg highlights a key belief about the welfare state and government overreach held by the center-right Moderate Party. Inspired by neoliberal ideas, the Moderates, in recent years, have favored a platform that advocates for lower taxes, less government intervention, and a dramatic reduction in the size and function of the Swedish welfare state. This position reflects neoliberal beliefs that generous and universal Nordic welfare states are too expensive and inefficient and hinder competition and economic growth. These promarket policies were a central feature of Moderate prime minister Fredrik Reinfeldt's conservative administration, which governed Sweden from 2006 until 2014. In the wake of the GFC, there have been rising tensions between the traditional Swedish welfare model, built on social democratic ideals, and neoliberal pressures to promote a more competitive and market-oriented social protection system. While the center-left Social Democrats embraced neoliberal reforms and social spending cuts in the decades before the GFC, the party has moved further to the left postcrisis and has advocated for greater investment in the welfare state.

In many respects, Sweden is the archetypal Nordic welfare system, where the state provides well-funded universal social benefits and services (Pierson 1996, 2001; Esping-Andersen 1990, 1999; Kvist 1999; Häusermann and Palier 2008). The principle of universal social rights is a cornerstone of the Swedish welfare state in which benefits are extended to the entire population rather than welfare being targeted toward the vulnerable lower class through means-tested programs, as in Liberal welfare states. A wider proportion of constituents thus are beneficiaries of welfare state assistance than in many other countries. Due to generous social benefits, Nordic states, such as Sweden, typically have lower levels of poverty, income disparity, and social exclusion than other EU member states (Häusermann and Palier 2008). Citizens in Nordic welfare states, however, face higher tax burdens than those in other countries to fund a strong social safety net.

This chapter will provide an analysis of Sweden before and after the GFC to see how this event altered domestic social spending patterns and affected welfare state politics. The first section will examine social spending trends in Sweden during the two decades prior to the crisis. This period was notable as neoliberal reforms to the welfare state were introduced by parties on both the left and the right. This embrace of neoliberal reforms by the left is surprising given that the welfare state was built upon social democratic values that encouraged generous social spending and a large and active role for government. The second section analyzes the stimulus package put forth by the Swedish government in response to the GFC. This section identifies how the welfare policies and social spending increases outlined in government stimulus measures were influenced by historical welfare state legacies. These measures represented a break from precrisis welfare liberalization and retrenchment. Finally, this chapter will investigate the critical role that partisan politics has played in defining long-term social spending in Sweden after the GFC. Despite the generous and universal nature of the traditional Swedish welfare state, conservative party control of government created pressure for social spending decreases and welfare liberalization postcrisis. While this does not indicate a convergence of the Swedish model with Liberal welfare states, it does speak to the powerful influence that political parties play in influencing social spending outcomes even within one of the most universal and generous welfare states in the EU.

Swedish Welfare State Precrisis (1990–2007)

Welfare State Liberalization

In the decades preceding the GFC, the Swedish government undertook a series of social policy reforms that included efforts to liberalize, privatize, and shrink the size of the welfare state. This move toward welfare state liberalization and retrenchment was, in part, triggered by a financial crisis that Sweden faced in the early 1990s (Haffert and Mehrtens 2015). Beginning in 1991, the Swedish economy was affected by a major crisis stemming from failures in the banking sector (European Commission 2009b). Efforts toward financial liberalization and capital market deregulation that were implemented in the mid-1980s had effectively removed quantitative restrictions on the volume of bank lending. As a result, the Swedish banking sector saw a credit boom starting in 1985 and large investments in housing, commercial real estate, and the stock market (European Commission 2009b). This led to asset overvaluation and the eventual collapse of the housing market in 1991, creating widespread liquidity problems in the banking sector.[1] These banking failures had broader consequences for the Swedish economy and led to a sizeable increase in unemployment, a sharp decline in tax revenues, and higher public debt and deficits. As a result of this banking crisis, the annual deficit of the Swedish government soared from approximately 45 percent of GDP in 1990 to over 80 percent in 1994 (Englund 1999). The crisis of the 1990s in Sweden was one of the worst economic downturns in the country's history. Not only was economic growth severely weakened, but the cumulative employment loss was even greater than during the Great Depression of the 1930s (European Commission 2009b).

In the wake of the crisis, Swedish political leaders faced enormous pressure to pursue far-reaching fiscal consolidation and make drastic cuts to public spending (Englund 1999). By mid-1995, austerity measures equivalent to 8 percent of GDP had been adopted, which represented considerable budgetary reductions (Haffert and Mehrtens 2015). The crisis-management response adopted by the Swedish government during this time was notable for a high degree of political unity. Political leaders from the center-right coalition government and the center-left Social Democratic opposition party accepted a neoliberal agenda that recommended extensive welfare state reforms and a restructuring of public finances to bring the crisis under control (European Commission 2009b; Haffert and Mehrtens 2015).

The logic of fiscal consolidation and the necessity of neoliberal reforms,

---

1. In many respects, the causes of the Swedish banking crisis of the early 1990s were remarkably similar to those that led to the 2008 subprime mortgage collapse in the United States that triggered the global financial crisis.

which grew out of crisis-management policies, led to more sweeping welfare reforms in Sweden throughout the 1990s and 2000s. As in the case of fiscal consolidation measures, in the aftermath of the banking crisis, neoliberal welfare reforms received widespread political support from both left- and right-leaning parties (Bergh and Erlingsson 2009). Whereas welfare liberalization and retrenchment were introduced by a center-right ruling coalition in the early 1990s, the center-left Social Democrats continued these neoliberal welfare reforms once they came into power in 1994.

One of the most significant reforms that the Swedish government undertook was the 1990 tax reform. This legislation has often been referred to as the "tax reform of the century" since it was the most extensive transformation of tax policies that any advanced industrialized state had undertaken since the end of World War II (Haffert and Mehrtens 2015). Introduced by a center-right government, changes to the tax code reduced public revenue streams by lowering income and corporate tax rates. These neoliberal-inspired policy changes were intended to stimulate economic growth by encouraging higher levels of foreign investment and creating a business-friendly environment. For example, under the new legislation, the corporate tax rate, which had been at 57 percent, was reduced to 30 percent (Auerbach, Hassett, and Sodersten 1995). These tax reforms, however, had profound consequences for the Swedish welfare state since they reduced revenue sources for social services. The reforms undermined the progressive tax system that ensured that wealth was efficiently transferred from the rich to the poor (Agell, Englund, and Söderstein 1996). Since the Swedish welfare state relies on taxation as a primary source of funding rather than workforce contributions, as in the case of Continental European welfare states, these revenue cuts constrained government social spending.

After the 1990 tax reform, similar neoliberal tax policies were implemented by both left- and right-leaning parties. For example, in 2004 the Social Democratic–led government abolished the inheritance tax after reducing it several times beforehand (Haffert and Mehrtens 2015). After taking office in 2006, the center-right government reduced tax rates further and even went so far as to eliminate some taxes altogether, such as wealth and property taxes (Haffert and Mehrtens 2015). In 2014, the conservative-led government once again announced that it would cut income taxes, the fifth time it had done so since coming to office in 2006 (Haffert and Mehrtens 2015).

A second major reform in Sweden was to the pension system. A series of pension reforms adopted between 1994 and 1998 made the system entirely independent from the national budget, meaning that public funds would no longer be used to cross-subsidize pensions (Haffert and Mehrtens 2015). In other words, only revenues raised by the pension system itself would be distributed, and if contributions declined then benefits would be adjusted downward accordingly (Haffert and Mehrtens 2015). The goal of the reform was to reduce government spending and encourage the development of a Swedish investment culture in private pensions (Belfrage and Ryner 2009). Since these reforms were enacted, nearly 90 percent of Swedes have felt the need to invest in some form of private insurance in addition to their public pensions (Edlund 2006).

In addition to sweeping changes to tax and pension systems, Sweden also made significant reductions to its public sector beginning in the 1990s. Between 1990 and 1998, the number of people employed in the public sector declined by more than 200,000 (Haffert and Mehrtens 2015). As in the case of pension reforms, the objective of public-sector cuts was to limit government expenditures and emphasize greater reliance on the private sector. These reforms were embraced not only by parties on the right but also by leaders such as Göran Persson, the former head of the Social Democratic Party, who served as prime minister from 1996 until 2006 (Haffert and Mehrtens 2015). The prevailing neoliberal belief, that fiscal consolidation and social investment strategies that focused on competition would lead to higher economic growth, was largely uncontested at the time. This resulted in left-leaning parties, traditionally in favor of a well-funded welfare state, to justify a certain degree of retrenchment as a way to improve efficiency and make funding more sustainable. It is important to note that while several neoliberal reforms were introduced to the Swedish welfare state prior to the GFC, these changes did not entail a convergence toward a Liberal welfare model. Although Sweden had implemented a number of cutbacks to its welfare system, the state still maintained higher levels of social protection and a larger public sector than many of its EU counterparts (Vis 2009).

Swedish Welfare State Postcrisis

Crisis-Management Stimulus Measures (2008–2010)

Whereas welfare liberalization and social spending reductions had become prominent in Sweden during the 1990s and 2000s, the severity of the GFC required immediate and substantial government intervention to stabilize domestic markets and minimize the social costs for citizens. In many respects, the crisis-management response of the Swedish government in the aftermath of the Great Recession was in line with traditional Nordic welfare strategies, predicated on generous social spending and a high degree of state involvement. This response highlights the influence of the Swedish welfare state in defining government social and economic policies immediately after the crisis. While the severity of the GFC led the Swedish government to intervene in the form of an extensive stimulus package, the makeup of these measures reflected traditional Nordic welfare state policies rather than liberal market-based crisis-management strategies, such as those adopted in states like the UK.

In the wake of the crisis, the Swedish government passed a stimulus package worth SEK15.5 billion (US$1.8 billion) (US Federal Government 2009). Subsequent stimulus measures were adopted worth SEK45 billion (US$5.21 billion) in 2009 and SEK60 billion (US$6.95 billion) in 2010 (Swedish Ministry of Finance 2009a). Reflecting the generosity of the Swedish welfare state, the size and scope of these stimulus measures was much larger than that of many other EU member states (Chung and Thewissen 2011). In composition, the stimulus package reflected traditional Nordic welfare state strategies and goals, placing a strong emphasis on the expansion of already generous and universal social programs. One of the major objectives of the stimulus measures was to promote full employment while also providing high levels of income protection and unemployment benefits for all citizens (Swedish Prime Minister's Office 2008).

To address rising unemployment, the Swedish government relaxed requirements for unemployment benefits and abolished work history eligibility requirements (EIRO 2008; Swedish Ministry of Finance 2008). Public funds were provided to expand social programs at the municipal level, including a SEK5 billion (US$580 million) increase per year and a further supplementary SEK7 billion (US$810 million) adopted in 2010 (Swedish Ministry of Finance 2008). A number of changes in tax benefits were also introduced to provide greater income security, including a lowering of in-work tax credits, an increase in income tax deductions, and a reduction in state income tax. In sum, these measures provided a tax reduction of more than SEK1,000 (US$115) per month for 97 percent of full-time workers (Swedish Ministry of Finance 2008). Taxes on marginal income-based pensions were also lowered, providing more income to 90 percent of Sweden's pensioners (Swedish Ministry of Finance 2008).

The Swedish government also invested in workforce activation policies intended to facilitate higher rates of employment. Swedish stimulus measures provided funding for a variety of job training and vocational workshops, with the goal of training 165,000 individuals by 2011 (Economy Watch 2010). To promote education and skill development, the study allowance grant for individuals over twenty-five was increased to 80 percent of the total cost, and additional public funds were dedicated to a range of employment programs (EIRO 2009g, 2009h). The Lyft program was introduced, which created 40,000 temporary jobs in the public sector, providing employment opportunities and skill development for those out of work (Swedish Ministry of Finance 2009b; EIRO 2009g, 2009h). To increase employment incentives, the Swedish government lowered the payroll tax for employers and reduced the level of unemployment contributions required by employees (EIRO 2008). Reductions were even greater for youth workers who faced higher rates of unemployment than other demographic groups postcrisis (EIRO 2008; Swedish Ministry of Finance 2008). As an incentive for firms to hire the long-term unemployed, the government cut employment tax requirements in half (Chung and Thewissen 2011).

Overall, Swedish stimulus measures resulted in an expansion of universal social benefits and greater investment in workforce activation and skill development (Chung and Thewissen 2011). It is important to note that these strategies to address unemployment differed in important ways from other welfare state types. Whereas Germany, as an example of a Continental welfare state, intervened directly in the labor market, the Swedish government did not do so, relying instead on negotiations between social partners to come up with tenable solutions to rising unemployment (Chung and Thewissen 2011). While Liberal welfare states, such as the UK, adopted a largely hands-off approach to social policy after the crisis, the Swedish government was directly involved in providing high levels of social protection. For example, although the UK relied primarily on market-based tax incentives to encourage firms to hire more workers and was less willing to increase spending on unemployment policies, Sweden combined workforce activation policies with generous increases in unemployment and other social benefits (Chung and Thewissen 2011; Clegg 2010). The crisis-management response in Sweden emphasizes how institutional welfare state legacies shaped the policy choices and decisions of the government at the start of the crisis. Although the Swedish welfare state underwent a series of neoliberal reforms before the GFC, the stimulus measures adopted immediately after the crisis led to increased social spending and government intervention.

In addition to the social spending stimulus measures adopted by the Swedish government, automatic stabilizers provided a high degree of social protection for citizens. In the wake of the Great Recession, automatic stabilizers in Sweden absorbed 42 percent of the income shock, well above the EU average of 38 percent (Dolls, Fuest, and Piechl 2012). Automatic stabilizers acted as an even stronger buffer against the negative effects of the crisis on the Swedish labor market, absorbing a remarkable 68 percent of the unemployment shock, more than twenty points higher than the EU average of 47 percent (Dolls, Fuest, and Piechl 2012). The strength of these automatic stabilizing mechanisms speaks to both the scale and scope of the Swedish welfare system. Generous social transfers, in combination with stimulus measures, played a key role in stabilizing disposable incomes and household demand within the Swedish economy.

The Politics of Austerity (2010–Present)

The combination of generous social spending stimulus measures and strong automatic stabilizers provided significant protection for Swedish citizens against the negative effects of the economic crisis. This resulted in more limited social unrest and a higher degree of political stability than in many harder-hit peripheral European countries. But, although Sweden has not seen the same degree of political upheaval as some other EU member states, political party control of government has played an important role in driving postcrisis social spending. Unlike many ruling parties who were unseated in the wake of the crisis, the conservative Moderate Party, which gained office in 2006 on a platform emphasizing tax cuts, job creation, and welfare reform, was able to remain in power after the 2010 election. This was fairly remarkable for a party that had introduced considerable welfare cuts and privatized a number of state-owned companies, including in the education and health care sectors (Huffington Post 2014a).

Since coming to power in 2006 in Sweden, Prime Minister Reinfeldt's center-right coalition accelerated the pace of neoliberal welfare and tax reforms started in the 1990s. A major focus of the conservative government's platform was to reduce income, wealth, and corporate taxes as a means to promote competition and job growth, focusing on supply-side economics rather than government interventionist strategies (*Spectator* 2012). Reducing the tax base also meant reducing welfare funding. To this end, the conservative-led government tightened eligibility requirements for unemployment benefits and sick pay (The Local 2014a). Public spending as a percent of GDP declined nearly 20 percent from a record high of 71.0 percent in 1993 to 53.3 percent in 2013 (The Local 2014a). To put these reforms in perspective, of all the Scandinavian countries, Sweden has gone the furthest in reducing the size of its welfare state (The Local 2014a).

The neoliberal-inspired policies of the center-right government led to some economic success. Under the leadership of the Moderate-led government, Sweden's GDP grew by 12.6 percent, disposable household income increased as a result of tax cuts, and a large budget surplus was achieved (Huffington Post 2014a). But while economic growth and public debt and deficit levels improved in Sweden after the crisis, social conditions worsened in terms of poverty and inequality. Between 2007 and 2010, income inequality in Sweden rose considerably (by 1.0 percentage points measured by the Gini index), an increase that was only exceeded by Spain (3.0 points) and the Slovak Republic (1.7 points) (Dølvik, Andersen, and Vartiainen 2014). The poverty rate in Sweden also increased from 7.4 percent of the population in 2007 to 9 percent in 2010 (OECD 2014b). To put this in perspective, in 2010 the poverty rate was 8 percent of the population in Germany and 10 percent in the UK. Despite increasing inequality, in 2010 Sweden was one of the few OECD countries in which the richest 1 percent of the population had the lowest share of pretax income, around 7–8 percent, compared with 13 percent in the UK and Germany (OECD 2014b). This indicates that while social conditions had worsened after the crisis, they were still more favorable than in many other countries.

Rising social inequality, however, has generated concerns among center-left parties that promarket reforms have undermined the country's welfare system and harmed the well-being of Swedish citizens (Huffington Post 2014a). Postcrisis the unemployment rate had risen to around 8 percent, the highest of any Nordic state, and the youth unemployment rate had increased to over 19 percent (*Bloomberg* 2014a; Policy Network 2013). After 2010, the Swedish economy also began to slow down, with an average of only 1.5 percent GDP growth during this time (OECD 2015a). This has led to greater criticism of center-right decisions to cut taxes and reduce social benefits. Although the Swedish economy has been one of the most resilient in the EU after the GFC, concerns about economic growth, unemployment, and the well-being of citizens have led to partisan conflicts over welfare. This is notable, as such debates were largely absent in the decades building up to the crisis.

Postcrisis Political Divisions

Although generous social spending provided a buffer for Swedish citizens against the crisis, thus limiting social unrest and political volatility, divisions have grown between political parties on the left and the right over welfare. These political divisions reflect a growing ideological divide between those who continue to support neoliberal welfare retrenchment and fiscal discipline and those who question the orthodoxy of this strategy and instead favor greater government intervention and higher social spending. Given this politicization of the welfare state, political party control of government has played a critical role in influencing postcrisis social spending in Sweden.

Despite recognizing the need for fiscal stimulus in the immediate wake of the GFC, as the crisis continued the conservative-led government reaffirmed its commitment to fiscal austerity and welfare state retrenchment. In an interview, Anders Borg, the conservative Swedish finance minister, stated that he was determined that the 2008 economic crisis would not stop him from cutting the size of government (*Spectator* 2012). To this end, Borg continued to recommend tax cuts and social spending reductions to stimulate growth. This included unpopular measures to cut property taxes for the wealthy as a way to entice entrepreneurs and investors to return to Sweden (*Spectator* 2012). These policies emphasized market-led investments, rather than government stimulus, to increase demand and reduce unemployment. Corporate tax cuts, it was argued, would encourage business investment and job creation, leading to economic growth and lower unemployment. Similarly, cuts to income tax, it was argued, would increase the disposable household incomes, leading to higher demand that would fuel growth.

While Social Democrats had been supporters of welfare state liberalization before the crisis, the position of the party has shifted considerably since the start of the GFC. In the wake of the crisis, Social Democrats have been far more skeptical of the promarket reforms advocated for by the conserva-

tive government. Rather than embracing neoliberal reforms, Social Democrats have argued that these policies have weakened the welfare state, which
has led to higher levels of poverty, unemployment, and social inequality,
while failing to create more jobs or stimulate economic growth. Stefan
Löfven, the Social Democratic party leader, criticized Prime Minister Reinfeldt's center-right government, arguing that after seven years in power conservative policies had not worked. The policies of Mr. Reinfeldt's administration, he argued, have instead led to rising social inequality and an
unemployment rate that was higher at the end of their term than when they
took office (Reuters 2014b). In an interview prior to the 2014 election, Mag-
dalena Andersson, the Social Democratic finance minister, stated that "the
[conservative] government has done completely the wrong thing when they
have pushed through big and ineffective and expensive tax cuts instead of
making important investments in jobs and education" (*Bloomberg* 2014b).
This statement reflects the concerns of left-leaning parties that the tax cuts
and social spending reductions adopted by the center-right government
have critically undermined the welfare system.

Social Democrats have also voiced their opposition to center-right initiatives to privatize the national healthcare and education systems, echoing
concerns among the public that such policies would weaken the social
safety net. This issue became a prominent concern after a series of scandals
appeared in the Swedish media involving the falling standards in schools,
reports of overcrowding in hospitals, and mistreatment in elder care facilities (Huffington Post 2014b; *Wall Street Journal* 2014). Anxiety also
increased after the 2014 OECD Programme for International Student
Assessment sent shock waves through Sweden as the report indicated that
educational standards over the past decade had dropped well below average
in math, reading comprehension, and the natural sciences (OECD 2014b).
Sweden's schools, once leaders in education, now ranked below the United
States and the UK (OECD 2014b). Growing concerns over the effects of
neoliberal welfare reforms in Sweden highlight the growing divide between
parties on the left and right. Since the start of the crisis, Social Democrats
have shifted further to the left on issues such as the welfare state and economic governance. This move parallels a larger political shift to the left
among the voters in the 2014 Swedish general election.

Despite remaining in power after the GFC, the center-right coalition
faced a major political challenge from the Social Democrats in the 2014
national election. The Social Democrats ran on a policy platform to undo

the tax cuts and welfare reductions the conservative coalition had enacted, pledging to increase the government's tax revenue to fund unemployment and sickness benefits, invest in education, and to promote job creation (*Bloomberg* 2014b). To this end, the Social Democrats pledged to reverse nearly one-third of the SEK 130 billion ($18.3 billion) tax cuts that the conservative Moderate-led government adopted and use the increased revenue to fund education, child benefits, pensions, public-sector jobs, unemployment policies, and sick-leave benefits (*Bloomberg* 2014b; The Local 2014b). The Social Democrats also stated that they would increase spending by SEK 40 billion (US$5.7 billion) for welfare programs, schools, and job creation initiatives (Reuters 2014b).

Sweden's 8 percent unemployment rate was a major focus in the 2014 election, as Social Democrats cited poor job market performance as a failure of conservative policies. To address this issue, the Social Democrat's manifesto outlined plans to give the long-term unemployed jobs in the public or voluntary sector, increase unemployment benefits to 80 percent of previous salary earnings, and guarantee young people a job, trainee position, or education within ninety days of unemployment (The Local 2014b). The stated goal of these policies was to make the Swedish unemployment rate the lowest in the EU by 2020 (The Local 2014b). Not only did these policies represent a commitment to higher social spending, but they were also informed by traditional social democratic beliefs that the state should play a greater role in promoting employment. The Social Democrats' platform to increase social spending was in stark contrast to their precrisis position that accepted the need for limiting the size and scope of the welfare state. This shift to the left is an indicator of ideological changes within the party over welfare.

Political and ideological differences over taxes and social spending remained prominent in the 2018 general election. For the center-right Moderate Party, their 2018 platform continued to favor a combination of tax cuts and public spending reductions. For example, the party platform included income tax cuts worth SEK43 billion ($4.7 billion) over four years, including higher in-work tax credits and lower taxes on pensions (Reuters 2018b). Similarly, the Moderates' plan included additional tax cuts, such as corporate and fuel tax rate cuts equivalent to SEK50 billion ($5.5 billion) over four years (Reuters 2018b). The Moderate platform also outlined public spending and welfare cuts, such as a reduction in employment scheme funding, which would save SEK20 billion ($2.2 billion) over four years

(Reuters 2018b). The platform of the center-right Moderate Party, therefore, underscored its continued commitment to austerity and promarket policies.

By contrast, the Social Democratic 2018 manifesto included commitments to increase social spending and raise taxes. Overall, the party promised to boost public spending by more than SEK70 billion ($7.7 billion) over four years to strengthen the welfare state (Reuters 2018b). This included a proposed SEK14.6 billion ($1.6 billion) for higher pension payments and reduced income taxes for retirees, as well as an additional SEK7.3 billion ($800 million) in education funding (Reuters 2018b). To offset some of these costs, Social Democrats outlined plans to impose a tax on banks and increase capital gains taxes, which would raise government revenues by SEK5 billion ($550 million) per year (Reuters 2018b). The contrasting visions outlined in the Moderate Party and Social Democratic manifestos highlight major differences on the left and right over social spending. Since the start of the GFC, Social Democrats have renewed their support for the welfare state, reflecting an embrace of their traditional left-wing values. This shift appears to be part of a broader pattern in the EU as social democratic parties across Europe have moved further to the left on issues of the welfare state and economic liberalism (Bremer 2018).

The Effects of Partisanship at the EU Level

The growing divide between center-left and center-right parties in Sweden over welfare and austerity has had consequences not only domestically but at the EU level. Conservative party leadership in Sweden, in the years following the crisis, was important in influencing social and economic policy-making in the EU. While not fully embracing austerity as a cure-all for Europe's woes, Prime Minister Reinfeldt and his conservative government were still an important ally for countries, like Germany and the UK, that advocated for fiscal discipline and structural reforms (Huffington Post 2014b). Prime Minister Reinfeldt was often a reliable partner for UK prime minister David Cameron and German chancellor Angela Merkel in advocating for more promarket EU policies to improve regional competitiveness (*Wall Street Journal* 2014). Under center-right Moderate Party leadership, Sweden was a strong advocate of supply-side economics and ideologically attuned to arguments favoring austerity. Former center-right Swedish finance minister Anders Borg, for example, was a high-profile champion of fiscal discipline in the EU who argued that to address its debt problems and facilitate the recovery of European markets, the EU needed to accept austerity measures (*Wall Street Journal* 2014). The promarket ideology of the ruling Moderate Party in Sweden influenced the country's position in EU social and economic policy negotiations and contributed to the strength of a proausterity coalition of EU member states, composed of other center-right governments such as Germany, the UK, and Finland.

The electoral success of Social Democrats in the 2014 national election marked an important shift for social and economic policies both in Sweden and at the EU level. Among the priorities of the Social Democrats has been a relaxing of EU austerity requirements and an emphasis on the need for stronger social protection across Europe. In 2017, Social Democratic prime minister Stefan Löfven cohosted a European Social Summit in Sweden along with the president of the European Commission, Jean-Claude Juncker. This was the first Social Summit in twenty years. The event brought together leaders of twenty-five of the twenty-eight EU member states, EU representatives, social partners, and civil society actors to discuss ways to improve social conditions in Europe (Government of Sweden 2017). A key part of the summit was the proclamation of the European Pillar of Social Rights, which outlined the EU's commitment to principles ranging from greater equality and social protection to fairer working conditions and encouraging lifelong learning (Government of Sweden 2017). The main objective of the Social Pillar, as well as the Social Summit, was to offset the negative effects of austerity, restore public trust in political institutions, and promote a more social Europe. These goals reflect the view of Sweden's Social Democrats that a greater focus must be given to social issues and strengthening the welfare state in the EU.

The left-leaning ideology of the Social Democrats is also reflected in Sweden's position in EU debates over how to promote economic growth in the region. Whereas his conservative predecessor, Mr. Reinfeldt, worked closely with center-right governments to promote fiscal discipline as a means to achieve growth, Mr. Löfven campaigned for EU investments in job creation and education to promote growth, which would be funded by higher taxes on companies and the wealthy (Huffington Post 2014b). In other words, while center-right parties favored fiscal consolidation, Sweden's center-left party encouraged increased EU investments for labor market development and higher social spending. In this regard, the electoral success of Sweden's Social Democrats stands out as a rebuke to austerity at home and throughout the EU.

The GFC was a catalyst for greater political contestation over social policies in Sweden that had important implications within the country and at the EU level. Signaling the increased level of politicization since the start of the crisis, Sweden has not only seen a growing divide between the policy positions of center-left and center-right parties but has also witnessed the rise of the far-right Sweden Democratic Party. While the 2014 national election saw the return of the Social Democrats to power, the Sweden Democrats, an anti-immigration party with neo-Nazi roots, also saw their share of the vote rise to nearly 13 percent, from 5.7 percent in the 2010 elections, making them the third-largest party in Parliament (*Wall Street Journal* 2014). This followed the Swedish Democrats' success in the 2014 European Parliament elections where the party gained 9.67 percent of the vote and earned two seats in the legislative body (European Parliament 2014). Sweden Democrats joined several anti-EU parties that gained seats in the 2014 European Parliament elections.

The 2018 Swedish national elections saw unprecedented political polarization and instability as voters turned away from traditional center-left and center-right parties. Although the Social Democrats won the highest number of seats in Parliament, their vote share declined to 28.3 percent, the party's worst results in more than a century (Parties and Elections 2018). The Moderate Party came in second in the election but saw their vote share decline to 19.8 percent, the party's worst result in fifteen years (Parties and Elections 2018). By contrast, the far-right populist Sweden Democrats saw their best electoral result to date, claiming 17.5 percent of the vote (Parties and Elections 2018). As a result of the election, neither the traditional center-left nor center-right party was able to form a majority government or even establish a coalition government as both parties refused to work with the far-right Sweden Democrats. Although the Speaker of Parliament has the power to nominate prime ministerial candidates under these circumstances, the Moderate leader Ulf Kristersson and the Social Democratic leader Stefan Löfven were both rejected by Parliament, bringing the country closer to a forced snap election (The Local 2018). The 2018 general election, and the notable success of Sweden Democrats, therefore, has led to a political crisis in Sweden. As a party dedicated to nationalism, protectionism, social conservatism, and anti-immigration, the strong showing of Sweden Democrats in national and European Parliamentary elections signals increased polarization and an electoral push toward the political fringes since the beginning of the GFC. Much of the foundation of this polarization lies in the disillusionment many voters feel with traditional parties and EU institutions, growing concerns among some citizens over immigration, and the negative consequences of worsening social and economic conditions.

Conclusion

Despite its long history favoring universal and generous social programs funded through progressive taxation, Sweden introduced a series of neoliberal welfare state reforms in the early 1990s. These reforms were adopted in response to a serious financial crisis that many at the time saw as a failure of the social democratic model. In response to this event, policymakers on both ends of the political spectrum agreed on the need for Sweden to adopt neoliberal social and economic reforms. Political party differences at this time were not significant in shaping social spending, as a growing consensus had formed among parties in support of welfare liberalization. Neoliberal ideas became more prominent among Social Democratic leaders, bringing them more in line with the views of center-right political parties (Bergh and Erlingsson 2009; Bremer 2018). The decades prior to the GFC saw increased welfare liberalization and retrenchment in Sweden as political divisions over social and economic policies narrowed. As a result, political conflict over social spending was more muted as parties on the center-left and center-right pursued similar policies (Bergh and Erlingsson 2009; Haffert and Mehrtens 2015).

The severity of the GFC, however, necessitated immediate government intervention and social spending increases. These measures represented a break from the welfare retrenchment that had been introduced in the decades before the crisis and reflected a more traditional Nordic welfare state approach. In addition to creating demand for increased social spending, the GFC led to greater political divisions over welfare. Although the center-right governing coalition was able to maintain political power and continue its policies of tax cuts and welfare reductions to promote economic growth, they faced growing challenges from center-left parties. Most notably, the Social Democrats began to question whether neoliberal reforms had gone too far in undermining the welfare system in Sweden. The success of the Social Democrats in the 2014 general election marked a significant shift as the party began to prioritize more government intervention and social spending increases. Welfare spending remained a prominent issue in the 2018 national election, with sharp divisions between parties on the right that favored fiscal conservatism and those on the left that favored higher taxes to fund additional social spending. The results of the 2018 election also underscored the high degree of political polarization in Sweden as mainstream parties lost ground to the far-right Swedish Democrats. This political polarization has been made worse by negative social and economic conditions such as rising inequality and poverty.

Ultimately, the GFC acted as a critical juncture that renewed partisan divisions over the welfare state and social spending in Sweden. Although the conservative Moderate Party has continued its support for promarket welfare reforms and social spending cuts, Social Democrats have moved further to the left since the crisis began, embracing their traditional beliefs in higher social spending and a larger role for the welfare state. Political party control of government has, therefore, played a key role in shaping postcrisis social spending in Sweden. The Moderate-led government, which remained in office during the crisis until 2014, made deep cuts to the welfare state. Once in office, beginning in 2014, the Social Democrats reversed many of the tax cuts and welfare reductions adopted by the previous center-right government. These political differences have also been important in defining Sweden's position in EU-level social and economic policy discussions. While the Moderate Party was an important ally for other center-right governments in encouraging fiscal discipline throughout the EU, Social Democrats have been less supportive of austerity and have instead emphasized the importance of addressing social issues in the EU.

CHAPTER 7

Spain

Southern European Welfare State

> "The primary menace is inequality, which has surged under the policies of austerity imposed by the European Union. Spain has suffered a profound socioeconomic crisis, which has led us to our current political crisis. This is because the elite want to codify a social model based on the ongoing impoverishment of the majority of the Spanish people."
>
> —Pablo Iglesias, Secretary General of Podemos (2014–2021)

The statement made by Pablo Iglesias, leader of the far-left Podemos party, could have been taken straight from the slogans and banners held aloft by the thousands of antiausterity protesters who took to the streets of Madrid, Barcelona, Valencia, and other cities and towns across Spain at the height of the Eurozone crisis. This should come as little surprise, as Podemos arose from these grassroots protest movements and drew its support from increasing public dissatisfaction with the social and economic costs of austerity. Dr. Iglesias' comments emphasize the point that poverty and inequality are the primary issues facing Spain and that these social problems have intensified as a result of the fiscal discipline imposed by EU institutions. As the leader of Podemos, Dr. Iglesias has demanded an end to neoliberal policies and called for stronger social protections for Spain's citizens. This position highlights the political polarization that has grown in Spain between parties on the left and right over social and economic policies. It also reflects the tensions that exist between domestic political actors and EU institutions. Partisan conflict has intensified in Spain after the GFC and will have a lasting impact on the politics of welfare at home and the country's relationship with the EU and other member states going forward.

In many respects, Spain is a prime example of the Southern European welfare state. While some scholars have viewed welfare states in southern Europe as a subgroup of the Continental welfare model (Esping-Andersen 1999), there are distinct institutional characteristics found in Italy, Spain, Greece, and Portugal that warrant a separate category for these countries (Castles and Obinger 2008; Dolls, Fuest, and Piechl 2009, 2010; Ferrera 1996). These institutional differences are significant in explaining the distinct social and political outcomes seen in southern Europe after the GFC. While sharing many of the institutional features of Continental European welfare states, including pension systems, unemployment benefits, and labor market policies based on a logic of strong employment and wage protections, there remain important differences (León and Pavolini 2014). For example, the education and healthcare systems in southern Europe are more universalistic than the corporatist models found in Continental European welfare states (Ferrera 1996; León and Pavolini 2014). Social assistance and family support are also far more limited in southern European welfare states than in western and northern Europe (León and Pavolini 2014). Limited welfare benefits has led to a greater reliance on the family as an informal source of social support in southern Europe than in other countries (Karamessini 2007; Palme et al. 2009).

Labor markets in southern Europe are strongly dualized, which results in large gaps in social benefits between standard and nonstandard workers (Moreno 2000; Picot and Tassinari 2014). Although there are similar labor market divisions between insiders and outsiders in Continental European welfare states, the disparity between these groups is far more pronounced in Southern Europe. This is due to the lower levels of social protection for labor market outsiders and the high incidence of nonstandard work contracts. Overall, the defining features of the Southern European welfare state include distinct institutions and principles that represent a unique model that is different from the systems found in Continental Europe (Ferrera 1996; León and Pavolini 2014; Moreno 2000).

To understand the unique characteristics of Southern European welfare states, it is important to note the relatively recent development of the social protection systems in these Mediterranean countries. While advanced welfare states emerged in most of western Europe at the end of World War II, it was not until the democratic transitions of the 1970s that the modern welfare state in southern Europe emerged. The experience of authoritarian rule in southern Europe limited economic growth and the modernization process, resulting in underdeveloped welfare states compared to the rest of Europe (Ferrera 1996; Moreno 2000). As a result of this late development, Southern European welfare states are much smaller and less generous than many of their EU counterparts (Moreno 2000; Scruggs, Detlef, and Kuitto 2014). The result is fewer social benefits and lower levels of protection for citizens against economic shocks. Since Continental European welfare states are much larger by comparison, they provide stronger automatic stabilizers, which protect citizens by increasing social spending during a crisis. By contrast, the smaller welfare states in Southern Europe have weaker automatic countercyclical responses (Dolls, Fuest, and Piechl 2010). As a result, social spending decisions, which rely on the use of discretionary budgets, are more likely to be subject to political debates and partisan divisions (Starke, Kaasch, and van Hooren 2012).

Spanish Welfare State Precrisis

Democratic Transition and Early Welfare Modernization (1975–1990)

After the death of Franco in 1975, Spain began a transitional period from authoritarian rule to full democracy. By 1980, social spending was only 17.1 percent of GDP, compared to the EU average of 21.9 percent of GDP (Guillén 2010). Throughout the 1980s and early 1990s, however, Spain saw significant expansion in terms of coverage and expenditures for welfare programs, particularly in universal education and health services (Guillén 2010; Moreno 2000). In 1986 the Spanish government adopted the General Health Act, which provided universal healthcare for all citizens, which by 1991 covered 99.8 percent of the Spanish population (Almeda and Sarasa 1996). Unemployment benefits were also expanded in the late 1980s and early 1990s to cover 50 percent of the unemployed population (Jeong 2010). The government during this time also expanded access to primary and secondary education and provided scholarship funding for low-income families to gain entry into higher education (Moreno and Arriba, 1998).

Social spending increases during this early democratic period far outpaced economic growth and represented a significant investment by the Spanish government in the welfare state, which lagged behind many other EU countries. From 1975 to 1980 social expenditures grew annually at 8.9 percent, while GDP only increased an average of 1.8 percent each year

(Moreno 2000). Social spending as a percentage of GDP continued to grow significantly between 1980 and 1992 by 4.4 percent, higher than the EU average of 2.7 percent (Moreno 2000). Although at 22.5 percent of GDP by 1992, social spending in Spain remained below the EU average of 27.1 percent, and the rate of social spending expansion represented a clear process of catch-up with the more established EU welfare states (Moreno 2000).

Efforts toward welfare state expansion and economic liberalization were largely driven by Spain's entry into the European Economic Community (EEC) in 1986 and its adoption of the Maastricht Treaty in 1992, which inducted Spain as a member of the European Monetary Union (Oliver-Alonso and Valles 2005). European integration put pressure on the Spanish government to bring the country's welfare state closer in line with EU social standards by extending universal health, education, and other social benefits (Guillén and Alvarez 2001; Oliver-Alonso and Valles 2005). At the same time, Maastricht Treaty convergence requirements stressed Spain's need to open its economy to international trade, adopt strict fiscal requirements, and liberalize aspects of its economy and labor market.

Welfare Expansion and Liberalization (1990–2007)

Beginning in the 1990s, Spain underwent a series of welfare state reforms that in addition to expanding social protection and closing welfare gaps, emphasized liberalization, efficiency, and budgetary discipline. The objective of these reforms was to introduce greater competitiveness to the Spanish economy and welfare state as well as to increase labor market flexibility. A particular area of focus was on the adoption of neoliberal labor market reforms and workforce activation measures to help increase employment for outsider groups. Due to a high degree of employment and wage protections for the core workforce and a traditional male-breadwinner model, Spain in the 1980s and early 1990s had one of the most rigid labor markets in western Europe (Guillén 2010). Between 1993 and 1994, a number of liberal reforms were introduced to the Spanish labor market. Policies that encouraged job creation and the greater workforce participation of labor market outsiders were put in place, including tax and social contribution exemptions for companies hiring youth workers, the long-term unemployed, workers forty-five years and older, and the disabled (Guillén 2010). Workforce development and job training programs were also introduced to improve the quality of the workforce. Family and care policies also saw a modest expansion in the 1990s, in part to ease the burden on women and encourage greater female workforce participation (Guillén 2010). These labor market reforms aimed to promote private investment and encourage economic competitiveness. These policies complemented efforts by the Spanish government to open the economy to international markets. A major feature of these reforms was the introduction of fixed-term contracts that allowed firms to hire and fire workers on a part-time basis more easily. Employment protection and social benefits, however, remained largely untouched for much of the core workforce.

Although fixed-term contracts, introduced in the 1980s and 1990s, allowed for greater labor market flexibility, the core workforce in Spain retained high levels of employment and wage protection. These temporary contracts, which quickly accounted for 30 percent of all salaried workers, allowed for cyclical employment during times of economic growth but did little to offer stable employment and benefits to labor market outsiders (Guillén 2010). As a result, the Spanish labor market became more dualized and was unable to effectively reduce long-term unemployment. Attempts to address the problem of dualization and to further liberalize the core labor market were introduced in 1994, 1997, 2001, and 2006, although significant protection gaps remained for the long-term unemployed, nonstandard workers, and new labor market entrants (Picot and Tassinari 2014). Due to the continuous entry and exit from the labor market of nearly a third of the workforce, the costs of unemployment benefits grew sharply. As a result, the National Institute for Unemployment (INEM) nearly faced bankruptcy in the 1990s, and cost containment and retrenchment became necessary.

While Spain had expanded social benefit access to a wider portion of its population in efforts to bring the welfare state in line with other EU members, cost containment pressures to meet Maastricht fiscal requirements led the government to introduce welfare cutbacks in some areas to achieve debt and deficit targets (Guillén 2010; Petmesidou 2019). Whereas social expenditures as a percentage of GDP had expanded significantly during the 1980s and early 1990s, by 1993 spending had peaked and would decrease throughout the rest of the decade. Certain social benefits were also reduced at this time. In 1992, for example, unemployment benefits became more restrictive and coverage rates fell dramatically from 80.3 percent in 1992 to 50.7 percent by 1995 (Ministerio de Trabajo 1996). This was the result of a government decree that introduced cuts to unemployment coverage, reduced the amount and length of benefits, tightened eligibility conditions, and increased work requirement periods from six months to one year (Royo 2006). Although unemployment coverage had increased significantly since the Franco era, in the 1990s benefit rates were lowered and means-tested benefits were introduced, rather than universal measures (Sanchez de Dios 1998). Legislation introduced in 1985 led to substantial cuts in the social security system equivalent to around US$ 600 million (Bermeo and Garcia-Duran 1994).

During the 1980s, pension costs grew by 23 percent in real terms in Spain. These rising costs put greater strain on Spanish finances. A series of rationalizing measures to reduce the cost of the pension system were also introduced in the 1980s and 1990s (Ferrera 2010). This included the expansion of minimum contribution periods from ten to fifteen years and changes to the formula used to calculate benefits, which lowered payments (Guillén 2010). The private sector also took on a larger role in the pension system, accounting for 40 percent of all workers (Guillén 2010).

During the 2000s and up until the GFC, the government expanded welfare benefits while at the same time implementing a series of cost-containment measures. In the area of family policy, the government introduced a paternity leave policy for public administration workers in 2006 and increased funding for public care facilities for children up to three years of age (Guillén 2010). A national law, the Ley de Dependencia, was also adopted in 2006 that established a universal right to long-term care for individuals with reduced autonomy (León and Pavolini 2014).

Overall, the development of the Spanish welfare state from its transition to democracy until the start of the 2008 economic crisis, can be characterized as one of both welfare expansion and liberalization. This evolution follows a very different trend from that of northern Europe and can best be understood as driven by a desire for Spain to catch up with the rest of the EU in terms of social benefit levels and coverage, while at the same time seeking to liberalize its economy, welfare state, and labor market. In the early years, from 1980 until 1991, Spain's integration into the EU allowed the government to justify increasing social spending to bring it in line with other EU members (Bernaciak 2015; León and Pavolini 2014). The signing of the Maastricht Treaty in 1992, however, marked a shift in Spanish welfare state development where the desire to expand social benefits was coupled with an emphasis on welfare efficiency and budgetary discipline. The convergence criteria required by the Maastricht Treaty to join the European Monetary Union put pressure on the Spanish government to focus on inflationary targets, deficits levels, and domestic spending limits. As a result, the objective of catching up on social spending often remained secondary to concerns about cost containment, efficiency, and competition (Bernaciak 2015). Maastricht Treaty rules not only emphasized liberalization but constrained domestic decision making on social policies (Ferrera 2005). The rising costs of new social programs and a shift in focus toward limiting public deficits led to a decline in social spending beginning in 1992. Overall, from the 1990s until the start of the GFC, Spain modestly expanded social benefits while at the same time introducing a series of neoliberal welfare state reforms.

Precrisis Political Support for Welfare Expansion and Liberalization

The perceived need to catch up with EU social standards and a desire to meet Maastricht Treaty requirements led to considerable consensus across political parties and among the public in general precrisis. After its accession into the EEC in 1986 and signing the Maastricht Treaty in 1992, there was a strong desire among government leaders and Spanish citizens to achieve social and economic convergence with other EU member states (León and Pavolini 2014; Moreno 2000). This desire to catch up with the rest of Europe led both the center-right People's Party (PP), which was in power from 1996 to 2004, and the center-left Spanish Socialist Workers' Party (PSOE), which was in power from 2004 to 2011, to introduce similar policies to expand the welfare coverage while at the same time introducing neoliberal reforms in areas such as labor market protection (León and Pavolini 2014). There was considerable cross-party support, for example, for promoting legislative and institutional changes that would allow for more female workforce participation (León 2011; Valiente 2013). In the area of family policies, both center-right and center-left governments increased funding during their time in office (León and Pavolini 2014), but this expansion in welfare coverage did not necessarily entail an improvement in the quality of social benefits nor did it prevent an increase in private-sector care providers, which reflects a liberalization of social support (León and Pavolini 2014).

During its tenure in office from 1982 until 1996 and again from 2004 to 2011, the left-wing PSOE-led government introduced reforms that expanded access to welfare while also lowering social benefit levels to bring the budget into balance (Magone 2004; Solsten and Meditz 1988). This included reducing employment and wage protections for the core work-force (León and Pavolini 2014). The PSOE introduced social benefit restrictions, including reducing the length of unemployment support, to cut welfare spending (Royo 2006). While dedicated to expanding the reach of the welfare state, many of the social and economic policies implemented by the PSOE-led government reflected prevailing neoliberal ideas (Guillén 2010). The conservative PP party, which ruled from 1996 until 2006, pursued similar social and economic policies. While embracing a neoliberal agenda focused on deregulation, market liberalization, economic competitiveness, and welfare cost containment, the PP did not make drastic cuts to the welfare state (Llamazares 2005).

Overall, parties on the left and right sought to strike a balance between welfare state expansion and social and economic liberalization in the pre-crisis period (León and Pavolini 2014; Moreno 2000). The desire for EU integration helps to explain continued public support for some of the harsh economic measures and social benefit restrictions that various governments adopted (Moreno 2000). The underlying logic of catching up with the rest of the EU allowed for significant restructuring of the labor market and the lowering of certain social benefits held by the core workforce. For example, the social pacts agreed upon by unions and other social partners in 1996 and 2006 introduced increased flexibility into the labor market by allowing for more open-ended contracts and modified part-time contracts, as well as reducing the costs of laying off workers (Guillén 2010).

By 2007, the Spanish welfare state had been vastly improved from the predemocratic period, with benefits extended to a broader population and social spending at higher levels. Pension and healthcare coverage by 2007 was around 80 to 85 percent of the total population, and unemployment benefits, despite some of the reductions in the 1990s, covered a much wider cross-section of the workforce (Guillén 2010). Labor market reforms also introduced some flexibility, although part-time contracts with limited social protection exacerbated issues of dualization and persistent unemployment (Picot and Tassinari 2014). By the eve of the GFC, the Spanish welfare state was significantly more developed in terms of coverage and expenditures than in the early democratic phase, with social spending as a percentage of GDP more than five points higher than in 1980 (OECD 2015b). Despite these improvements, however, the welfare state remained small by EU standards, with social spending in 2007 at 20.3 percent of GDP, well below the EU average of 25.3 percent (Eurostat 2015). While GDP per capita had improved in the decades before the Great Recession in Spain, as well as Portugal and Greece, per capita social spending had not kept pace, indicating that these southern European welfare states underspent on welfare compared to their European counterparts (Petmesidou 2019). As the negative effects of the GFC became widespread, the consequence of the smaller and less far-reaching Spanish welfare state would have profound effects on social conditions in the country as unemployment rose precipitously and social protections remained limited. Spain would also see much higher levels of political volatility and polarization than in many other EU member states.

Spanish Welfare State Postcrisis

Crisis-Management Stimulus Measures (2008–2010)

In the decade before the GFC, Spain had seen steady economic gains, with an average GDP growth rate of nearly 3.8 percent from 2000 to 2007 (OECD 2015b). This was significantly higher than the Eurozone average of 2.2 percent at this time (OECD 2015b). Although Spanish unemployment in 2007 was at 8.2 percent, higher than the 7.1 percent EMU average, this represented a decade low for the country (OECD 2015b). The onset of the Great Recession, however, had a considerably negative effect on the Spanish economy. In the first two years of the crisis, GDP fell by 7.3 percent, which, though significant, was slightly better than the 7.6 percent average drop across the Eurozone (OECD 2015b). In part due to a high degree of labor market dualization and an overreliance on short-term contracts, however, unemployment rose precipitously from 8.2 percent in 2007 to a staggering 26.1 percent by 2013 (OECD 2015b; Picot and Tassinari 2014). The unemployment rate for labor market outsiders, which had always been higher than for the core workforce in Spain, was far worse. Workers who were hired on short-term contracts faced mass layoffs in the wake of the crisis. As a result, certain populations, notably youth workers, were disproportionately affected by the severe economic slowdown in terms of employment and social protection (Dellepiane and Hardiman 2012; OECD 2010b). In 2006, perpetually high youth unemployment had reached a ten-year low of 17.9 percent (OECD 2015b). By 2013, youth unemployment had risen to a shocking 55.5 percent (OECD 2015b).

As the crisis progressed, many short-term contracts, which covered a large proportion of Spanish workers, were not renewed, resulting in large-scale unemployment (Picot and Tassinari 2014). The collapse of the housing market contributed to worsening economic conditions and poor employment outcomes as workers in the construction sector faced massive layoffs (Bentolila et al. 2012; Royo 2006). In response to this drastic economic downturn, the center-left PSOE government adopted generous stimulus measures beginning in 2009 to offset the social and economic consequences of the crisis. The stimulus package introduced by the PSOE government was one of the largest of any EU member state as a percent of GDP, worth €12.31 billion ($17.1 billion) equivalent to around 1.1 percent of GDP (European Parliament 2009; Watt and Nikolova 2009). Nearly half of these funds, €5.9 billion ($8.2 billion), worth 0.5 percent of GDP, were dedicated to employment policies and household benefits (European Parliament 2009). The PSOE-led government also adopted a temporary €420 ($584) monthly payment for long-term unemployed workers who had exhausted standard welfare benefits (EIRO 2009i; Picot and Tassinari 2014). These measures passed despite opposition from the conservative PP party, which argued that these measures would be too costly and do little to address the underlying causes of unemployment (EIRO 2009i). This opposition highlights growing political divisions between parties on the left and right over welfare and appropriate fiscal responses to the recession.

Whereas concerns over cost containment were pervasive across parties precrisis, the center-left government believed that the severity of the crisis necessitated a strong government response in the form of fiscal stimulus. The stimulus package introduced by the PSOE combined tax cuts and social spending increases as a way to provide countercyclical support that would improve demand, encourage growth, and reduce unemployment. The types of measures and generosity of the social spending response reflected the government's partisan orientation, as Prime Minister Zapatero stressed the social democratic values behind these policies (Dellepiane and Hardiman 2012). These Keynesian policies were in stark contrast to the fiscal adjustment strategies adopted by liberal countries, such as Ireland and the UK, which sought to reduce public expenditures and implement austerity (Dellepiane and Hardiman 2012). The stimulus response by the Spanish government was consistent with the European Economic Recovery Plan put forth by the European Commission, which emphasized the necessity of countercyclical spending increases to reduce the social and economic consequences of the crisis (European Commission 2008).

Although the stimulus response of the Spanish government was considerable, as a percentage of GDP it was still smaller in total value than that of wealthier EU members such as France, Germany, and the UK (European Parliament 2009). Due to the smaller size of Spain's welfare state, the crisis was met in Spain by weaker automatic stabilizer effects. In fact, automatic stabilizers in Spain accounted for only 28 percent of income shock absorption (Dolls, Fuest, and Piechl 2012). This was far below the EU average of 38 percent and among the lowest in the region (Dolls, Fuest, and Piechl 2012). The automatic stabilizer response for the job market was similarly weak, accounting for only 38 percent of the unemployment shock after the crisis, compared with an EU average of 47 percent (Dolls, Fuest, and Piechl 2012). The automatic stabilizer effects on unemployment in Spain were also considerably lower than in states in northern Europe. For instance, automatic stabilizers accounted for 82 percent of the unemployment shock absorption in Denmark, 68 percent in Sweden, and 62 percent in Germany (Dolls, Fuest, and Piechl 2012). As we have seen in other EU cases, automatic stabilizers played a key role in offering an immediate buffer against the effects of the GFC. Whereas countries in northern Europe were able to limit unemployment and income loss through automatic social spending increases, Spain, and many of its southern European neighbors, had much more limited responses. As a result, we see far higher levels of unemployment and social instability in this region compared to other parts of the EU with more mature welfare states. The weaker automatic stabilizer response in Spain also meant that social spending increases had to come from discretionary budgets. This allowed for more political contestation over decisions to expand or reduce social spending and helps to explain the pronounced political divisions that have emerged in Spain between parties on the left and right over welfare and fiscal discipline after the crisis.

The Politics of Austerity (2010–Present)

While the center-left PSOE government was able to increase social spending at the start of the GFC, slow growth and continued problems with soaring unemployment led to a sharp rise in public expenditures (Picot and Tassinari 2014). This led to a considerable increase in Spanish public debt as the crisis continued. Whereas Spanish debt was a mere 41.7 percent of GDP in 2007, by 2014 it reached 117.7 percent (OECD 2015b). As it became clear that the Spanish economy was facing more than a temporary downturn, the government came under intense pressure, especially from EU institutions, to reduce debt and deficit levels (Dellepiane and Hardiman 2012; Petmesidou 2019). As the crisis persisted and concerns over sovereign debt repayments increased, the European Commission, which had initially encouraged stimulus, began to argue that fiscal increases should be temporary and that by 2010 member states should begin to cut spending to balance budgets (European Parliament 2009). In 2010, the Eurogroup, an informal collection of Eurozone finance ministers, met and demanded that Spain adopt austerity measures to lower public deficits and debt (Picot and Tassinari 2014).

This pressure came to a head in 2010 as fears over Greek sovereign debt repayments led to growing EU financial market uncertainty. In response to this international pressure, in 2010 the Spanish government began to phase out stimulus. The PSOE, however, initially sought to make deficit reductions not by cutting spending but through tax increases such as ending a tax rebate scheme and raising the VAT, which increased tax revenue by about 1.5 percent of GDP (Dellepiane and Hardiman 2012). The goal of this approach was for the left-leaning government to lower the budget deficit and still maintain high levels of social spending to support the large number of unemployed citizens. This agenda was in contrast to the conservative PP opposition party, which argued for large spending reductions, including welfare cuts (Dellepiane and Hardiman 2012). The policies of the left-wing PSOE government in the face of austerity differs from conservative-led governments in other EU member states, such as the UK, which implemented widespread and deep cuts to their welfare systems to balance their budgets (Dellepiane and Hardiman 2012).

Despite attempts to insulate citizens from welfare cuts, however, the PSOE was eventually encouraged, under pressure from the European Commission and ECB, to lower social spending (León and Pavolini 2014). In line with Eurogroup recommendations, in May 2010 the Spanish government adopted an emergency budget that included €15 billion ($20 billion) in public spending cuts from 2010 to 2011 (Dellepiane and Hardiman 2012). These measures included cuts to public-sector wages by 5 percent and 15 percent to politicians' wages, along with reductions in child welfare and pension benefits (*Guardian* 2010). These social spending cuts highlighted the stress placed on the center-left government to introduce fiscal reductions, despite the PSOE's attempts to resist such pressures. Even though cuts were eventually adopted, the PSOE maintained its ideological commitment to the welfare state rather than embracing a proausterity agenda. Although cuts were eventually introduced, the PSOE was able to rely on revenue from tax increases for about 60 percent of fiscal adjustments (Dellepiane and Hardiman 2012). In other words, even after mounting pressure from EU institutions to reduce deficit spending, the center-left PSOE government sought to insulate social programs from severe cuts and to protect core features of the welfare state.

Postcrisis Political Divisions

The Great Recession was a major economic shock in Spain that transformed political competition and introduced new issues into the policy agenda. Whereas economic issues were less salient and depoliticized in the precrisis period, they were by far the most salient and politically charged topic in the wake of the crisis. Party competition and political debates postcrisis largely focused on fiscal discipline and welfare (Vidal and Sánchez-Vítores 2019). Welfare became a highly politicized issue structured along a left-right dimension. At the right-hand side of the political spectrum, the PP advocated for austerity and welfare liberalization. On the other end of the spectrum, the PSOE supported greater social spending and government intervention to address rising economic inequality (Vidal and Sánchez-Vítores 2019). But while the PSOE initially resisted pressure to implement austerity measures, eventually it conceded to some reforms that further polarized Spanish politics and created an opportunity for the far-left Podemos to organize on an antiausterity and prowelfare platform.

Fiscal consolidation measures, while prudent to address Spain's debt and deficit problems, took their toll on the PSOE, which lost the support of many unions and other left-leaning parties. The adoption of fiscal discipline led to a loss of confidence in the government among the public and increased support for the conservative PP party. Throughout this time frame, the PSOE faced opposition from the PP, even after giving in to pressure to adopt spending cuts (Dellepiane and Hardiman 2012). This culminated in significant electoral losses for the PSOE in the 2011 general election, the party's worst performance ever, and resulted in a clear majority for the PP (*Guardian* 2011). This election result would lead to a clear shift toward fiscal conservatism.

Whereas the PSOE had resisted making cuts to the welfare state, the PP embraced austerity measures and social spending reductions. With a clear majority, the PP government, under the leadership of Mariano Rajoy, started implementing budgetary cuts and structural reforms. These measures were dissimilar to the policies adopted by the PSOE in the earlier phase of the crisis, which increased social spending to offset the negative effects of the economic downturn (Picot and Tassinari 2014). This policy change reflects ideological differences as the conservative led-government pursued austerity and a reversal of the social spending increases adopted by the PSOE (León and Pavolini 2014). Even when the PSOE eventually conceded to modest spending cuts, the party remained committed to social democratic values and agreed to welfare retrenchment out of necessity, rather than preference, and taking efforts to insulate core social programs from cuts. The PP legislative agenda, by contrast, reflected a neoliberal strategy to reduce social spending.

In July 2012, the PP-led government adopted sweeping social spending cuts and tax increases worth €65 billion ($83 billion) (*Guardian* 2012a). These austerity measures included reductions in unemployment benefits, an increase in the retirement age to sixty-eight years, and cuts in public-sector wages, as well as the closure of state-owned industries and the privatization of national ports, railroads, and airports (*Guardian* 2012a). These austerity measures, while the largest and most sweeping, were the fourth set of cuts implemented by the PP since coming into office seven months earlier (*Bloomberg* 2012). These reforms came as Spain's economy continued to struggle and fiscal concerns mounted. Spanish public debt had risen to 92 percent of GDP by 2012, up from 41.7 percent in 2007, and the government budget deficit for the previous year was 8.9 percent of GDP (OECD 2015b; *Wall Street Journal* 2012c).

Along with pressure from international financial markets to adopt fiscal consolidation, the EU had a strong influence over the types of policies that the PP adopted. In the days preceding the July 2012 adoption of austerity measures, the Spanish government was in negotiations with the EU for €100 billion ($128 billion) in bailout funds to prop up its struggling banking sector (*Guardian* 2012a). The bailouts included strict debt and deficit requirements, to be achieved through tax increases and social spending cuts (*Guardian* 2012b). These requirements reflected a shift in EU policy-making from stimulus toward austerity beginning in 2010. As sovereign debt concerns, particularly in Europe's periphery, grew, the European Commission and the ECB along with the IMF put considerable pressure on member states with high deficits to make deep across-the-board public spending cuts (León and Pavolini 2014). These bailout conditions strengthened arguments that austerity was the only viable policy response to the crisis, a stance already embraced by the conservative PP government. The influence of EU institutions in Spain underscores their ability to shape policymaking in member states. Spain's bailout negotiations confirm the indirect influence that the EU has over national social policies (Del Pino 2013; Pavolini et al. 2016). The talks also highlight the importance that economic concerns had over social concerns.

Along with the social spending reductions that were part of the 2012 austerity package, the PP introduced €6 billion ($7.7 billion) in cuts to the National Health Service (Social Europe 2012). Drastic cuts were also made to gender equality policies, childcare, long-term elderly care, and other family support benefits (León and Pavolini 2014). The center-right government was able to use the crisis and external pressure to push through deregulatory reforms in line with its neoliberal agenda (Picot and Tassinari 2014). For example, in 2012 the PP introduced far-reaching labor market reforms with the aim of introducing greater labor market flexibility and reducing labor costs. Collective bargaining was decentralized, giving priority to firm-level over industry-wide agreements, which shifted the balance of power in favor of employers rather than unions (Picot and Tassinari 2014). Employment protection was lowered for workers with permanent contracts, and the cost gap between firing full-time and temporary employees was decreased (Picot and Tassinari 2014). These policies represented a liberalization of the Spanish labor market and an attempt by the government to address dualization. At the same time that employment protections were weakened, however, these measures were not coupled with higher social support for labor market outsiders or restrictions in the use of temporary contracts (Picot and Tassinari 2014). There was also no increase in unemployment benefits or an expansion of active labor market policies, such as job skill training programs (Picot and Tassinari 2014). Highlighting the significance of partisanship, while Spain enacted neoliberal labor market reforms coupled with reduced social protection coverage for workers, Italy implemented more modest labor market reforms and adopted enhanced social protection for workers. A key driver of these divergent outcomes was the stronger influence of the center-right in Spain versus a stronger center-left influence in Italy (Picot and Tassinari 2017). Overall, the policies pursued by the center-right PP government in Spain constituted the largest welfare cuts since democracy was established in Spain and included some of the most transformative liberal labor market reforms in recent history (Social Europe 2015).

While successful in lowering budget deficits and making the labor market more flexible, the austerity measures implemented by the PP government led to political tensions fueled by high unemployment and rising inequality. In opposition to the PP, the PSOE adopted a platform in 2013 that included commitments to remove income tax requirements for the unemployed and pensioners, repeal the labor market reforms introduced by the PP, and increase funding for pensions, healthcare, family care, and education (Euro Intelligence 2013). This new platform represented a shift further to the left for the PSOE and highlighted the division between its policies and those of the conservative PP. The PP also faced opposition from far-left parties that capitalized on growing public disenchantment with austerity measures and welfare cuts.

In response to the PP's 2013 budget, which outlined €150 billion ($200 billion) in public spending cuts between 2012 and 2014, including welfare cuts, thousands of protesters took to the streets of Madrid and other towns and cities around Spain (BBC 2012a). These protests were in opposition to what many perceived as a systematic dismantling of the welfare state by the PP government (Social Europe 2012). These rallies were part of a larger grassroots movement called Los Indignados that organized ongoing protests and demonstrations against the austerity measures put forth by the PP government and promoted by the EU (BBC 2012b). These protests were part of an antiausterity movement that swept through much of southern Europe as citizens disenchanted with worsening social and economic conditions demanded more social assistance rather than welfare retrenchment. There has been an increased politicization of social and economic policies throughout the region as public dissatisfaction with austerity has grown in countries such as Greece, Italy, and Spain.

In addition to popular unrest in the streets, Spain has also seen greater contention in the political arena and the rise of the populist far-left Podemos party, which received support at the expense of traditional center-left and center-right parties. PSOE's perceived inability to manage the crisis and its concessions to EU pressure to implement fiscal discipline opened up a political space for Podemos as a leftist antiausterity alternative (Hutter, Kriesi, and Vidal 2018). Podemos was established in 2014 with the publication of its founding manifesto, which outlined the need to adopt radically different policy solutions to the issues of poverty, inequality, unemployment, and slow growth (Caballero and Alvarez-Diaz 2015). In particular, Podemos called for the end to austerity, the restructuring of Spanish debt, and an increase in social protection for all citizens, including an increase in the minimum wage, a return of the retirement age to sixty-five, and the annulment of the PP labor market reforms (Junor 2015; Open Europe 2014). Podemos is a political party that grew out of the Los Indignados movement and capitalized on rising public discontentment with Spain's mainstream parties. According to a November 2014 public opinion poll administered by Spain's leading newspaper, *El Pais*, Podemos was supported by 27.7 percent of the population, compared with 26.2 percent for the center-left PSOE and 20.7 percent for the conservative PP party (Junor 2015). This was the first time that the new party had come in ahead of its two traditional opponents in polls, indicating a large shift in Spanish politics. In fact, within a year of its founding, Podemos had more than 283,000 members, making it the second-largest party in Spain after the PP (Junor 2015).

Podemos's success, at the expense of the traditional PSOE and PP parties, has been part of a rising trend of public dissatisfaction with the two mainstream parties. The PP and PSOE saw their joint share of the national vote decline nearly 10 percent, from 83.3 percent in 2008 to 73.4 percent by 2011 (Funke, Schularick, and Trebesch 2015). This trend continued in regional elections, where, although the PSOE and PP were able to maintain their status as the two leading parties, they saw a sharp decline in their share of the votes. Whereas the PP and PSOE accounted for 65 percent of the vote in the 2011 regional and municipal elections, this had fallen to 52 percent of the vote in 2015 (*Economist* 2015). This was the worst local election result for the PP in twenty years as the party saw its share of the vote drop by ten percentage points (Reuters 2015d, *Wall Street Journal* 2015a). This loss of the vote share can be attributed to the entrance of alternative parties, like Podemos and the newly established right-wing Ciudadanos, into Spanish politics and the radicalization of the electorate (*Wall Street Journal* 2015a). The antiausterity message put forward by Podemos resonated with the Spanish people and reflects significant changes in the public's faith in the government after the crisis.

The introduction of Podemos into Spanish politics has led to a significant reordering of the political landscape in the country and has increased tensions between advocates and opponents of austerity (Vidal and Sánchez-Vítores 2019). The party has been highly critical of the conservative PP government, arguing that the austerity measures they implemented led to an impoverishment of the Spanish people and growing social, political, and economic crises. Podemos has also criticized the PSOE for its earlier embrace of neoliberal ideas and policies. Podemos leaders have argued that the neoliberal welfare and labor market reforms that PSOE supported before the crisis only served to undermine the Spanish welfare state and remove worker protections (*Nation* 2018). PSOE has also been blamed by Podemos for bowing to EU pressures to introduce budgetary cuts while in office after the start of the GFC (*Nation* 2018).

Podemos has taken on an even greater role in Spanish politics in the wake of a 2018 vote of no confidence, which saw the conservative PP leader Mariano Rajoy ousted from power and replaced by PSOE leader Pedro Sánchez. To strengthen his minority government, which only holds 84 of the 176 seats needed for a majority, Mr. Sánchez has worked more closely with Podemos (*El País* 2018a). A highlight of this new progressive alliance is a 2019 budget deal that includes several social spending measures, such as raising the minimum wage by 22 percent, the largest increase in forty years (*El País* 2018b). The budget also includes commitments to increase pensions by €1 billion ($1.14 billion), education funding by €1.3 billion ($1.5 billion), unemployment and disability benefits by €850 million ($970 million), housing benefits by €600 million ($685 million), and paternity leave by €300 million ($342 million) (*El País* 2018b). Although this budget may face opposition from the PP-controlled Senate and would require a negotiation with EU officials to raise public spending, the agreement signals a shift to the left in Spanish politics. The deal may also pave the way for a left-wing PSOE-Podemos coalition government after the 2020 national election (*El País* 2018b). The possibility of governing in partnership with the PSOE is a remarkable outcome for Podemos, a party that only a few years earlier was organizing street protests and had little formal power in Spanish politics. The new partnership also highlights the PSOE's shift further to the left on social and economic issues, with the party favoring the expansion of welfare programs and social spending increases.

The Effects of Partisanship at the EU Level

In addition to the impact that the emergence of Podemos has had on Spanish politics, the party has also influenced politics at the EU level. In the 2014 European Parliamentary elections, Podemos received nearly 8 percent of the vote and earned five seats in the EU body, a surprising outcome for a party that was formed less than half a year earlier (European Parliament 2014). As a result of this election, for the first time the two main parties, the PP and PSOE, had been denied a majority of votes (*New York Times* 2015b). Podemos's electoral success reflected a larger upset of the status quo within the European Parliament as parties on the far left and far right made significant gains over traditional centrist parties. In Greece, the far-left Syriza party won a large majority in the European Parliamentary elections, garnering 26.6 percent of the vote and earning six seats (European Parliament 2014). Aligning himself with Syriza, Pablo Iglesias, the leader of Podemos, made statements after the European Parliamentary elections that by pursuing austerity in Greece and other indebted member states, EU institutions and the IMF were threatening the European project and undermining democracy in the region (Reuters 2015e). These statements were a sign of solidarity with other far-left parties in the EU and a challenge to the austerity policies promoted by EU institutions and conservative governments such as Germany. The success of far-left parties, like Podemos in Spain and Syriza in Greece, marks an important shift in the EU political landscape as resistance to austerity measures has become fiercer and calls for alternative policies that acknowledge the importance of social problems have grown. The emergence of Podemos as a major player in Spanish politics reflects the politicization of social and economic policies and an electoral push toward the political fringes since the start of the GFC.

Conclusion

While dissimilar from many of its northern European counterparts, the development of the Spanish welfare state followed a path similar to many countries in southern Europe. After a transition to democracy in the mid-1970s, the government was dedicated to an expansion and modernization of the social protection system to bring it closer in line with the more advanced welfare states of other EU member states. During the 1990s and 2000s, welfare state development followed a process of social benefit expansion in terms of coverage, and liberalization in terms of cost containment and efficiency. The adoption of the Maastricht Treaty in 1992 created incentives for government leaders to pursue social and economic convergence with other EU members that led to considerable policy consensus across political parties and among the public (León and Pavolini 2014; Moreno 2000). The desire to catch up with the rest of the EU in terms of social and economic standards led parties on the left and the right to adopt similar policies to expand welfare coverage and introduce neoliberal reforms in areas such as the labor market (León 2011; León and Pavolini 2014; Valiente 2013). Overall, the social policies introduced in the precrisis period were relatively depoliticized, as there was agreement by the main political parties in Spain on the need to expand social benefits and reform the welfare state.

Whereas cost-containment concerns dominated Spanish policymaking before the GFC, in the immediate wake of this event the center-left PSOE government adopted a series of stimulus measures that included higher welfare spending, to offset the social and economic costs of the crisis. A high degree of labor market dualization and an overreliance on flexible part-time contracts, however, led to large-scale layoffs as economic conditions deteriorated. Unemployment in Spain soared after the crisis, with nearly a quarter of the population out of work. The results were far worse for labor market outsiders, such as youth workers, who faced an unemployment rate above 50 percent. Due to the small size of the Spanish welfare state and weak automatic stabilizer response, limited social protection was offered to unemployed citizens, who faced poor prospects of returning to work. As economic conditions worsened and demand for unemployment benefits and other types of social assistance continued to rise, the government was faced with difficult fiscal circumstances.

In 2010, fears over a possible Greek default on its national debt created instability in European markets, which led EU institutions to emphasize austerity as a means to bring domestic finances back in order. Despite adopting a generous stimulus package, the center-left PSOE was gradually pressured to implement austerity measures that led to welfare retrenchment. The PSOE, however, attempted to resist introducing welfare reductions by using tax increases, rather than social spending cuts, to lower its deficit. Although eventually capitulating to demands for fiscal discipline, the PSOE maintained its commitment to social democratic beliefs, emphasizing that austerity measures were being adopted out of necessity and not out of an ideological commitment. These policies, however, led to considerable unpopularity for the PSOE, resulting in an electoral victory for the conservative PP party in the 2011 general election. Unlike the PSOE, the PP was ideologically more attuned to neoliberal policy recommendations. Under PP leadership, Spain accelerated its fiscal consolidation process, and severe cuts were made to the welfare state. This marked a considerable turn away from stimulus and reflected a growing emphasis on austerity.

While helping to reduce debt and deficit levels, austerity measures resulted in increasing social and political volatility in Spain. High unemployment, slow economic growth, labor market dualization, and a limited welfare response resulted in increasing political polarization in Spain. Since the crisis began, the PSOE has adopted a more progressive policy platform, indicating growing differences between the two main political parties (Euro Intelligence 2013). Increasing popular unrest over austerity measures has led to a politicization of social and economic policies and a radicalization of the electorate, with newly established parties, such as the far-left Podemos, taking support away from the traditional PP and PSOE parties. This shift to the far left has not only transformed Spanish politics but has led to considerable contestation at the EU level over austerity. The success of Podemos and other antiausterity parties, such as Syriza in Greece, in the 2014 European Parliamentary election reflected tensions between advocates of fiscal discipline and opponents, especially in indebted peripheral EU members, who perceived austerity as counterproductive to economic recovery, social stability, and well-being.

In sum, Spain has witnessed a high degree of political conflict not seen before the crisis. There has been a growing divide between mainstream centrist parties as PSOE has shifted its platform further to the left on issues such as the welfare state and economic governance. Domestically, there have been high levels of support for new antiestablishment parties at the political extremes, which have undercut the traditional party support. While the long-term influence of Podemos has yet to be determined, political dynamics in Spain are likely to be influenced by nontraditional parties at least for the foreseeable future. This political sea change will likely continue to have an important influence on social and economic policymaking in Spain and throughout the EU in coming years.

CHAPTER 8

Czech Republic

Eastern European Welfare State

> "The European economic and social model [is one] characterized by government overregulation and by the unproductive welfare state."
> —Václav Klaus, Czech Republic Prime Minister (1996–1998) and President (2003–2013)

The statement made by the Czech Republic's first prime minister speaks to the centrality of neoliberal ideas at the heart of his center-right Civic Democratic Party (ODS) platform. Mr. Klaus is an avowed free-market advocate and Euroskeptic whose administration oversaw the early days of democratic and economic transition. Promarket ideas and policies were highly prevalent before the GFC in the Czech Republic and gained widespread support across parties who saw liberalization as essential to modernizing the economy and the welfare state. Mr. Klaus's comments reflect a neoliberal view of the European welfare state as an "unproductive" hindrance to economic competition and growth. It also speaks to Mr. Klaus's belief in the importance of deregulation and a reliance on the market, rather than on the government or EU institutions, to provide positive economic and social outcomes. Although there were pressures to bring Czech social spending and benefits in line with the more developed and generous welfare states of other EU member states before the GFC, there were also pressures, both internal and external, to introduce sweeping neoliberal reforms. Neoliberalism was highly influential during the early postcommunist transition in many central and eastern European countries and influenced the development of their markets and welfare states. These ideas have been challenged postcrisis by left-leaning parties who, although once supportive of these reforms, have started to push back against conservative austerity policies and instead supported higher social spending. Government social and economic policymaking became more structured along the left-right political dimension after the crisis across central and eastern European countries, including the Czech Republic, Hungary, Poland, and Slovakia (Myant, Drahokoupil, and Lesay 2013). After the GFC, the Czech Republic has seen a polarization and fragmentation of its political system and the emergence of left-right blocs with competing economic and social policy agendas that will be highly influential in the years to come.

The social protection system that developed in the Czech Republic after the fall of the "Iron Curtain" is representative of a distinct Eastern European welfare state type that emerged in the region (Aidukaite 2009a, 2009b, 2011; Arts and Gelissen 2002; Cerami 2010; Cerami and Vanhuysse 2009; Fenger 2007; Golinowska, Hengstenberg, and Żukowski 2009). While there are of course some variations in welfare state development between eastern European countries (see for example Hacker 2009; Lauzadyte-Tutliene, Balezentis, and Goculenko 2018), there are important similarities in terms of the institutions and policies that were adopted by national governments in response to the challenges of the postcommunist transition. The institutional features of the Eastern European welfare state provide an important explanation for the social spending patterns and political dynamics in the Czech Republic after the GFC.

Perhaps the most important historical precedent for the contemporary welfare state in eastern European countries, such as the Czech Republic, is the Bismarckian social protection system, with its corporatist structures and generous social and health insurance schemes funded largely through compulsory employee contributions (Potůček 2009; Żukowski 2009). This system was present prior to communist rule in the Czech Republic and its influence can be seen in present-day social provisions, including the pension system, unemployment benefits, and labor market policies, based on a logic of employment and wage protection rather than social equality and universal coverage (Deacon 1997; Jinsoo and Sojeung 2008). In the case of the health insurance system that was adopted after 1989, the Czech government and public opinion overwhelmingly supported a system of health coverage financed by compulsory employee, employer, and state contributions, rather than a more universal system funded through general taxation (Potůček 2009).

But whereas eligibility for benefits in Continental European welfare states is primarily based on labor market participation, the social protection system in the Czech Republic exhibits more universal tendencies (Aidukaite 2011; Potůček 2009). This embedded universal approach to welfare reflects the legacies of the communist system, in which social protection was part of the centrally planned economy. The welfare state in communist-led states in eastern Europe was predicated on a mix of corporatism and universalism (Saxonberg and Sirovátka 2009). Due to near full employment, the corporatist communist welfare system was effectively able to achieve universal coverage (Cerami 2010; Standing 1996). In the case of pensions, for example, although benefits were supposed to be linked to professional status, wage equalization in the communist system led to flat-rate benefits for everyone (Cerami 2010). Healthcare under communist rule was also universal and free to all citizens through a centralized national health care system (Kornai 2001). Household social support and family benefits were also extensive and aimed at encouraging full employment for men and women (Cerami 2010). These universal policies have continued in some areas of the modern Czech welfare state, including old-age pensions, disability payments, and healthcare, where full coverage is provided for all citizens (Żukowski 2009). After the fall of the "Iron Curtain," maintaining universal access to social security continued to be a central objective of the Czech government's response to the challenges of high unemployment and low economic growth (Aidukaite 2011).

It is important to note, however, that while the Czech Republic offers more universal welfare coverage than many of its continental European neighbors, benefit levels are far lower (Aidukaite 2011). Social spending as a percentage of GDP in 2007, before the GFC, was 17.5 percent, well below the EU average of 25.3 percent (Eurostat 2015). During the 1990s and 2000s, there were also efforts to introduce promarket social policies across eastern European welfare states, which coincided with wider neoliberal economic reforms (Aidukaite 2011; Potůček 2001, 2009; Saxonberg and Sirovátka 2009). The Czech welfare state, therefore, incorporates many features of other welfare state types, while maintaining certain arrangements that constitute a distinct Eastern European welfare model. This regime offers high social protection coverage, low social spending, limited means-tested benefits, and residual neoliberal elements throughout the social protection system (Aidukaite 2011).

Beyond examining the unique mix of characteristics present in Eastern Europe welfare states, it is vital to look at the postcommunist transition of these systems. Whereas welfare states in western Europe were founded at the end of World War II, it was not until the postcommunist democratic and economic transitions of the 1990s that modern welfare states developed in eastern Europe. The fall of the "Iron Curtain" in 1989 had a profound impact across eastern Europe, which fundamentally altered the social and economic context under which citizens lived and governments operated. Countries in eastern Europe at this time underwent an abrupt shift from centrally planned communist systems to free-market economies and from authoritarian rule to democratic pluralistic forms of government. During this transition, economic growth and labor market concerns became major issues. Whereas the communist system ensured near full employment, the transition toward a free-market economy led to huge changes in the labor market, including decreased demand for workers and rising unemployment. To address these concerns, welfare programs were introduced, such as compulsory health and social insurance, active labor market policies, and means-tested minimum social protections for all citizens (Potůček 2001). At the same time that states sought to provide comprehensive social protection for their citizens, rising unemployment taxed these new welfare states, and pressure to liberalize grew (Potůček 2001).

A legacy of communist rule was that by the start of the GFC, welfare states in eastern Europe were much smaller and less generous than social protection systems in western Europe (Eurostat 2015). After the crisis, citizens in these countries had fewer welfare benefits and lower levels of social protection against economic shocks than many of their western European neighbors. Since Nordic and Continental European welfare states are much larger and more comprehensive by comparison, they provide significant automatic stabilizers, which protect citizens by increasing social spending during a crisis. In contrast, the smaller Eastern European welfare states lack these automatic countercyclical responses and offer less of an immediate buffer against the negative consequences of economic downturn (Dolls, Fuest, and Piechl 2010). Welfare responses to the Great Recession in eastern Europe, therefore, relied on government discretionary spending. Therefore the decision to increase or decrease social spending was more heavily influenced by ideological beliefs and subject to partisan conflict.

Czech Welfare State Precrisis

Welfare Expansion and Liberalization (1990–2007)

Czechoslovakia transitioned from a communist-led state to a liberal democracy in late 1989 after a series of nonviolent protests known as the "Velvet

Revolution." This political reordering led to the end of forty-one years of communist rule and a transition from an authoritarian government to a parliamentary republic and a free-market economy. Shortly after gaining independence, the Czech government adopted a plan to offer universal compulsory social insurance and health coverage combined with means-tested welfare assistance to all citizens (Potůček 2009). Effectively, this system sought to replace state paternalism with a more decentralized and efficient welfare state. These reforms were informed by the social protection systems in place in other EU member states and the neoliberal economic reforms that were being implemented in the country at the time (Potůček 2009). This restructuring of the welfare state coincided with serious social problems resulting from the postcommunist transition, including an economic recession, high inflation rates, rising unemployment, widespread poverty, and deteriorating living standards (Aspalter, Jinsoo, and Sojeung 2009; Cerami 2010). As a consequence, many of the early welfare policies adopted by the Czech government after 1989 can be characterized as emergency responses to the social costs of political and economic transitions (Horibayashi 2006; Offe 1993). In other words, the social policies put in place were intended to provide a safety net for citizens during a time of intense political and economic upheaval. These measures included the establishment of a new compulsory social insurance system that provided universal benefits for the unemployed, families, the disabled, and pensioners (Potůček 2009). Bills adopted in the early 1990s, including the State Social Support Act, Subsistence Level Act, and the Social Need Act, established a commitment of the state to guarantee a basic standard of living for citizens above a minimum level of subsistence (Orenstein 1995; Potůček 2009).

While the first few years of the postcommunist transition saw the introduction of emergency measures to address social concerns such as rising unemployment, during the early to mid-1990s the Czech government began to implement a series of neoliberal welfare reforms. These policies can be attributed to internal and external reform pressures. By 1992,[1] a new government came into power that emphasized the need to embrace neoliberal economic reforms and a more limited welfare state (Potůček 2009). Decisions to reduce social spending reflected increasing budgetary pressures domestically, and the growing acceptance of neoliberal ideas and poli-

---

1. During this same year, Czechoslovakia peacefully divided into two independent states, the Czech Republic and the Slovak Republic.

cies throughout eastern Europe advocated for by international organizations such as the IMF and World Bank (Horibayashi 2006). The neoliberal welfare agenda for the region emphasized means-tested benefits and the privatization of pensions and healthcare (Deacon 1997). Eligibility requirements for unemployment benefits in the Czech Republic, for example, became more restricted during the 1990s. Whereas unemployment benefits were paid for an entire year in 1991 at 90 percent of earnings for the first six months and 60 percent of earnings thereafter, the length and generosity entitlements were reduced so that by 1999 only 50 percent of earnings were paid in the first three months and 40 percent of earnings for the next three months (Horibayashi 2006). Due to these higher restrictions, those eligible for unemployment benefits declined from 72 percent in 1991 to 50 percent by 1996 (Adam 1999).

In 1995, there was a significant legislative change in the structure of pensions that saw the retirement age increase for women from between fifty-three and fifty-seven to between fifty-seven and sixty-two (depending on the number of children) and from sixty to sixty-two for men (Potůček 2009). This age limit was raised again in 2003 to sixty-three for men and women without children (Potůček 2009). This followed the introduction of voluntary private pensions in 1994, which offered a market-based alternative to public pensions. Average pensions compared to average net wages decreased from 66 percent in 1990 to 52.7 percent in 2006. Similarly, average pensions compared to average gross wages decreased from 52.7 percent in 1990 to 40.8 percent in 2006 (Potůček 2009). So not only did pension eligibility become more restricted, but benefits decreased relative to wages, leaving the possibility that some retirees could fall below the subsistence level.

Similar neoliberal welfare reforms were introduced in 1995 to family and child benefits. Although benefits had previously been guaranteed to families with dependent children, the 1995 State Social Support Act introduced means-tested measures that limited eligibility to families whose income was up to 1.8 times the social minimum (Horibayashi 2006). In 1996, cuts were made to the social insurance system and eligibility restrictions were introduced as the Czech government sought to limit universal access (Orenstein and Haas 2005). Many healthcare facilities were also privatized at this time and voluntary private health insurance was introduced in 1993, reflecting a liberalization of the health services in the country (Potůček 2009).

Although Czech social policymaking during the 1990s and 2000s favored liberalization, this did not constitute a convergence with Liberal welfare states, and some social benefits were even expanded. While economic liberalization was a core feature of the postcommunist transition throughout eastern Europe, many countries, including the Czech Republic, increased social spending to a degree. While social spending as a percentage of GDP was at 14.6 percent in 1990, it reached a high of 19.6 percent by 2003 (OECD 2015b). It is important to note, however, that although social spending grew in the Czech Republic and other eastern European states, it fell in absolute levels corresponding with overall declines in GDP (Orenstein and Haas 2005). Despite this decline in absolute terms, during the period from independence until the start of the GFC, the Czech Republic saw limited welfare retrenchment. Instead, social spending increased, representing a process of catch-up with other more established welfare states in other EU countries. By the start of the Great Recession, however, the Czech welfare state remained smaller than many of its EU counterparts in terms of social spending.

Orenstein and Haas highlight a significant "Europe effect" that explains the continued support for social spending in the Czech Republic despite internal and external pressures to liberalize (2005). First, integration into the EU may have provided important incentives for eastern European states to pursue higher social spending (Orenstein and Haas 2005). This argument follows the compensation hypothesis, namely, that in response to economic openness governments will raise social spending to protect citizens against rising inequality and to limit political instability (Cameron 1978, Garrett 2001; Frye 2002). Second, prospective EU membership may have led governments to embrace EU norms and levels of social expenditure (Orenstein and Haas 2005). In the case of economic and political reforms, the influence of EU norms was clear. The 1993 Copenhagen Criteria of Accession, for instance, outlined requirements for candidate countries to adjust national economies and build democratic institutions to bring them into accordance with existing EU member state practices (Potůček 2009).

EU integration played a significant role in shaping social policy discourse, agenda setting, instruments, and norms across eastern Europe (Orenstein and Haas 2005; Potůček 2009). The EU's influence over social policies in eastern Europe only increased further in 2002 with the adoption of the Lisbon Strategy (Cerami 2010; Potůček 2009). While social objectives remained secondary to economic and political integration goals, the Lisbon

Strategy encouraged eastern European states to embrace the European social model. Candidate countries, such as the Czech Republic, were required to introduce policies that focused on social activation and inclusion (Potůček 2009). Additionally, EU structural funds provided an important revenue source for some Czech welfare programs. For example, EU funds made up nearly a third of Czech active employment spending in 2006 (Potůček 2009). Overall, the "Europe effect" helps to explain the maintenance of a strong welfare state in the Czech Republic despite the introduction of neoliberal reforms in some areas.

In sum, welfare development in the Czech Republic from the early post-communist transition until the start of the GFC can be characterized as one of welfare modernization, expansion, and liberalization. Much like in southern Europe, the welfare state in eastern Europe followed a process of catching up with the rest of the EU. In the Czech Republic, there was a desire to bring social spending and welfare policies in line with other EU welfare states, and also to introduce neoliberal economic reforms. Social policy, in the first few years of independence, entailed the introduction of comprehensive welfare coverage as an emergency measure to address the costs of political and economic transitions (Horibayashi 2006; Offe 1993). As domestic and international pressures to liberalize the economy and the welfare state grew beginning in the 1990s, the universality of early social programs became more targeted, and eligibility was tightened. Neoliberal concerns of cost containment, efficiency, and competition also came to the fore at this time. But while the Czech welfare state underwent neoliberal reforms during the 1990s and 2000s, EU integration encouraged the government to bring social spending in line with the rest of the EU (Cerami 2010; Orenstein and Haas 2005; Potůček 2009). Compared to many of its EU neighbors, however, the Czech welfare state remained smaller and offered less protection against the effects of the GFC.

Precrisis Political Support for Welfare Expansion and Liberalization

Reflecting the dominance of neoliberal ideas and policies, the promarket welfare reforms introduced in the Czech Republic in the 1990s and 2000s were met with a high degree of political consensus. Within corporatist arrangements at the central government and regional levels, there was a considerable level of trust and collaboration between trade union representatives, employees, and government officials (Potůček 2009). In addition to agreement between social partners, there was also a strong consensus between political parties over welfare reforms at this time. In the early years of the postcommunist transition, emergency social benefits were introduced as a necessary means to protect citizens against the potential harms of political and economic reform. As these systems became burdened by high unemployment and slow economic growth, arguments in favor of liberalization gained traction across parties. The tightening of welfare benefit eligibility and social spending cuts were seen by many on the left as necessary to maintain the welfare state and by those on the right as the best policy approach from a neoliberal ideological perspective (Müller-Rommel, Fettelschoss, and Harfst 2004; Potůček 2001).

Neoliberal thinking was particularly pronounced in the Czech Republic under the conservative government of Václav Klaus, who served as prime minister from 1993 to 1998. During his tenure in office, Prime Minister Klaus called for significant cuts to unemployment benefits and other social programs (Cerami 2010). To highlight the influence that neoliberal thinking had on policy discourse during these years, some government officials argued that unemployment was natural and beneficial for the country (Cerami 2010). This suggested that unemployment was part of a normal functioning market and that government efforts to promote employment may even prove harmful to economic efficiency. But while neoliberal thinking was influential in economic and social reforms in the Czech Republic in the decades after the postcommunist transition, this did not result in a wholesale dismantling of the welfare state. While some welfare programs were liberalized, the Czech government also undertook efforts to increase social spending and bring it more in line with other EU members. As the "Europe effect" hypothesis suggests, prospective EU membership may have led parties on the left and right to embrace EU norms and levels of social spending (Cook, Orenstein, and Rueschemeyer 1995). This provides an important explanation for why the conservative ODS party under Václav Klaus did not pursue more sweeping welfare retrenchment despite its strong neoliberal ideological leanings.

Despite a transition from conservative to social-democratic government leadership in the late 1990s, neoliberal welfare reforms continued (Potůček 2009). Political divisions between the left and right over welfare were fairly muted at this time as a strong consensus had formed over the necessity of neoliberal reforms. In fact, left-right political divisions and party ideology appear to have had little effects on welfare policies and social spending in the Czech Republic at this time (Cerami 2010; Cook, Oren-stein, and Rueschemeyer 1995; Lipsmeyer 2000; Orenstein and Haas 2005). In terms of social spending, there were only minor fluctuations between the conservative ODS government, which was in power from 1992 until 1997, and the social-democratic government led by the Czech Social Democratic Party (ČSSD) from 1998 until 2006 (Potůček 2009). In other words, precri-sis social spending in the Czech Republic was not driven by political party control of government, but rather by dual pressures to liberalize aspects of the welfare state while at the same time bringing the social protection sys-tem more in line with EU-wide standards.

Czech Welfare State Postcrisis

Crisis-Management Stimulus Measures (2008–2010)

During its first two decades of independence, the Czech Republic under-took a number of macroeconomic structural reforms that led it to be one of the strongest economies in eastern Europe by the start of the GFC. Between 2003 and 2005 real GDP growth averaged around 5 percent and GDP per capita grew from 73 percent to 80 percent of the EU average (European Commission 2009a). Unlike a number of its European neighbors, the Czech Republic was not immediately affected by the GFC and the long-term impact was more moderate overall (OECD 2010a). This insulation from the effects of the financial crisis was owed largely to sound fundamentals in the Czech economy, including limited reliance on foreign currency loans,[2] high levels of bank capitalization, a flexible exchange rate, credible monetary policy, and the lack of major asset bubbles (IMF 2012). The exposure of Czech banks to subprime securities at the start of the crisis was fairly negli-gible, which contributed to the resilience of the banking sector (European Parliament 2009). The Czech government also maintained healthy spend-ing levels, with government debt at 27.1 percent of GDP in 2008 with a

---

2. Whereas foreign currency loans accounted for nearly 80 percent of private-sector funding in some eastern European countries, such as Estonia and Latvia, the Czech economy was far less reliant on external credit. Foreign currency loans to the private sector only accounted for 10 percent of funding in the Czech Republic prior to the GFC, making the country far less vulnerable to the postcrisis drop in international lending (European Commission 2009a).

budget deficit of 2.2 percent for the same year (OECD 2015a). But despite being more modestly affected by the initial macroeconomic shock than many other EU members, the Czech Republic still faced weakened demand and a loss of output as the crisis wore on. This led to higher unemployment, limited economic growth, and increasing social problems.

Since the Czech economy is largely export-oriented, there was a slow-down of growth beginning in 2008, stemming from the collapse in global demand. In 2009, exports and industrial production each fell by 18 percent (European Commission 2009a). Although less reliant on international credit than many of its neighbors, the Czech Republic was still negatively affected by tightening credit availability and lower levels of foreign direct investment, which resulted in a 7.4 percent reduction in investment in 2009 (European Commission 2009a). This had the effect of exacerbating economic decline and generating further social problems. By 2009, GDP had fallen by nearly 5 percent and unemployment rose rapidly to 8 percent, representing the biggest increase in a decade (Clasen, Clegg, and Kvist 2012). In response to these worsening social and economic conditions, the Czech government adopted two stimulus packages in 2009 worth CZK75.6 billion (US$3.9 billion) equaling over 2 percent of GDP (European Commission 2009a; UNDP 2010).

Social spending increases were a sizeable part of these stimulus measures worth more than CZK18.4 billion (US$ 950 million) and making up 24.34 percent of the overall package (UNDP 2010). In addition to introducing measures aimed at addressing unemployment, these measures also lowered social security contribution requirements for citizens (European Commission 2009a). Despite the introduction of neoliberal reforms during the precrisis period, early crisis-management responses by the Czech government reflected a corporatist approach. Such responses highlight the path-dependent nature of the welfare state and the influence of Bismarckian social protection legacies similar to those found in Continental European welfare states. For example, in the aftermath of the crisis, the Czech government undertook tripartite deliberations with unions and employers to address concerns of slow growth and rising unemployment. One of the major labor market measures adopted by the Czech government, as a result of these negotiations, was a government-subsidized short-time working scheme, closely resembling the programs introduced in Germany (Clasen, Clegg, and Kvist 2012; Glassner and Keune 2012; Heyes 2011). This scheme is estimated to have benefited nearly 2 percent of the Czech workforce in

2009 and helped to stem the rise of unemployment (Hijzen and Venn 2011; OECD 2010c). This corporatist response differs from the measures undertaken by Liberal welfare states, such as the UK, that were far more reliant on market-based policies, rather than state negotiations with social partners (Heyes 2011).

In 2009, the Czech government introduced the "Education Is a Chance" and the "Educate Yourself" programs that offered financial incentives for employers to support training activities for workers, particularly those on short-time work schemes, to improve employee skill sets and reduce the need for layoffs (Clasen, Clegg, and Kvist 2012; Heyes 2011). These programs were funded largely by EU structural funds indicating an important connection between EU and domestic policymaking (Clasen, Clegg, and Kvist 2012). As with the short-time work schemes, these programs were established through tripartite negotiations and were similar to policies put in place by Austria and Germany (Heyes 2011). The government also increased spending on job search support programs and active labor market policies to encourage higher levels of employment (Marchal, Marx, and Van Mechelen 2014).

As in Continental European welfare states, the emphasis that these stimulus measures placed on ensuring employment protection and increasing social benefits for core workers led to greater problems of dualization within the Czech workforce. Full-time regular employees were the primary beneficiaries of measures aimed at protecting employment in the wake of the crisis (Clasen, Clegg, and Kvist 2012). By contrast, vulnerable workers, such as temporary workers, immigrants, and youth, who did not benefit from the same employment protections, were far harder hit by the crisis and faced much higher unemployment rates (Heyes 2011). The policies adopted by the Czech government in response to the crisis further exacerbated this problem. While a number of measures were implemented to cushion the effects of the crisis on core workers, few measures were taken to support the long-term unemployed, and several entitlement programs for labor market outsiders were even cut (Clasen, Clegg, and Kvist 2012). For example, while unemployment benefit rates were increased from 50 percent to 60 percent of salary earnings for the first two months of unemployment, the length of eligibility was reduced by one month (European Commission 2010). In other words, while the short-term unemployed enjoyed better benefits, those who remained out of work for longer periods received less generous social support (Clasen, Clegg, and Kvist 2012).

The Czech government also made greater allowances for the use of temporary contracts, in response to concerns over rising unemployment (Heyes 2011). While these policies allowed many job seekers to return to the labor market, these workers did not enjoy the same level of employment protection or social benefits as their core worker counterparts. Additionally, although temporary contracts allowed for greater labor market flexibility, these measures were not accompanied by policies that would allow low-skilled and part-time laborers to receive the training or support needed to transition into the full-time core workforce (Clasen, Clegg, and Kvist 2012; EIRO 2010). In sum, although the unemployment policies and labor market responses adopted by the Czech state alleviated joblessness in the short term, they may have created further problems of dualization in the long term (Clasen, Clegg, and Kvist 2012; Heyes 2011).

While the stimulus packages adopted by the Czech government were large as a percentage of GDP, in overall value they were far smaller than those implemented by wealthier EU welfare states, such as France, Germany, the UK, and Sweden (European Parliament 2009). The smaller size of the welfare state also meant that the automatic stabilizers in place to protect citizens against the economic downturn were weaker (Dolls, Fuest, and Piechl 2012). While data for the effects of automatic stabilizers in the Czech Republic is limited,[3] available evidence indicates that, as in the case of southern Europe, automatic stabilizers in eastern Europe were far lower than in northern and western Europe states (Dolls, Fuest, and Piechl 2009). In terms of income absorption, automatic stabilizers across eastern Europe ranged from 25 percent in Estonia to 32 percent in Slovenia, below the EU average of 38 percent and far lower than the effects in countries like Demark at 56 percent, Belgium at 53 percent, and Germany at 48 percent (Dolls, Fuest, and Piechl 2009, 2012). Automatic stabilizer responses were similarly weak in labor markets across eastern Europe, accounting for only 23 percent of the unemployment shock in Estonia, 33 percent in Poland, and 43 percent in Slovenia (Dolls, Fuest, and Piechl 2009, 2012). Again, the effects of these automatic social spending increases were lower in eastern Europe

---

3. To give perspective, automatic stabilizers in the Czech Republic closely parallel that of Poland and fall somewhere between those in Estonia on the low end and Slovenia on the high end (Eller 2009). In this regard, Poland serves as a useful proxy for Czech automatic stabilizer responses in the wake of the GFC. It is useful, however, to provide a range to understand that this is only an estimate and the true value lies somewhere between the given lower and upper bounds.

than the EU average of 38 percent and considerably lower than some western and northern European states, such as 61 percent in Belgium, 62 percent in Germany, 68 percent in Sweden, and a staggering 82 percent in Denmark (Dolls, Fuest, and Piechl 2009, 2012).

As discussed in earlier chapters, these automatic stabilizers provide a buffer against the negative effects of an economic downturn, particularly during a crisis when consequences are sudden and severe and require a rapid response. While many welfare states in western Europe were able to effectively lessen the negative consequences of the crisis in terms of unemployment and income loss, countries throughout eastern Europe, such as the Czech Republic, had much more limited responses. As a result, we see higher levels of unemployment and social instability in this region compared to other parts of the EU with more mature and comprehensive welfare systems. Overall, the weaker automatic stabilizer response meant that social protection measures to address the effects of the GFC in the Czech Republic had to be addressed through discretionary spending. This opened up the possibility for greater political contestation over social spending and helps to explain the polarized political conflicts that have emerged between parties on the left and right over welfare after the crisis.

The Politics of Austerity (2010–Present)

Although stimulus measures were initially implemented by the Czech government to limit the effects of the GFC, fiscal consolidation and budgetary concerns became the main focus of the government not long after these measures went into effect (ECB 2010). Despite a vote of no confidence, which saw a conservative ODS-led government removed from office in 2009 and a strong showing for the social democratic ČSSD party in the 2010 elections, center-right parties were able to stay in power. The conservative ODS-led government used the crisis as a justification to further liberalize the welfare state and introduce a series of austerity measures (Blum, Formánkováb, and Dobrotic 2014; Clasen, Clegg, and Kvist 2012). In other words, by 2010 there was a reversal in the Czech government's response to the GFC from a strategy of stimulus and social spending expansion to one of fiscal austerity and welfare cuts (Richardson 2010).

While the effects of the GFC were less severe in the Czech Republic than in some other EU member states, this event served as an excuse for the right-wing government to adopt welfare cuts and implement fiscal discipline (Blum, Formánkováb, and Dobrotic 2014). The logic behind these austerity measures was that public debt and deficit levels needed to be reduced and individual responsibility encouraged to decrease reliance on the welfare state (Blum, Formánkováb, and Dobrotic 2014). The 2011 budget, for example, reduced public spending by 10 percent of GDP, primarily through welfare state cuts (European Commission 2009a; Pietras 2009). The center-right ODS government also implemented a series of widespread public-sector wage cuts and employment reductions. This included a 2011 bill that reduced public employee salaries by 10 percent (Glassner and Keune 2012). Measures were also taken to freeze minimum wages between 2009 and 2011 (Glassner and Keune 2012).

In addition to wage cuts and public-sector layoffs, significant reductions were introduced by the conservative Czech government to several social programs. In the case of healthcare, the budget for the Ministry of Health was reduced by CZK2 billion (US$83 million) in 2010, representing a 30 percent decrease from 2008 funding levels (Mladovsky et al. 2012). Individual charges were also increased for health services, including the introduction of patient charges for hospitals and drug prescriptions. Inpatient fees, for example, were increased from CZK60 to CZK100 per day in 2012 (Mladovsky et al. 2012). The reimbursement rate of prescription drugs by national health insurance funds was also cut by 7 percent between 2009 and 2011, resulting in higher patient copayments (Mladovsky et al. 2012). Overall, these reductions in the Czech healthcare sector were among the most severe in Europe and similar to those taken by southern European countries, which were much harder hit by the crisis, such as Greece and Spain (Euractiv 2014).

The conservative Czech government also introduced several reductions to family benefits. In August 2010, for instance, the government introduced Act No. 347/2010 Coll., which reduced funding for family benefits by CZK1.3 billion (US$53.6 million) (Blum, Formánkováb, and Dobrotic 2014). The ODS-led government also adopted legislation that lowered maternity and paternity allowances and reduced eligibility duration (Richardson 2010). These social spending cuts were informed by neoliberal ideology as reductions in welfare benefits, and a greater reliance on private care was promoted as a means to increase individual responsibility and introduce market alternatives to state support (Blum, Formánkováb, and Dobrotic 2014). This is unsurprising, as the ODS has had strong free-market leanings since its foundation. For example, Václav Klaus, a cofounder of ODS and the first prime minister of the newly independent Czech Republic, was an avid supporter of neoliberalism. The austerity measures and social spending cuts of the ODS government postcrisis, therefore, represent a continuity of the party's commitment to its core neoliberal ideology.

Postcrisis Political Divisions

Since the start of the GFC, political polarization and instability have increased in the Czech Republic, and divisions between parties on the left and right have grown over the welfare state. The shift from stimulus to austerity, for instance, reflects the importance that political party control of government had postcrisis (Myant, Drahokoupil, and Lesay 2013). Whereas the period from independence until the beginning of the crisis was largely defined by the unifying goal of EU accession, which guided policymaking toward neoliberal reforms, welfare state modernization, and catch-up with the rest of the EU, the GFC seriously challenged this political consensus (*Economist* 2010b). Slow economic recovery from the Great Recession, credited by some as a consequence of austerity measures, led to growing political divisions between the main political parties, mass protests on behalf of citizens, and the rise of new parties on the political extremes.

Although stimulus packages were implemented by the Czech government in 2009 as an emergency response to the crisis, it was not long before the conservative ODS government, led by Prime Minister Mirek Topolanek, began to pursue a proausterity agenda. Mr. Topolanek was appointed by Czech president Vaclav Klaus in 2007, and like Mr. Klaus harbored strong neoliberal ideological leanings. As the crisis progressed, policies were implemented to introduce sweeping public finance reforms and social spending cuts to reduce government expenditures (Radio Prague 2007; Reuters 2007). These plans, however, were limited by strong opposition in Parliament led by the center-left ČSSD and faced considerable resistance from trade unions and civil society actors who came out against the legislation (Radio Prague 2007). Opposition to Prime Minister Topolanek's government culminated in a 2009 vote of no confidence led by the ČSSD, which saw the ousting of the conservative ruling coalition and the establishment of a temporary nonpartisan placeholder government under the leadership of economist Jan Fischer. The vote of no confidence highlighted tensions between mainstream political parties on the left and right. This dissent between advocates of austerity and proponents of stimulus on how best to address the crisis became even clearer in the June 2010 general election.

In the buildup to the national election, the Social Democrats ran on a platform of protecting the welfare state from cuts and preserving popular social benefits, like the pay-as-you-go pension system (Reuters 2010a). Jiri Paroubek, the head of the ČSSD, who led the call for a vote of no confidence against the ODS, made several pledges to raise taxes on the wealthy and businesses as a means to expand welfare benefits (Clasen, Clegg, and Kvist 2012; *New York Times* 2009a; Reuters 2010b). To lower the national debt, the ČSSD proposed raising government revenue by CZK70 billion (US$2.2 billion) through a combination of higher taxes on the wealthy and an increase in the corporate tax rate from 19 percent to 21 percent (Reuters 2010a). By contrast, the center-right ODS ran on a platform emphasizing budgetary responsibility as a means to prevent a debt crisis similar to that faced by the Greek government (Reuters 2010b). The ODS's goal of cutting the national deficit from 5.9 percent in 2010 to 3 percent of GDP by 2012, as recommended by the EU, would be achieved by reducing social spending and privatizing aspects of the healthcare and pension systems (Reuters 2010b).

The election platforms of the ODS and ČSSD, therefore, underscored the contrasting beliefs that the main Czech parties had about appropriate government responses to the crisis. Economic stability and management were a major concern for Czech voters in this election. While the ČSSD emphasized the need for higher welfare state spending (LeDuc and Pammett 2013), the right-wing ODS used fear of economic uncertainty to justify the need for austerity measures and welfare cuts (Linek 2011).

Despite receiving more votes than any other party, at 22.1 percent of the electorate, the social democratic ČSSD was unable to secure a parliamentary majority after the 2010 election (Reuters 2010b). This failure to form a coalition government represented a considerable blow to left-wing parties and the ČSSD in particular. Instead, with 20.2 percent of the vote, the ODS successfully formed a center-right governing coalition, along with the newly established conservative TOP 09 Party and the centrist Public Affairs Party (Reuters 2010b). Petr Nečas, the head of the new ODS-led government, made clear his neoliberal leanings by stating that his administration would focus on promoting "a government of budget responsibility" and arguing that the policies of left-leaning parties would lead the state into bankruptcy (Dvorakova and Stroleny 2012; Reuters 2010b).

Although successful in forming a conservative coalition based on fiscal responsibility, the ODS-led government faced an increasingly unstable political environment. Upon taking office, the ODS sought to fulfill its campaign promises by implementing substantial budgetary cuts. The 2011 budget, for example, reduced public spending by over CZK35 billion (US$1.4 billion) through a series of tax increases, welfare state reductions, and a 10 percent cut to public-sector wages (Contiguglia 2011; Dvorakova and Stroleny 2012). To implement these austerity measures, in October 2010 the ODS and its allies declared a legislative state of emergency that allowed them to bypass opposition in Parliament and forgo negotiations with social partners (Freedom House 2013). These legislative actions, along with a growing public dissatisfaction with austerity, led to mass protests in Prague, with tens of thousands of citizens taking to the streets (BBC 2015e; EPSU 2011). The CMKOS trade union confederation organized these antiausterity rallies against welfare state and public wage cuts, arguing that proper social dialogue had not occurred around these measures (Dvorakova and Stroleny 2012; EPSU 2011). These protests represented an alliance of social democratic groups and other left-leaning political actors with a growing civil-society coalition united against the perceived neoliberal undermining of social rights in the country (Potůček 2012; Ripka and Mares 2016).

Political resistance increased in October 2010, when the Social Democrats won control of the Senate in midterm elections, which allowed them to obstruct the proposed austerity measures (BBC 2015e). In addition to facing a veto by the ČSSD-controlled Senate, conservatives were also dealt a considerable setback in 2011 when the Constitutional Court declared that the emergency legislative procedures undertaken by the government were unconstitutional, thereby preventing the proposed austerity measures from moving forward (Freedom House 2013). The Constitutional Court has become a more significant political actor postcrisis, occasionally serving as a veto point for contentious legislation (Ripka and Mares 2016). The ČSSD, for example, made several appeals to the Constitutional Court to block conservative welfare cuts, including in areas such as pensions and healthcare (Ripka and Mares 2016). Despite extensive political hostility, in June 2011 the ODS was able to successfully push through neoliberal welfare reforms, in areas such as healthcare and unemployment benefits, in the lower house (Freedom House 2013). In November 2011, the lower house was also able to implement major changes to the pensions, which partially privatized the system (Freedom House 2013).

This legislation was once again met with substantial backlash by the public. In April 2012, some of the largest protests seen since the fall of communism took place in Prague, with eighty to ninety thousand citizens coming out against austerity and recent corruption scandals (*Guardian* 2012c). These protests were part of ongoing mass resistance organized by trade unions and civil society groups who opposed the social spending cuts and neoliberal policies of the conservative government. The ODS-led government under Prime Minister Nečas lost a tremendous amount of popularity in the wake of these demonstrations. Shortly afterward the Nečas government faced two parliamentary votes of no confidence, in April and November 2012, and narrowly avoided losing power in both (Freedom House 2013). Political opposition also gained momentum in the October 2012 elections, as the ČSSD secured further seats in the Senate (Freedom House 2013; *Wall Street Journal* 2012d). With public scrutiny at an all-time high, in June 2013 Prime Minister Nečas resigned amid a corruption scandal, leading to the establishment of a temporary placeholder government (BBC 2015e).

Taking advantage of public dissatisfaction with austerity, loss of faith in conservative party leadership, and the longest economic recession on record in the Czech Republic, the ČSSD gained control of the government in 2013, forming a left-wing ruling coalition (BBC 2015e; *Bloomberg* 2013b). The outcome of the 2013 national election represented a clear shift to the left in Czech politics. Upon taking office, the ČSSD and its allies introduced policies that increased the minimum wage, offered tax breaks to families with children, ensured that pensions were tied to inflation rates, and eliminated the healthcare fees put in place by the ODS (*Economist* 2013). Legislation was also adopted that reversed many of the neoliberal reforms made by the Nečas government to the pension system, including abolishing policies that allowed retirement savings to be diverted from state programs into private funds (*Economist* 2013).

The ascendance of the political left in the Czech Republic beginning in 2013 marked a significant turning point for the welfare state. Whereas the conservative ODS government pursued fiscal discipline and implemented broad cuts to several welfare programs, the ČSSD, under Prime Minister Bohuslav Sobotka, increased social spending. The 2015 budget, for example, included provisions to increase social spending by CZK450 million (US$18.66 million), bringing an end to a series of budgetary cuts to the welfare state (Radio Prague 2014). In addition to overall social spending increases, the budget included specific measures to increase pensions by an average of CZK200 (US$8.25), which although modest was five times higher than the previous ODS budgetary increase (Radio Prague 2014). Public-sector employee wages were also increased by 3.5 percent to 5 percent, and tax breaks were introduced for families with children along with cuts to value-added taxes on prescription drugs (Radio Prague 2014). Reflecting the desire to promote generous labor market and social policies, the ČSSD also dedicated the largest share of funding in the entire budget to the Ministry of Labour and Social Affairs (Radio Prague 2014). These policies were met with strong resistance by right-wing parties, who claimed that these plans would cause problems for government finances. Miroslav Kalousek, a prominent member of the conservative TOP 09 Party, claimed that under the 2015 budget investment would suffer, and he criticized high state spending (Radio Prague 2014). These sharp political divisions between parties on the left and right after the GFC were in contrast to the long-standing political accord over social and economic policies that prevailed before the crisis.

Along with divisions between center-left and center-right parties, there has been a rise of new parties in Czech politics since the start of the crisis. The rise of these new parties represents a higher degree of domestic polarization and public disillusionment with traditional parties. This change is surprising as the party system in the Czech Republic was one of the most stable in eastern Europe after the fall of communism. Compared with other countries in the region, such as Poland and Slovakia, public support for mainstream parties in the Czech Republic before the crisis remained relatively consistent (Havlík 2015; Spáč 2013). Whereas the two mainstream parties in Czech politics, the ČSSD and ODS, collectively received more than two-thirds of the vote in the 2006 general election, by the 2010 elections their vote share was only 42 percent percent and had dropped to a mere 28 percent in the 2013 elections (Havlík 2015). These election results represent a considerable loss of public support for traditional parties and a large-scale change of the party system in the Czech Republic (Havlík 2020).

The 2010 general election saw the introduction of two new political parties, TOP 09 and Public Affairs, into the Czech Parliament. TOP 09, a conservative party, emerged in 2009 and capitalized on the crisis to call for austerity measures to avoid a Greek-style debt crisis. Although established in 2001 as a regional party, Public Affairs also emerged on the national political scene during the 2010 elections, running on an antiestablishment and anticorruption platform (Havlík 2015). Both upstart parties were able to take advantage of the ongoing crisis to make significant gains in Parliamentary elections, together receiving nearly one-third of the vote (Havlík 2015). Not only did the 2010 election represent a significant victory in terms of public support for both TOP 09 and Public Affairs, it also gave these parties considerable political power as they each ended up serving as the main partners in the ODS conservative coalition (*Economist* 2010b; Euractiv 2010; Havlík 2015).

The 2013 general election also saw the introduction of two new antiestablishment populist parties, the Action of Dissatisfied Citizens (ANO) and the Euroskeptic Dawn of Direct Democracy (Usvít), into the Czech Parliament (*Economist* 2013). The newly formed ANO party received an impressive 23.5 percent of the seats in Parliament and became a partner in the ruling coalition led by the ČSSD (Havlík 2015). Collectively, ANO along with Usvít and TOP 09 accounted for 43.5 percent of the seats in Parliament after the 2013 election (Havlík 2015). While a presence in Czech politics since independence, the far-left KSČM communist party also increased its vote share, receiving 16.5 percent of the seats in Parliament in 2013, up from 13 percent in 2010 (Havlík 2015).

The 2017 general election resulted in an even more significant upset to the Czech political order, as antiestablishment parties made substantial gains. The recently formed ANO party, led by populist billionaire Andrej Babis, won the largest vote share of any party at 29.6 percent (Parties and Elections 2018). The antiestablishment Czech Pirate Party saw its vote share increase from 2.7 percent in 2013 to 10.8 percent in the 2017 election (Parties and Elections 2018). The newly established right-wing populist Freedom and Democracy Party secured 10.6 percent of the vote (Parties and Elections 2018). Although the ODS came in second with 11.3 percent, they fell far short of being able to form a working right-wing coalition (Parties and Elections 2018). The social democratic ČSSD saw a sharp decline in its support and its worst electoral outcome ever at 7.3 percent, down from 20.5 percent in the 2013 election. The ČSSD went from governing with the largest share of the vote in 2013 to sixth place in the 2017 election. One argument for the poor performance of the ČSSD is that ANO was able to co-opt many of the party's key issues such as increasing the minimum wage, pensions, and public-sector wages. Although the ČSSD was the main party in government, Mr. Babiš, who served as finance minister, managed to take credit for many of the social and economic improvements made in the country (*Washington Post* 2017). Recent elections indicate that there has been a sea change in the Czech political landscape, with voters moving away from the mainstream ODS and ČSSD in favor of new parties.

Although there has been a considerable disruption of the electoral politics status quo, ANO was able to form a left-wing ruling coalition with the social democratic ČSSD and the communist KSČM party. The coalition is similar in composition to the previous government, as the ČSSD had worked with ANO in an alliance after the 2013 elections. As a result, the policies of the new coalition government are similar to the previous left-wing alliance. This continuity is reflected in the 2018 budget, which includes social spending increases for healthcare, public wages, education, sick pay, and other welfare programs (OSW 2018; Reuters 2018c). Pensions, for example, are expected to increase by around 8 percent (Reuters 2018c). In 2017, the previous ČSSD-led government introduced an amendment to the Pension Act that sought to ensure the adequacy of pension payments (Emerging Europe 2018). The new ANO-led government agreed to build on the work of the previous coalition by introducing legislation that increased pension wages (Emerging Europe 2018). This legislation is designed to assist poorer and older pensioners who are at higher risks of living in poverty (Emerging Europe 2018). The ANO-led government highlights the rise of new political forces in the Czech Republic and a fragmentation of its party system, as well as the influence of partisanship on social spending after the GFC.

The Effects of Partisanship at the EU Level

The high degree of political instability in Czech politics, and the sharp left-right divisions over welfare after the crisis, have had important implications at the EU level. The debate over austerity versus stimulus, for example, came to the forefront in 2009, when conservative Czech prime minister Mirek Topolanek, who held the rotating position as president of the EU at the time, denounced US president Barack Obama's stimulus plan as "a way to hell" that would "undermine the stability of the global financial market." (*New York Times* 2009b). These provocative comments were met with discomfort by many EU leaders, who did not believe that this sentiment reflected the EU consensus and could potentially undermine solidarity for regional and global efforts to address the crisis (*New York Times* 2009b).

The neoliberal position of the ODS, therefore, had important implications at the EU level, shedding light on ideological differences between countries over the benefits and costs of stimulus. Despite the relatively small size of the Czech economy, as acting head of the EU Topolanek was granted an outsized voice in EU policymaking and diplomacy, which added further support to members favoring austerity, such as Germany and the UK. German officials for, example, echoed concerns that the American stimulus program would lead to financial instability and argued that EU countries must pursue a path of fiscal discipline instead (*New York Times* 2009b).

Prime Minister Topolanek's statements not only highlighted divisions between the policy positions of EU member states, but also the growing divide between parties on the left and the right within countries. His comments, for example, were not only met with resistance by left-wing parties in the Czech Republic but also by other left-leaning parties in other countries such as Germany. Martin Schulz, a leading German Social Democrat, for example, criticized the Czech prime minister's comments, arguing that they were undiplomatic and did not reflect the position of the EU as a whole (*New York Times* 2009b). Topolanek's controversial statements, and the reactions they evoked, laid bare the political separation that had emerged across parties on the left and right throughout the EU. Unlike the cross-party neoliberal consensus that had prevailed before the crisis, the postcrisis period has been characterized by increased political polarization over social and economic policymaking.

The increasing volatility of the Czech party system after the crisis has also played out in European Parliamentary elections. Whereas mainstream parties dominated the 2009 European Parliamentary elections, with the ODS receiving 31.45 percent of the vote and the ČSSD coming in second place with 22.38 percent, each faced significant losses in the 2014 elections (European Parliament 2009). The 2014 European Parliamentary elections represented a big victory for newly established parties, as ANO came in first with 16.13 percent of the vote followed in second place by a coalition between TOP 09 and STAN, a right-leaning party focused on local issues (European Parliament 2014). ČSSD came in third with 14.17 percent of the vote, representing an 8.21 percent loss of the vote share compared with its 2009 results (European Parliament 2014). The far-left KSČM communist party came in fourth place 10.98 percent of the vote (European Parliament 2014). Finally, the ODS came in a distant sixth place with a mere 7.67 percent of the vote, representing a remarkable 23.78 percent drop from its 2009 election results (European Parliament 2014). Overall, 2014 European Parliamentary election outcomes paralleled the loss of support for mainstream parties domestically in the Czech Republic, a notable change from the high degree of stability that existed in the party system prior to the crisis (Brusis 2004; Havlík 2015; Spáč 2013).

In addition to a loss of support for mainstream parties in lieu of newly formed alternatives, the 2014 European Parliamentary elections also saw an uptick in anti-EU sentiment among Czech parties. In the buildup to the 2014 European Parliamentary elections, the center-right ODS made a rejection of the euro as the national currency the main theme of its campaign (*Economist* 2014a). Even the pro-European ČSSD rejected EU austerity plans, indicating that the party was less willing to accept the necessity of neoliberal policies (*Economist* 2014a). The far-right Usvít party ran on an anti-EU platform and advocated for the closing of European borders to immigrants (*Economist* 2014a). The conservative No to Brussels—National Democracy (National Democracy) party, established in 2014 from the earlier Law and Justice Party, ran a provocative anti-EU campaign ad that was banned from Czech state television due to, among other issues, its perceived anti-Semitic content (*Economist* 2014b). Although many of these parties, for example, Usvít and National Democracy, did not gain seats in the European Parliament, their presence indicates a clear Euroskepticism within Czech politics (*Economist* 2014a; Hornát 2014).

The strong anti-EU sentiment and rise of new Czech political parties largely stem from the ongoing effects of the economic crisis. The foundation for much of the political conflict has been competing visions for how to improve economic growth and address rising social problems between advocates and opponents of austerity. At the same time that the ODS lent strength to a proausterity agenda at the EU level, the legitimation of this strategy by powerful conservative actors, such as Germany and the ECB, reinforced the domestic austerity plans of the right-wing government (Ripka and Mares 2016).

Conclusion

While sharing some of the key institutional features of its continental European neighbors, the Czech welfare state represents a distinct combination of social protection arrangements that are characteristic of eastern

European history and development. The welfare state in the Czech Republic, like many of other eastern European states, has a strong corporatist tradition, based on Bismarckian social protection policies, similar to those found in the continental European welfare states. This system was present in the Czech Republic prior to communist control of the country and continues to have important legacies in present-day social protection measures, including pension systems, unemployment benefits, and labor market policies (Deacon 1997; Potůček 2009; Żukowski 2009). Unlike continental European regimes, however, the Czech welfare state exhibits more universalistic tendencies, reflecting the high degree of coverage that existed under the Soviet system (Aidukaite 2011; Potůček 2009). Another important aspect of the development of eastern European welfare states is the historical postcommunist transition to liberal market economies that these countries underwent beginning in the early 1990s. After the fall of the "Iron Curtain," considerable efforts were made to liberalize various aspects of eastern European welfare states that coincided with broader economic restructuring. It is important to note, however, that this process did not constitute a wholesale dismantling of the welfare state or convergence toward a Liberal welfare state (Aidukaite 2011; Potůček 2001, 2009; Saxonberg and Sirovátka 2009).

The welfare state in the Czech Republic, therefore, encapsulates a unique mix of social protection arrangements that incorporate certain features of other regimes, while constituting a distinct Eastern European welfare type (Aidukaite 2009a, 2009b, 2011; Arts and Gelissen 2002; Cerami 2010; Cerami and Vanhuysse 2009; Fenger 2007; Golinowska, Hengstenberg, and Żukowski 2009). Generally, social protection is characterized by a high degree of coverage, low levels of social spending and benefits, and residual liberal tendencies, particularly in recent years (Aidukaite 2011). The period after the transition to democracy until the crisis was largely defined by a desire to liberalize the Czech economy and modernize the welfare state by bringing it closer in line with other EU members. Welfare reforms during this period from independence until the start of the GFC were largely driven by the unifying goals of integration into the global economy and EU accession, which led to considerable political stability and consensus between parties over reform trajectories.

This consensus is exemplified by the fact that welfare reforms and social spending remained relatively stable in the Czech Republic during the 1990s and 2000s, even as control of government shifted between conservative and social-democratic leadership (Potůček 2009). Political party divisions and ideological differences appeared to have had very little influence over social spending during this time (Cerami 2010; Cook, Orenstein, and Reusche-meyer 1995; Lipsmeyer 2000; Orenstein and Haas 2005). Instead, social reforms were guided by neoliberal pressures to make the welfare state more efficient and the belief that social policies and expenditures needed to be brought more in line with other EU member states.

The GFC, however, led to considerable political instability and conflict between parties in the Czech Republic over social and economic policies. Shortly after adopting emergency stimulus measures, the conservative ODS-led coalition government switched tactics and embraced a series of neoliberal-inspired budgetary cuts and welfare state retrenchment. These conservative policies, however, were met with considerable resistance by left-wing parties postcrisis. The proausterity agenda of the ODS and its con-servative allies, for instance, was met with strong opposition in Parliament by the ČSSD, who not only worked to block proposed cutbacks to social spending but organized several votes of no confidence, successfully ousting ODS governments in 2009 and 2013. By contrast Social Democrats, upon taking office in 2013, pursued an alternative agenda that saw the expansion of social spending and a reversal of many of the cuts implemented by the ODS (Clasen, Clegg, and Kvist 2012; *New York Times* 2009a; Reuters 2010b). The ascendance of the political left in the Czech Republic marked a signifi-cant turning point for social spending and highlighted the ideological dif-ferences that informed the decision making of parties on both ends of the political spectrum. In short, the GFC appears to have ended the political agreement that had formed between parties precrisis around social and economic reforms, leading to greater political conflict.

As the economic crisis persisted more and more citizens began turning to new alternative parties, which resulted in a splintering of the Czech party system. This was a remarkable change in domestic political dynamics, as the Czech party system had been one of the most stable in eastern Europe after the fall of communism (Havlík 2015; Spáč 2013). These new parties have been highly effective in drawing support away from the two main parties, the ODS and ČSSD, who saw their collective share of the popular vote drop from 77.5 percent of parliamentary seats in 2006 to only 33 percent in 2013 (Havlík 2015). In fact, the ODS went from eighty-one seats in Parliament in 2006, the highest share of any party, to only sixteen seats in 2012, the second-lowest of any party (Havlík 2015). The newly formed Public Affairs,

TOP 09, and ANO all served as coalition partners in government, and the latter two parties came in first in the 2014 European Parliamentary elections, indicating that these parties wielded considerable political power. ANO's fortunes have only improved over time as they became the ruling party after the 2017 election.

Slow recovery from the worst recession since independence led to popular unrest over austerity measures, as tens of thousands of citizens took part in mass protests in Prague and other cities around the country. These demonstrations indicated an increased politicization of social and economic policies and a disenchantment with political leadership. The postcrisis period also saw a radicalization of public opinion, with anti-EU and anti-immigrant sentiments gaining ground (BBC 2015e; *Economist* 2014a; *Independent* 2015c; Radio Prague 2016). Coinciding with these more extreme sentiments among some citizens has been the rise of far-right parties, such as Usvít, Freedom and Direct Democracy, and the Bloc against Islam. Although overall support for these parties has remained minimal, their formation represents an increase of political extremes in Czech politics. In contrast to the decades after independence, the postcrisis period represents a time of intense political contestation and ideological division within the Czech Republic.

Changing domestic political dynamics in the Czech Republic have also influenced the EU austerity debate. While holding the rotating Presidency of the EU, the center-right ODS party acted as a strong advocate of neoliberal principles and pushed the necessity of fiscal austerity. These arguments in the early phases of the crisis contributed to a growing coalition of actors at the EU level who favored austerity as a regional response to the crisis and saw continued stimulus as potentially destabilizing to financial markets and economic growth. While in office from 2006 until 2013, the center-right ODS government remained a strong proponent of austerity, embracing EU calls for fiscal discipline to reduce debt and deficits. The ascendance of the left-leaning parties starting in 2013, however, represented a turning point toward greater stimulus and social spending. This leftward shift may potentially undermine the austerity coalition, spearheaded by countries like Germany and the UK, that has been influential in informing EU policymaking postcrisis. The 2014 European Parliamentary elections also saw the induction of several new Czech political parties into the body, indicating a loss of influence for the ODS and ČSSD at the EU level. This change in the political makeup of the Czech party system and its representation in the European

Parliament may make achieving political consensus over social and economic policies more difficult in the future both at home and regionally.

In sum, there has been a high degree of conflict and instability in Czech politics since the beginning of the GFC, which was not seen in the decades preceding this event. There has been a growing divide between mainstream parties as the precrisis consensus that existed over social and economic reforms has fallen apart. The center-right ODS party has embraced austerity measures as a means to reduce debt. By contrast, the center-left ČSSD has advocated for increased social spending and welfare benefit expansion. Along with growing ideological divisions between the ODS and ČSSD, there has been a high level of support for newly established parties that have undercut the traditional party system in the Czech Republic. This political shift has had important implications domestically and at the EU level that may affect the policy agenda for the entire region. The foundation of this political fracturing lies in the wider debate over the merits and disadvantages of neoliberal policies that has arisen in the wake of the GFC. Ideological differences have led parties on the left and right to pursue very different social spending that has further fueled the politicization of the welfare state.

CHAPTER 9

Conclusion

The Great Recession was one of the worst economic disasters that the world had seen in nearly a century. The crisis resulted in the loss of trillions of dollars in GDP and millions of jobs around the globe. This event represented an unprecedented and massive shock to the entire global economy that not only challenged the resiliency of the welfare state, but undermined the very ideas, policies, and practices upon which the precrisis social and economic policy consensus had rested. The magnitude and effects of the GFC on political, economic, and social dynamics cannot be overstated. This final chapter will analyze the postcrisis realignment of the politics of social spending that has taken place across advanced capitalist economies, a change in which the partisan composition of government once again matters for welfare state policymaking. A review of key findings from the statistical analysis and case studies will highlight that this shift has taken place across a diverse set of welfare states. Finally, the chapter will investigate some of the possible long-term consequences that the renewed influence of partisanship on social and economic policymaking may have going forward in Europe and beyond.

Crisis as a Catalyst for Change

As evidence from the previous chapters of this book has demonstrated, the GFC was a powerful catalyst for a shift in social spending dynamics across advanced economies. In the wake of this event, intense political conflict has arisen over economic regulations, redistribution, social spending, and the role of the welfare state (Starke, Kaasch, and van Hooren 2012). This highly politicized postcrisis environment stands in stark contrast to the depoliticized nature of precrisis social and economic policymaking. As discussed in

169

chapter 2, there are several theoretical reasons as to why the GFC led to such a dramatic realignment of welfare state politics. First, the severity of the crisis raised social issues to the top of the policy agenda, creating pressure for governments to increase social spending to offset the negative distributional effects of this event. While social spending on average increased sharply across the OECD at the start of the GFC, this stimulus led to higher public debt and deficit levels. Growing budgetary concerns as the crisis wore on forced political actors to make difficult choices about whether to expand or cut social spending, giving rise to intense partisan conflicts over the social and economic consequences of these decisions (Singer 2011a; Vis, Van Kersbergen, and Hylands 2011).

Second, the GFC seriously challenged the logic of market fundamentalism and the need for more limited state intervention, which had been ascendant before the crisis. The crisis exposed some of the weaknesses of neoliberal policies, thereby undermining the precrisis consensus that had formed around these ideas. As a result, after the crisis, there have been more pronounced ideological divisions between political parties on the left and the right over the welfare state. While conservative parties have largely embraced the need for fiscal discipline and social spending cuts, many parties on the left have begun to raise concerns that such policies may limit long-term growth and lead to deteriorating social conditions. As ideological polarization between parties on the left and right has increased over the welfare state postcrisis, partisan differences have become more influential for social spending (Bremer 2018; Finseraas and Vernby 2011; McManus 2019).

Third, as social and economic concerns became more important to voters after the GFC (Margalit 2013; Tavits and Potter 2015; Traber, Giger, and Häusermann 2018), political parties were incentivized to respond to the material needs of their constituents. Left-wing parties tended to favor social spending increases that benefit their core low- and middle-income constituents, while right-wing parties, who represent medium- and higher-income voters, tended to favor welfare retrenchment and fiscal discipline (Ahrend, Arnold, and Moeser 2011; Bremer 2018; Starke, Kaasch, and van Hooren 2014). The GFC provided a window of opportunity for left-wing parties to embrace higher social spending and distance themselves from the neoliberal policies that were viewed as a major cause of the crisis (Bremer 2018). At the same time that center-left parties moved further to the left in response to voter demands after the crisis, center-right parties, seeking to highlight their commitment to fiscal conservatism to their constituents, moved further to the right. As support for antiestablishment far-left and far-right parties has increased, signaling growing public dissatisfaction with centrist policies, mainstream parties have shifted further to the left and right respectively on issues such as social spending and economic governance (Hobolt and Tilley 2016).

Finally, the economic crisis created political opportunities for opposition parties to gain power by claiming that responsibility for the GFC fell onto ruling governments. The clear winners of this political transition in the EU were center-right parties who were swept into power in the early years of the crisis. The conservative political landscape in the EU after the crisis not only legitimized a proausterity agenda but also defined political conflict lines as the crisis wore on. Conservative actors, including political parties, EU representatives, think tanks, and economists influenced social and economic policies domestically and EU-wide (Brunnermeier, James, and Landau 2016; Carstensen and Schmidt 2018). This has led to increased ideological polarization between parties over the welfare state and a backlash by left-leaning parties, which have questioned the benefits of austerity and advocated instead for greater government intervention and social protection. While the varieties of capitalist literature argues that distinct economic growth models in northern versus southern European countries explain EU-level differences over fiscal austerity (Hall 2014; Iversen et al. 2016; Regan 2017), it is unclear that countries fall into two distinct clusters (Hay 2019). For example, although France and Belgium are export-oriented northern member states, both countries were more favorable to fiscal transfers to indebted peripheral states (Lehner and Wasserfallen 2019). Although institutions such as the economic system and welfare states may play an important role in shaping government preferences, these structures are not deterministic, and ideational and partisan variables are argued to have an important influence over decision making. The next sections will analyze the pre- and post-crisis periods to identify how the GFC altered the politics of social spending, paying close attention to ideological and partisan conflict in the post-crisis period.

Precrisis Social and Economic Policy Consensus

The precrisis period was characterized by a political consensus among parties on the left and the right over the necessity of neoliberal social and eco-

nomic reforms (Hendrik, Schäfer, and Manow 2004; Häusermann and Palier 2008; Leschke and Jepsen 2012). Whereas historically, EU countries had
been associated with generous social spending and welfare benefit expansion, beginning in the 1990s, reforms were introduced to liberalize welfare
states and reduce social spending. During this time, governments led by
parties on both the left and right began to subscribe to the belief that the
welfare state should be more limited in scope and should serve primarily in
a market-supporting role (Begg, Draxler, and Mortensen 2008; Rodrik
2011; Scharpf and Schmidt 2000). Along with national governments, EU
institutions also encouraged neoliberal reforms (Hemerijck 2013; Leschke
and Jepsen 2012; Scharpf 2002). The influence of neoliberal ideas in EU
policymaking during the precrisis period is evidenced by the negative correlation between EU membership and social spending at this time. Although
nearly all countries liberalized some aspects of their welfare state and lowered social spending to encourage economic competition, the pressure to
implement neoliberal reforms was greater for EU member states whose
generous social protection systems were portrayed as inefficient drags on
growth (European Commission 1997; OECD 1994, 1997).

Perhaps the most surprising aspect of the dominant neoliberal policy
agenda at this time is the high degree to which parties on both sides of the
political spectrum incorporated these ideas into their platforms. Social
spending during the precrisis period was largely depoliticized as parties on
the left and right across countries introduced a variety of promarket welfare
reforms and corresponding social spending cuts. Analysis of party manifestos during the 1990s and 2000s reveals that left-leaning parties moved further to the right on issues of social welfare and economic governance
(Bremer 2018; Hendrik, Schäfer, and Manow 2004). In fact, in the late
1990s, when social democratic parties were in control of a majority of governments in the EU, they pursued far less interventionist policies than they
had in the past and seemed far more willing to accept neoliberal-inspired
social and economic reforms (Hendrik, Schäfer, and Manow 2004). The
prevailing belief that fiscal consolidation and market-based social investments would result in higher levels of economic growth and well-being for
citizens led many left-wing parties, traditionally in favor of generous social
spending, to accept welfare state retrenchment. This depoliticization of precrisis welfare reforms can be seen in each of the case studies analyzed in this
book, indicating that this was a widespread phenomenon.

In the UK by the mid-1990s, the New Labour party, under the leadership of Prime Minister Tony Blair, began to rethink its commitment to a well-funded welfare state and instead adopted a series of neoliberal reforms (Labour Party 1994, 1997). Upon taking office in 1997, New Labour adopted many of the conservative welfare policies of the previous center-right Tory government, including fiscal discipline, social spending cuts, and neoliberal welfare reforms, such as the partial privatization of pension schemes (Hodson and Mabbett 2009; Taylor-Gooby 2001). In Germany, the left-leaning Social Democratic and Green Party coalition government introduced the Hartz IV reforms to the labor market and welfare state that built upon earlier neoliberal legislation adopted by conservative parties (CEPS 2014; Zohlnhöfer and Herweg 2012). Even in the case of Sweden, a traditional haven for social democratic support of a well-funded and extensive welfare state, neoliberal reforms were embraced not only by conservative parties but also by Social Democrats, who introduced legislation to liberalize the welfare state and reduce social spending while in office from 1996 until 2006 (Haffert and Mehrtens 2015). Finally, in both Spain and the Czech Republic, pressure to liberalize their economies, promote welfare state efficiency, and bring social spending in line with other EU members led to considerable consensus between parties on the left and right over the need for reforms (Cerami 2010; Cook, Orenstein, and Reuschemeyer 1995; León and Pavolini 2014; Moreno 2000; Müller-Rommel, Fettelschoss, and Harfst 2004; Orenstein and Haas 2005; Potůček 2009).

Postcrisis Political Divisions and Polarization

In contrast with the period preceding the GFC, there has been a high degree of polarization and political conflict over social and economic policies postcrisis. Between mainstream political parties on the center-left and center-right, there have been growing divisions over social spending and the role of the welfare state. In Sweden, for example, the Social Democrats introduced several neoliberal social policy reforms precrisis that sought to limit the size and scope of the welfare state. Since the start of the GFC, however, they have once again embraced traditional left-wing ideas that emphasize the need for higher social spending and welfare benefit expansion (Bergh and Erlingsson 2009; Bremer 2018; Haffert and Mehrtens 2015; Reuters 2014b). Sweden's Social Democratic Party has also been vocally opposed to conservative policies of austerity and welfare retrenchment after the crisis. Even in Germany, where the center-right CDU party remained in power after the crisis and political stability has been relatively high, left-leaning parties such as the SPD have moved further to the left and drawn clearer distinctions between their policy platforms and those of their conservative counterparts (ECFR 2012). While the center-right CDU has been a leader in promoting austerity measures in Germany and at the EU-level, the SPD and other left-wing parties, such as the Green Party and the Liberal Party, have challenged these policies and called for greater public investments in the welfare state (Armingeon and Baccaro 2014; Hübner 2013). In the UK, the Labour Party, which had embraced neoliberal-inspired Third Way policies during the 1990s and 2000s, has moved further to the left, particularly under the leadership of Jeremy Corbyn, opposing welfare cuts and calling to limit austerity (Labour Party 2015a, 2015b). By contrast, the Conservative Party continued its support for fiscally conservative policies by introducing the most sweeping cuts to the UK welfare state in modern history (Gardiner, Bromund, and Foster 2010; *New York Times* 2010a).

In addition to divisions between traditional parties, there has been a splintering of the party system in several countries and the rise of new anti-establishment parties. This includes the introduction of far-left and far-right political parties into national elections in many states. Spain, for example, has seen a high degree of political volatility since the start of the GFC, including popular unrest in the streets and a considerable loss of support for the center-left PSOE and center-right PP parties, who saw their joint share of the national vote decline by nearly 10 percent between 2008 and 2011 (Funke, Schularick, and Trebesch 2015). In 2014, the populist far-left Podemos party was formed on a platform to end austerity, restructure Spanish debt, and increase social spending (Caballero and Alvarez-Diaz 2015; Junor 2015; Open Europe 2014). According to a 2014 public opinion poll, Podemos was supported by 27.7 percent of the population, compared with 26.2 percent for PSOE and 20.7 percent for the ruling conservative PP party, representing the first time that a new party had come in ahead of the two mainstream parties (Junor 2015). Podemos has taken on an even greater role in Spanish politics after the 2018 vote of no confidence that led to the ouster of the conservative PP leader Mariano Rajoy and his replacement by PSOE leader Pedro Sánchez. To shore up support for his minority government, Prime Minister Sánchez has worked closely with the far-left Podemos party to craft a progressive budget deal. This partnership helped paved the way for a left-wing PSOE-Podemos coalition government after the national election in 2020.

The two main parties in the Czech Republic have also lost a considerable amount of public support postcrisis. Whereas the ČSSD and ODS collectively received more than two-thirds of the vote share in the 2006 general election, by the 2010 elections their vote share had shrunk to 42 percent. By the 2013 election it was 28 percent, and by the 2017 general elections it had shrunk to a mere 19 percent of the vote (Havlík 2015). These election results represent a significant loss of public support for the two mainstream parties and a transformation of the party system in the Czech Republic. Riding the wave of public discontent over political responses to the crisis, newly formed parties including TOP 09, Public Affairs, and ANO all made significant gains in national elections and served as ruling coalition partners (*Economist* 2010b; Havlík 2015). The 2017 general election resulted in an even more substantial upset to the Czech political system, as the recently established ANO party received the largest percentage of the vote and was able to form a coalition government with support from the left-leaning ČSSD party. The rise of ANO, at the expense of the mainstream ČSSD and PP parties, is especially surprising, as the Czech Republic party system was one of the most stable in eastern Europe before the start of the GFC.

The success of antiestablishment parties over traditional mainstream parties in countries such as Spain and the Czech Republic speaks to the considerable disruption of the political status quo that has occurred postcrisis. The growing influence of nontraditional parties on the far left and far right reflects a high degree of polarization and public disillusionment with traditional party leadership. The emergence of these parties has resulted in a substantial reordering of the political landscape within each country. The success of far-left and far-right parties has put further pressure on mainstream parties to move further to the left and right ends of the political spectrum on issues such as welfare and economic governance to gain the support of voters who have moved away from the center (Hobolt and Tilley 2016).

Partisanship has been a decisive factor in influencing social and economic policymaking in postcrisis Europe. Strong conservative political representation after the start of the GFC helped to legitimize a proausterity policy agenda in the EU postcrisis (EUCE 2013; Regan 2012). At the start of the crisis, EU institutions, including the European Commission and the ECB, also advocated for this conservative approach. The influence of neoliberal ideas and policies are evident in the strict debt and deficit requirements present in the European Fiscal Compact and in the structural reforms and austerity measures that were conditions of bailout funds for Ireland, Greece, Portugal, and Spain (European Commission 2012a, 2012b). But even though conservative parties and beliefs dominated EU policymaking postcrisis, opposition by left-leaning parties has grown. Left-wing governments in countries such as Spain, the Czech Republic, and Sweden have questioned the efficacy of austerity measures and welfare state retrenchment. Political divisions have become particularly pronounced in southern Europe as widespread public discontent over austerity has led to the rise of antiestablishment parties, such as Syriza in Greece and Podemos in Spain. Overall, social and economic policymaking has become highly politicized postcrisis, which has weakened support for traditional centrist parties and led to the rise of antiestablishment parties on the far left and far right. Worsening social conditions, slow economic recovery, and growing discontent with fiscal consolidation have helped to strengthen these radical parties. The result is a far more politically volatile environment in the EU.

The new political map of Europe, characterized by a high degree of polarization, may indicate a period of prolonged partisan conflict over social spending and greater instability, as agreement between parties may be more difficult to achieve. The foundation of this disagreement has been a serious re-evaluation of neoliberal policy orthodoxy and fierce political debates over the distributional consequences of austerity. Whereas the precrisis period saw widespread support for deregulation, market liberalization, and welfare state cuts, these measures have been seriously challenged after the crisis. While partisan politics have been of paramount importance in explaining the divergent social spending patterns of states postcrisis, other variables have also been influential, namely welfare state institutions and EU membership and policies.

Welfare State Influence

In line with theoretical expectations, welfare state types are correlated with different levels of social spending (see chapter, 2 table 1). Continental European and Nordic welfare states, for instance, are associated with higher social spending than their Liberal, Southern European, and Eastern European counterparts. In the immediate aftermath of the GFC, these welfare institutions played an important role in influencing the content of the stimulus measures adopted by national governments. The degree to which welfare states were able to protect citizens against the negative distributional effects of the crisis, particularly the size of automatic stabilizer responses, helped to mediate political conflict over social spending. Although government leaders and EU officials saw an immediate need to introduce stimulus measures to limit the social and economic costs of the crisis, the size and content of national fiscal responses differed considerably (OECD 2010a). Welfare state institutional legacies help to explain some of these divergent outcomes.

Whereas wealthier welfare states were able to introduce generous stimulus packages, other countries with less well-funded welfare states were unable to provide the same degree of social protection. Austria, Germany, Sweden, and Finland, for example, all introduced generous stimulus measures equivalent to more than 3–4 percent of GDP (European Commission 2009a; Leschke and Jepsen 2012, 291). By contrast, Hungary, with its smaller economy and less well-funded welfare state, was unable to increase social spending in response to the GFC (European Commission 2009a; Leschke and Jepsen 2012). Overall, stimulus packages were notably lower in southern and eastern Europe than in other EU regions. This shows that even at the early stages of the crisis there was considerable variation in national crisis-management responses that corresponded with the size and generosity of domestic welfare states.

Beyond the sheer size of stimulus packages, the crisis-management responses adopted by governments were largely in line with welfare state type. Germany, Spain, and the Czech Republic, for example, all adopted stimulus measures that were negotiated between government officials and social partners (Chung and Thewissen 2011; Clasen, Clegg, and Kvist 2012, Glassner and Keune 2012; Heyes 2011; Möller 2010). This strategy reflected the corporatist traditions of the welfare state in each country. Short-time work schemes introduced in the Czech Republic and Germany, for instance, were built upon an agreement that firms would limit layoffs if workers would agree to reduced wages. The state played an important role by providing tax breaks and other incentives for firms to maintain employment levels. The governments in both countries also offered social support to workers with reduced wages and the unemployed. These tripartite negotiations are in stark contrast to the UK crisis-management response, which relied more heavily on market-based policies rather than direct government negotiations with firms and employee associations (Chung and Thewissen 2011). Rather than negotiating short-time work schemes directly with firms, the UK government adopted workforce activation policies, including job search initiatives and training programs, designed to get unemployed laborers back to work. This response, which relied more on market mechanisms than on state intervention, was in keeping with the UK's Liberal welfare state traditions. Finally, reflecting the well-funded and universal characteristics of the Nordic welfare state, Sweden's stimulus response was much larger than many other EU member states (Chung and Thewissen 2011). Sweden's stimulus package also included policies that sought to promote full employment, provide income protection, and offer substantial unemployment benefits for out-of-work citizens (Swedish Prime Minister's Office 2008). These types of policies are all in keeping with the traditional social democratic ideals that underpin the Nordic welfare model. The Swedish government also played a much larger role in providing social support and protection in Sweden than in many other member states, such as the UK.

Overall, the composition of stimulus packages and the varying degrees of state intervention point to path dependencies based upon different welfare state institutional legacies. The social protection arrangements found within states, in other words, were influential in defining the kinds of early crisis response strategies adopted by governments. This is important because even though neoliberal reforms were introduced across welfare states during the precrisis period, the stimulus responses of governments did not follow a uniform liberal approach. This is contrary to the expectations of theorists who argue that international pressures and EU integration will lead to greater cross-national convergence of social policies in line with a Liberal welfare state type (Clayton and Pontusson 1998; Fulcher 1994; Gilbert 2002; Goodman and Pauly 1993; Korpi 2003; Korpi and Palme 1998; Mishra 1999). In fact, not only is there evidence for the existence of distinct welfare state types but that the differences between these systems have become more pronounced over time rather than less, despite increased globalization and EU integration (Castles and Obinger, 2008; Dolls, Fuest, and Piechl 2009, 2010). The divergent nature of initial postcrisis responses highlights the continued importance that welfare state differences play in shaping social policies.

The size of automatic stabilizers in different welfare states also played an important role in limiting or exacerbating political conflict over social spending postcrisis. For instance, automatic stabilizer responses in Nordic and Continental European welfare states were much larger than in Liberal, Southern European, and Eastern European welfare states. Due to the automatic nature of these mechanisms, social spending was increased without the need for discretionary budgetary decisions. As a result, there was less need for political debate over social spending increases in countries with stronger automatic stabilizers compared to those with weaker automatic stabilizers (Cohen and Follette 2000; Dolls, Fuest, and Piechl 2010).

Countries with less well-funded welfare states had weaker automatic stabilizer responses to the crisis. In Spain, for example, automatic stabilizers accounted for only 28 percent of income shock absorption and 38 percent of the unemployment shock absorption (Dolls, Fuest, and Piechl 2012). By comparison, automatic stabilizers accounted for 53 percent of income shock absorption in Belgium and 56 percent in Denmark (Dolls, Fuest, and Piechl 2009, 2012). Automatic stabilizers accounted for 68 percent of the unemployment shock absorption in Sweden and a remarkable 82 percent in Denmark (Dolls, Fuest, and Piechl 2009, 2012). Whereas welfare states in northern and western Europe were able to limit unemployment and income loss through automatic social spending increases, many countries in southern and eastern Europe had more limited responses. As a result, the social costs of the crisis, such as rising unemployment and poverty, were higher in these regions. Weak automatic stabilizer responses in Southern and Eastern European welfare states meant that a higher percentage of social spending came from discretionary budgets, which were subject to political debate. This allowed for greater political contestation over social spending and helps to explain the high degree of polarization and partisan conflict in many of these countries, such as the rising influence of far-left and far-right parties in national politics.

Beyond Welfare State Influence

While an important intervening variable, the differences in welfare state type alone cannot explain the divergent social spending outcomes we see across countries as the crisis continued. For example, although Sweden is a classic example of the Nordic welfare state, known for high social spending and universal benefits, as the GFC wore on the Swedish government pursued a series of welfare cuts and neoliberal reforms. This included extensive cuts to social programs and the tightening of eligibility for unemployment benefits and sick pay (The Local 2014a). To put these reforms into perspective, since the start of the crisis Sweden has gone the furthest in reducing the size of its welfare state than any other Scandinavian country (The Local 2014a). A key explanation for these social spending cuts, which seem counterintuitive for a Nordic welfare state, is the center-right coalition that held control of the government at the time. Under the leadership of Prime Minister Reinfeldt, Sweden's conservative-led government focused on fiscal discipline and social spending reductions. While these measures did not entail the transformation of the Swedish social protection system into a Liberal welfare state, they speak to the powerful influence that political parties play postcrisis in influencing social spending, even in traditionally one of the most well-funded and universal welfare states in Europe.

Political party control of government also helps to explain differences in social spending among countries with similar welfare states. For instance, at the same time that the United States introduced substantial social spending increases and implemented one of the most significant expansions of the American healthcare system in decades, the UK undertook a series of extensive budget cuts and welfare state reductions (*Economist* 2013; ILO 2011; OECD 2009). Political parties have been the key driver of these social spending differences between these two cases since the onset of the GFC (McManus 2018). The 2008 US general election saw the center-left Democratic Party, under the leadership of President Barack Obama, come into power. President Obama ran on a platform that emphasized government spending increases to encourage growth, promote job creation, and increase social spending (McCarty 2012; *New York Times* 2012). By contrast, the 2010 general elections in the UK saw the success of the Conservative Party under the leadership of David Cameron, who ran on a platform that stressed the need for fiscal discipline and welfare reductions (*New York Times* 2010a). As a consequence of these electoral results, while the United States continued stimulus social spending, by 2010 the UK began to introduce some of the most significant cuts to its welfare state since the end of World War II (*New York Times* 2010a). Differences between center-left and center-right party control of government in the United States and the United Kingdom help to explain why each state pursued such dissimilar long-term social spending, despite similarities in their welfare states and economic circumstances (McManus 2018). Partisan influence on social spending postcrisis offers an important counterargument to theories that argue that welfare state policymaking is strictly path-dependent and insulated from political pressures for change (Myles and Pierson 2001; Pierson 1996, 2001).

EU Membership and Policies

EU membership and policymaking have also had an important influence on social spending pre and postcrisis. Although EU member states maintain governing authority over social policies, decision making is embedded within a larger European institutional context. In the years prior to the crisis, EU membership was negatively correlated with social spending (see chapter 2, table 1). This effect corresponded with greater EU economic integration and a neoliberal emphasis on competition, efficiency, and increased market freedom (Leschke and Jepsen 2012). Expanded EU authority over economic matters, such as Maastricht Treaty convergence criteria, not only reduced the capacity of member states to determine economic policies but limited the ability of governments to define social policies (Hemerijck 2013; Scharpf 2002). The spillover effects of EU economic policies onto social policy areas resulted in greater pressure for welfare state liberalization and social spending reductions at this time.

Since the GFC, EU membership is no longer negatively correlated with social spending (see chapter 2, table 1). This change can be explained, in part, by the fact that during the early stages of the GFC, EU institutions and member states agreed on the need to implement strong and rapid stimulus measures, including social spending increases, to offset the negative consequences of the crisis.

Before the crisis, EU members made deeper cuts to social spending than nonmembers. In the wake of the GFC, however, the social spending of the two groups of countries was comparable. This is evidenced by the fact that that EU membership did not have a statistically significant effect on social spending postcrisis. Yet specific EU policies put pressure on member states to lower welfare spending. The European Fiscal Compact, which included binding rules that governments must maintain balanced budgets and lower their debts and deficits, for example, increased pressure on signatories to reduce social spending (De la Porte and Heins 2015; European Commission 2012a, 2012b).

Although EU membership and policies have influenced the social spending of member states, these factors alone cannot explain the variation that we see throughout the region. A great deal of the changes which occurred at the EU level relate to important shifts in the political map of Europe. Unlike the depoliticized precrisis policymaking environment in which neoliberal welfare state reforms were introduced across states with little resistance, social spending postcrisis has been subject to much sharper political divisions domestically and at the EU level.

The EU has been an important voice in the debate over austerity in Europe. It has also been subject to many of the political changes that have occurred since the onset of the crisis. On the one hand, the EU serves as the originator and enforcer of much of the region's austerity policies, for example, the European Fiscal Compact and bailout agreement conditions for indebted member states including Greece, Ireland, and Portugal. Yet on several occasions, EU institutions have also broken with fiscal policy conservative hardliners. The ECB's decision, for example, to implement a program of Eurozone government bond purchasing in 2015 led to tensions with proausterity governments in member states, such as Germany and the UK, who opposed quantitative easing measures aimed at buying public debt (*Wall Street Journal* 2015b). While acknowledging the importance of fiscal restraint, European commissioners José Manuel Barroso and Jean-Claude Juncker each noted the limits of austerity and the need to focus on growth and to address social issues (*Spiegel* 2013a; RTE 2014). President Juncker cited a lack of "political and social support" for austerity and the need to adopt policies that had "a stronger emphasis on growth" (*Spiegel* 2013a). This statement reflects growing antiausterity sentiments in EU politics and speaks to how political constraints have affected the decision making and policies at the EU level. It is vital, therefore, to acknowledge the powerful role that political and ideological shifts have had in influencing the policies and practices of both member states and EU institutions.

Conclusion

Since the start of the Great Recession, there has been a momentous realignment of welfare state politics across advanced capitalist economies. Whereas the partisan composition of government held little sway over social spending decisions in the decades leading up to the crisis, this event acted as a critical juncture that resulted in a repoliticization of the welfare state. In response to this event, left-wing parties have moved further to the left in support of the welfare state and greater government intervention. By comparison, right-wing parties have shifted further to the right on issues of the welfare state and economic governance, seeking to emphasize their commitment to fiscal conservatism. The transformation of the political landscape has had a profound influence on postcrisis social and economic policymaking.

The electoral success of center-right parties in the EU following the GFC allowed fiscally conservative policies to be promoted as the most reasonable and effective response to the recession. In other words, the ascendance of conservative actors in the EU postcrisis lent strength to a proausterity agenda supported by member states and EU institutions. Countries led by conservative governments, which by 2012 were the majority of states in the EU, were correlated with lower social spending than those ruled by center-left parties. Politically driven decisions to encourage austerity throughout the EU also had the effect of putting further pressure on member states to lower social spending. EU economic policies, such as the European Fiscal Compact, required governments to reduce public spending, with welfare states being a major target for cuts. Despite the dominance of conservative parties postcrisis, however, there has been growing opposition by left-leaning parties who have challenged the proausterity policy agenda and highlighted the negative distributional effects of social spending cuts.

Beyond reshaping political dynamics within states, partisan divisions have had important consequences for EU policymaking, as consensus over social and economic policies has been more difficult to achieve. At a time when agreement over socioeconomic goals is most needed, the high levels of political polarization present in the EU may hinder long-term unity (Lindqvist and Östling 2010). Contentious debates between the far-left Greek government and its creditors, for example, led to considerable instability in EU markets. Intensifying antiausterity sentiments have also limited the ability of member states and EU institutions to adopt common social and economic policies for the region, as differences between actors have widened.

In the long term, political challenges to neoliberalism may lead to a more significant re-evaluation of social and economic policies. While a proausterity agenda defined policymaking in the EU after the GFC, there have been growing critiques about the effectiveness of this approach. Austerity measures, for example, have been cited by critics as the cause of slow economic recovery in the EU and continued problems with high unemployment and low consumer demand (ECFR 2012; European Parliament 2013). This has led to a reassessment of neoliberal ideas and policies both domestically and at the supranational level. Although the EU and the IMF were instrumental in promoting austerity, for example as a requirement for bailout funds, these institutions have since acknowledged some of the negative economic and social consequences of fiscal cuts (*Bloomberg* 2013a; IMF 2013; *Washington Post* 2013). The European Commission, for instance, has identified the possible threats that rapid and sustained public spending reductions can have on social, political, and economic stability (RTE 2014; *Spiegel* 2013a).

In addition to questions about the effectiveness of austerity measures, there has also been an emerging focus on the negative effects of social inequality on economic growth and a renewed call for greater investment in the welfare state. A 2014 IMF report, for example, identifies the negative effects that social inequality has on health, education, investment, political stability, and economic growth (IMF 2014). Recent OECD reports have also identified the relationship between rising income inequality and low levels of economic growth and urged states to adopt policies that not only focus on growth but include mechanisms for more redistribution to help reduce inequality (OECD 2014a, 2015a). These findings mark a considerable about-face from precrisis arguments that blamed welfare states for hindering economic competition and growth. Instead, these new reports identify the importance of social spending as a tool for governments to encourage growth and address social issues, such as rising inequality and poverty. The renewed focus on the welfare state as a powerful mechanism to achieve social and economic objectives has gained acceptance by many left-leaning parties. For example, this belief was a central component of Sweden's Social Democrats' policy platform in recent national elections (*Bloomberg* 2014a, 2014b).

Historically, acute financial crises have produced broader paradigmatic shifts in thinking about the significance and role of the welfare state. The postwar period saw the rise of Keynesian economic theories and the development of the modern welfare state. The stagflation and oil crisis of the late 1970s saw a weakening of support for Keynesianism and a turn toward neoliberal ideas, which by the end of the Cold War had become the prevailing economic paradigm worldwide. As a result, there was a strong cross-national welfare liberalization trend at this time. While the Great Recession did not signal an end to the neoliberal paradigm, it has called into question many of its underlying ideas, and this has resulted in intense political conflict over market regulation, redistribution, and the role of the welfare state. Given this new postcrisis context, the importance of the welfare state and its relationship with the market is being re-evaluated. Rather than being seen as a hindrance to competition and prosperity, welfare states have been reconceptualized by advocates as essential for achieving positive social and economic ends. This is true not only for the market-supporting role that the welfare state plays through social investment but also for the vital redistributive function that it has in reducing inequality and poverty. Rising inequality has been increasingly recognized as a threat to social well-being and economic prosperity. Welfare states may, therefore, be a key instrument through which governments can address these pressing concerns.

As evidence from this book has demonstrated, the GFC fundamentally altered the politics of social spending across advanced welfare states, resulting in postcrisis dynamics that are far different from those that had existed in the precrisis period. These changes not only influenced the decisions taken by governments and EU institutions throughout the crisis, but they will have a profound effect on social and economic policymaking in the years to come. The fact that partisan conflict over welfare has arisen even in countries less affected by the economic downturn, such as Sweden and Germany, indicates that these political differences were not just an immediate reaction to the GFC, but reflect the re-emergence of deeper ideological divisions that are likely to last. Partisan divisions over social spending, for instance, have persisted in party platforms up until the present day, indicating that the welfare state is still a salient issue influenced by left-right ideological differences. Although the Great Recession has ended, many of the negative social and economic conditions that stemmed from the crisis persist. Issues such as rising income inequality and poverty remain high on the policy agenda and important to many voters. At the same time, concerns about budget deficits and public debt continue to garner significant attention. Governments will, therefore, continue to face pressures to balance the need for fiscal responsibility with providing adequate social protection for their citizens. This dynamic is highly relevant in light of the current COVID-19 pandemic. While governments quickly increased social spending in areas such as unemployment and healthcare to address the negative consequences of this public health and economic crisis, as time goes on, debt and deficit concerns may create pressure for governments to once again adopt austerity. The IMF, for example, has already signaled concerns about rising government debt due to COVID stimulus measures and emphasized the need for fiscal discipline once the pandemic ends (Reuters 2021). This indicates that political debates over austerity and welfare spending are likely to be highly relevant in the coming years. This policy balancing act will require governments to make difficult decisions over whether to expand or cut social spending to achieve economic growth and ensure social well-being. Partisan politics have played a critical role in shaping postcrisis social spending across advanced capitalist economies and are likely to continue to influence social and economic policymaking in the years to come.

REFERENCES

Abou-Chadi, Tarik. 2016. "Niche Party Success & Mainstream Party Policy Shifts." *British Journal of Political Science* 46, no. 2: 417–36.

Adam, J. 1999. *Social Costs of Transformation to a Market Economy in Post-Socialist Countries.* Macmillan Press.

Adler-Nissen, R., and K. Kropp, eds. 2016. *A Sociology of Knowledge of European Integration: The Social Sciences in the Making of Europe.* Routledge.

Agell, J., P. Englund, and J. Söderstein. 1996. "Tax Reform of the Century—The Swedish Experiement." *National Tax Journal* 49, no. 4: 643–64.

Ahrend, R., J. Arnold, and C. Moeser. 2011. *The Sharing of Macroeconomic Risk: Who Loses (and Gains) from Macroeconomic Shocks.* Paris: OECD.

Aidukaite, J., ed. 2009a. *Poverty, Urbanity and Social Policy: Central and Eastern Europe Compared.* New York: Nova Sciences Publishers.

Aidukaite, J. 2009b. "Old Welfare State Theories and New Welfare Regimes in Eastern Europe: Challenges or Implications." *Communist and Post-Communist Studies* 42, no. 1: 23–39.

Aidukaite, J. 2011. "Welfare Reforms and Socio-Economic Trends in the 10 New EU Member States of Central and Eastern Europe." *Communist and Post-Communist Studies* 44, no. 3: 211–19.

Akdede, S. 2012. "Income Inequality and Political Polarization and Fracturalization: An Empirical Investigation of Some European Countries." *Bulletin of Economic Research* 64, no. 1: 20–30.

Algan, Y., S. Guriev, E. Papaioannou, and E. Passari. 2017. "The European Trust Crisis and the Rise of Populism." Brookings Papers on Economic Activity.

Allan, J., and L. Scruggs. 2004. "Political Partisanship and Welfare State Reform in Advanced Industrial Societies." *American Journal of Political Science* 48: 496–512.

Almeda, E., and S. Sarasa. 1996. "Growth to Diversity." In *European Welfare Policy: Squaring the Welfare Circle*, edited by V. George and P. Taylor-Goody. London: McMillan.

Amable, B., D. Gatti, and J. Schumacher. 2006. "Welfare-State Retrenchment: The Partisan Effect Revisited." *Oxford Review of Economic Policy* 22, no. 3: 426–44.

Armingeon, K. 2012. "The Politics of Fiscal Responses to the Economic Crisis, 2008–2009." *Governance* 25, no. 4: 543–65.

Armingeon, K., and L. Baccaro. 2015. "The Crisis and Germany: The Trading State Unleashed." In *Complex Democracy: Varieties, Crises, and Transformations*, edited by V. Schneider and B. Eberlein. 165–83.

Armstrong, K., I. Begg, and J. Zeitlin. 2008. "JCMS Symposium: EU Governance after Lisbon." *Journal of Common Market Studies* 46, no. 2: 413–50.

Arts, W., and J. Gelissen. 2002. "Three Worlds of Welfare Capitalism or More? A State-of-the-Art Report." *Journal of European Social Policy* 12, no. 2: 137–58.

Aspalter, C., K. Jinsoo, and P. Sojeung. 2009. "Analysing the Welfare State in Poland, the Czech Republic, Hungary and Slovenia: An Ideal-Typical Perspective." *Social Policy & Administration* 43, no. 2: 170–85.

Atkinson, T., D. Luttrell, and H. Rosenblum. 2013. "How Bad Was It? The Costs and Consequences of the 2007–09 Financial Crisis." Dallas Federal Reserve. Staff Papers. No. 20. July 2013. Available at https://dallasfed.org/assets/documents/research/staff/staff1301.pdf.

Auerbach, A., K. Hassett, and J. Sodersten. 1995. "Taxation and Corporate Investment: The Impact of the 1991 Swedish Tax Reform." NBER Working Paper #5189, July 1995.

Bache, I., and M. Flinders. 2004. *Multi-Level Governance*. Oxford: Oxford University Press.

BBC. 2010. "David Cameron Launches Tories' 'Big Society' Plan." Available at http://www.bbc.com/news/uk-10680062.

BBC. 2012a. "Spain Austerity: Thousands Join New Budget Cuts Protest." Available at www.bbc.com/news/world-europe-20113664.

BBC. 2012b. "Spain's Indignados Protest Here to Stay." Available at www.bbc.com/news/world-europe-18070246.

BBC. 2014a. "Vote 2014: UK European Election Results." Available at http://www.bbc.com/news/events/vote2014/eu-uk-results.

BBC. 2014b. Europe Elections: Spain's Podemos Party Challenges System." Available at http://www.bbc.com/news/world-europe-27572663.

BBC. 2015a. "Greece: The Dangerous Game." Available at http://www.bbc.com/news/world-europe-31082656.

BBC. 2015b. "Greece Bailout: EU 'Mediating' Greek Row with Spain and Portugal." Available at http://www.bbc.com/news/world-europe-31696596.

BBC. 2015c. "Spain Rally: Podemos Holds Madrid Mass 'March for Change.'" Available at http://www.bbc.com/news/world-europe-31072139.

BBC. 2015d. "Election 2015." Available at http://www.bbc.com/news/election/2015/results.

BBC. 2015e. "Czech Republic—Timeline." Available at www.bbc.com/news/world-europe-17220571.

Begg, I. 2015. "Can EU Countries Still Afford Their Welfare States?" Available at https://www.bbc.com/news/world-europe-34272111.

Begg, I., J. Draxler, and J. Mortensen. 2008. "Is Social Europe Fit for Globalisation?: A

Study of the Social Impact of Globalisation in the European Union." CEPS special reports, The Centre for European Policy Studies (CEPS), Brussels, Belgium.

Bekker, S. 2015. "European Socioeconomic Governance in Action: Coordinating Social Policies in the Third European Semester." OSE Research Paper 19, Brussels, OSE. Available at www.ose.be/files/publication/OSEPaperSeries/Bekker_2015_OseResearchPaper19.pdf.

Béland, D., and R. H. Cox (eds.) 2011. Ideas and Politics in Social Science Research. New York: Oxford University Press.

Bélanger, E., and B. Meguid. 2008. "Issue Salience, Issue Ownership, and Issue-Based Vote Choice." Electoral Studies 27, no. 3: 477–91.

Belfrage, C., and M. Ryner. 2009. "Renegotiating the Swedish Social Democratic Settlement: From Pension Fund Socialism to Neoliberalization." Politics & Society 37, no. 2: 257–87.

Bentolila, S., P. Cahuc, J. Dolado, and T. Le Barbanchon. 2012. "Two-Tier Labour Markets in the Great Recession: France Versus Spain." The Economic Journal 122, no. 562: 155–87.

Bergh, A., and G. Erlingsson. 2009. "Liberalization without Retrenchment: Understanding the Consensus on Swedish Welfare State Reforms." Scandinavian Political Studies 32, no. 1: 71–93.

Bermeo, N., and J. Garcia-Duran. 1994. "Spain: Dual Transition Implemented by Two Parties." In Voting for Reform: Democracy, Political Liberalization and Economic Adjustment, edited by S. Haggard and S. Webb, 89–124. New York: Oxford University Press.

Bernaciak, M. 2015. Market Expansion and Social Dumping in Europe. Routledge.

Bloomberg. 2012. "Rajoy Outlines Budget Cuts as Protests Hit Madrid." Available at www.bloomberg.com/news/articles/2012-07-11/rajoy-outlines-65-billion-euros-of-cuts-as-protests-hit-madrid.

Bloomberg. 2013a. "IMF Officials: We Were Wrong About Austerity." Available at http://www.bloombergview.com/articles/2013-01-04/imf-officials-we-were-wrong-about-austerity.

Bloomberg. 2013b. "Czech Economy in Record-Long Recession as Austerity Bites." Available at www.bloomberg.com/news/articles/2013-02-13/czech-economy-in-record-long-recession-as-austerity-bites.

Bloomberg. 2014a. "Sweden's Reinfeldt Fights for Survival as Polls Show Defeat." Available at www.bloomberg.com/news/articles/2014-09-12/sweden-s-reinfeldt-fights-for-survival-as-polls-signal-defeat.

Bloomberg. 2014b. "Swedes Seek Regime Change as Tax Cuts Turn Into Poison Pill." Available at www.bloomberg.com/news/articles/2014-01-20/swedes-seek-2014-regime-change-as-tax-cuts-turn-into-poison-pill.

Bloomberg. 2018. "The Center Must Hold in Germany." Available at https://www.bloomberg.com/opinion/articles/2018-01-18/the-center-must-hold-in-germany.

Blum, S., L. Formánkováb, and I. Dobrotic. 2014. "Family Policies in 'Hybrid' Welfare States after the Crisis: Pathways between Policy Expansion and Retrenchment." Social Policy & Administration 48, no. 4: 468–91.

Blyth, M.2001."The transformation of the Swedish model: economic ideas, distributional conflict, and institutional change." World Politics 54, no. 1: 1–26.

Blyth M. 2002. *Great Transformations: Economic Ideas and Institutional Change in the Twentieth Century.* Cambridge: Cambridge University Press.

Blyth, M. 2013. *Austerity: The History of a Dangerous Idea.* New York: Routledge.

Boeri, T., A. Boersch-Supan, and G. Tabellini. 2001. "Would You Like To Shrink the Welfare State? The Opinions of European Citizens." *Economic Policy* 32: 7–44.

Bofinger, P., L. Feld, W. Franz, C. Schmidt, and B. Weder di Mauro. 2011. "A European Redemption Pact." Vox CEPR November 9, 2011. Accessed July 13, 2020. Available at https://voxeu.org/article/european-redemption-pact.

Boix, C. 2000. "Partisan Governments, the International Economy, and Macroeconomic Policies in Advanced Nations, 1960–93." *World Politics* 53, no. 1: 38–73.

Boltho, A. and W. Carlin. 2012. "The Problems of European Monetary Union." *Vox EU.* Available at: https://voxeu.org/article/problems-eurozone

Bonoli, G., and B. Palier. 2000. "How Do Welfare States Change? Institutions and Their Impact on the Politics of Welfare State Reform." *European Review* 8: 333–52.

Bradley, D., E. Huber, S. Moller, F. Nielsen, and J. D. Stephens. 2003. "Distribution and Redistribution in Postindustrial Democracies." *World Politics* 55: 193–228.

Bremer, B. 2018. "The Missing Left? Economic Crisis and the Programmatic Response of Social Democratic Parties in Europe." *Party Politics* 24, no. 1: 23–38.

Bruegel. 2012. "Germany: What About Eurobonds?" May 31, 2012. Accessed July 13, 2020. Available at https://www.bruegel.org/2012/05/germany-what-about-eurobonds/.

Brunnermeier, M., H. James, and J. Landau. 2016 *The Euro and the Battle of Ideas.* Princeton, NJ: Princeton University Press.

Brusis, M. 2004. "Europeanization, Party Government or Legacies? Explaining Executive Governance in Bulgaria, the Czech Republic and Hungary." *Comparative European Politics* 2, no. 2: 163–84.

Bulmer, S. 2014. "Germany and the Eurozone Crisis: Between Hegemony and Domestic Politics." *West European Politics* 37, no. 6: 1244–63.

Caballero, G., and M. Alvarez-Diaz. 2015. "Institutional Change in Spain from Francoism to Democracy." In *The Political Economy of Governance: Institutions, Political Performance,* edited by N. Schofield and G. Caballero. Springer.

Cameron, D. 1978. "The Expansion of the Public Economy: A Comparative Analysis." *American Political Science Review* 72, no. 4: 1243–61.

Cameron, D. 2010. "Big Society Speech." July 19, 2010. Available at https://www.gov.uk/government/speeches/big-society-speech.

Cameron, D. 2011. "A Confident Future for Europe." Davos Speech. World Economic Forum.

Capoccia, G. 2015. "Critical Junctures and Institutional Change." In *Advances in Comparative-Historical Analysis,* edited by J. Mahoney and K. Thelen. Cambridge: Cambridge University Press.

Capoccia, G., and R. Kelemen. 2007. "The Study of Critical Junctures: Theory, Narrative, and Counterfactuals in Historical Institutionalism." *World Politics* 59, no. 3: 341–69.

Carstensen, M., and V. Schmidt. 2018. "Power and Changing Modes of Governance in the Euro Crisis." *Governance* 31, no. 4: 609–24.

Castles, F., and D. Mitchell. 1992. "Identifying Welfare State Regimes: The Links Between Politics, Instruments and Outcomes." *Governance* 5, no. 1: 1–26.

Castles, F., and H. Obinger. 2008. "Worlds, Families, Regimes: Country Clusters in European and OECD Area Public Policy." *West European Politics* 31, no. 1–2: 321–44.

CEPS (Centre for Policy Studies). 2014. "The Hartz Reforms . . . and Their Lessons for the UK." Available at www.cps.org.uk/files/reports/original/141024133732 -TheHartzReforms.pdf.

Cerami, A. 2010. "The Politics of Social Security Reforms in the Czech Republic, Hungary, Poland and Slovakia." In *A Long Goodbye to Bismarck? The Politics of Welfare Reform in Continental Europe*, edited by B. Palier. Amsterdam: Amsterdam University Press.

Cerami, A., and P. Vanhuysse. 2009. *Post-Communist Welfare Pathways. Theorizing Social Policy Transformations in Central and Eastern Europe*. Palgrave Macmillan.

CFR (Council on Foreign Relations). 2010. "Eurozone Crisis as Historical Legacy: The Enduring Impact of German Unification, Twenty Years On." Available at http://www.cfr.org/world/eurozone-crisis-historical-legacy/p22932.

Cho, Y., and D. Newhouse. 2013. "How Did the Great Recession Affect Different Types of Workers? Evidence from 17 Middle-Income Countries." *World Development* 41, no. 1: 31–50.

Chung, H., and S. Thewissen. 2011. "Falling Back on Old Habits? A Comparison of the Social and Unemployment Crisis Reactive Policy Strategies in Germany, the UK and Sweden." *Social Policy and Administration* 45, no. 4: 354–70.

Clasen, J., D. Clegg, and J. Kvist. 2012. "European Labour Market Policies in (the) Crisis." European Trade Union Institute. Working Paper 2012.12. Available at www.etui.org/Publications2/Working-Papers/European-labour-market-polici es-in-the-crisis.

Clayton, R., and J. Pontusson. 1998. "Welfare-State Retrenchment Revisited: Entitlement Cuts, Public Sector Restructuring and Inegalitarian Trends in Advanced Capitalist Societies." *World Politics* 51, no. 1: 67–98.

Clegg, D. 2010. "Labour Market Policy in the Crisis: The UK in Comparative Perspective." *Journal of Poverty and Social Justice* 18, no. 1: 5–17.

CNBC. 2013. "Germany Plans More Austerity Measures: Report." Available at http://www.cnbc.com/id/100353656.

Cohen, D., and G. Follette. 2000. "The Automatic Fiscal Stabilizers: Quietly Doing Their Thing." *Federal Reserve Bank of New York Economic Policy Review* 6, no. 1.

Conservative Party. 2015. "The Conservative Party Manifesto 2015." London. Available at www.conservatives.com/manifesto.

Conservatives. 2019. "Conservatives Announce Range of Measures to Take Back Control of Our Borders." November 17, 2019. Accessed June 11, 2020. Available at https://www.conservatives.com/news/conservatives-announce-range-of-me asures-to-take-back-control-of-our-borders.

Contiguglia, C. 2011. "Austerity Measures Take Effect." *Prague Post*. Available at www.praguepost.cz/business/7017-austerity-measures-take-effect.html.

Cook, L., M. Orenstein, and M. Rueschemeyer, eds. 1999. *Left Parties and Social Policy in Postcommunist Europe*. Boulder, CO: Westview Press.

Cox, R.H. 2001. "The social construction of an imperative: why welfare reform happened in Denmark and the Netherlands but not in Germany." World Politics 55, no. 3: 463 – 98.

Crespy, A., and G. Menz. 2015. *Social Policy and the Eurocrisis*. Palgrave Macmillan.

Crouch, C. 2011. *The Strange Non-Death of Neoliberalism*. Cambridge: Polity Press.

Cusack, T., T. Iversen, and P. Rehm. 2008. "Economic Shocks, Inequality, and Popular Support for Redistribution." In *Democracy, Inequality, and Representation*, edited by P. Beramendi and C. Anderson. Russell Sage Foundation.

Dalton, R., D. Farrell. and I. McAllister. 2011. *Political Parties and Democratic Linkage: How Parties Organize Democracy*. Oxford: Oxford University Press.

De Grauwe, P. 2008. "Cherished Myths Fall Victim to Economic Reality." *Financial Times*. Available at www.ft.com/cms/s/0/b89eb5b2-5804-11dd-b02f-000077b0 7658.html#axzz3cle8bsgV.

De Grauwe, P. 2011. "Balanced Budget Fundamentalism." CEPS Commentary, Centre for European Policy Studies. Available at https://www.ceps.eu/publicati ons/balanced-budget-fundamentalism.

Deacon, B. 1997. "International Organizations and the Making of Post-Communist Social Policy", In *Global Social Policy*, edited by B. Deacon, M. Hulse, and P. Stubbs. London: Sage.

De la Porte, C., and E. Heins. 2015. "A New Era of European Integration? Governance of Labour Market and Social Policy Since the Sovereign Debt Crisis." *Comparative European Politics* 13, no. 1: 8–28.

De la Porte, C., and E. Heins. 2016. *The Sovereign Debt Crisis, the EU and Welfare State Reform*. UK: Palgrave Macmillan.

Della Porta D., H. Kouki, and J. Fernández. 2017. "Left's Love and Hate for Europe: Syriza, Podemos and Critical Visions of Europe During the Crisis." In *Euroscepticism, Democracy and the Media. Palgrave Studies in European Political Sociology*, edited by M. Caiani and S. Guerra. Palgrave Macmillan.

Dellepiane, S., and N. Hardiman, N. 2012. "The New Politics of Austerity: Fiscal Responses to the Economic Crisis in Ireland and Spain." UCD Geary Institute Discussion Paper Series; WP2012/07. University College Dublin. Geary Institute. Available at www.ucd.ie/geary/static/publications/workingpapers/gearyw p201207.pdf.

Del Pino, E. 2013. "The Spanish Welfare State from Zapatero to Rajoy: Recalibration to Retrenchment." In *Politics and Society in Contemporary Spain: From Zapatero to Rajoy*, edited by A. Botti and B. Field, 197–216. New York: Palgrave.

De Wilde, P., A. Leupold, and H. Schmidtke. 2016. "Introduction: The Differentiated Politicisation of European Governance." *West European Politics* 39, no. 1: 3–22.

DSS (Department of Social Security). 1998. *New Ambitions for Our Country: New Contract for Welfare*. London: Department of Social Security.

Deutsche Bank. 2012. "European Party Landscape in Transition." Published November 14, 2012. Available at www.dbresearch.com/PROD/DBR_INTERN ET_EN-PROD/PROD0000000000296927/European_party_landscape_in_tra nsition.pdf.

Deutsche Welle. 2012. "Debt Crisis Lays Waste to European Governments." Available at http://www.dw.de/debt-crisis-lays-waste-to-european-governments /a-15915310.

Dieckhoff, M., and D. Gallie. 2007. "The Renewed Lisbon Strategy and Social Exclusion Policy." *Industrial Relations Journal* 38, no. 6: 480–502.

Dolls, M., C. Fuest, and A. Peichl. 2009. *Automatic Stabilizers and Economic Crisis: US vs. Europe*. Cambridge, MA: National Bureau of Economic Research.

Dolls, M., C. Fuest, and A. Peichl. 2010. *Automatic Stabilizers, Economic Crisis and Income Distribution in Europe*. Cambridge, MA: National Bureau of Economic Research.

Dolls, M., C. Fuest, and A. Peichl. 2012. "Automatic Stabilizers and Economic Crisis: US vs. Europe." *Journal of Public Economics* 96, no. 1: 279–94.

Doluca, H., M. Hübner, D. Rumpf, and B. Weigert. 2012. "The European Redemption Pact: Implementation and Macroeconomic Effects." *Intereconomics* 47, no. 4: 230–39.

Dølvik, J. E., J. G. Andersen, and J. Vartiainen. 2014. "The Nordic Social Models in Turbulent Times: Consolidation and Flexible Adaptation." In *European Social Models from Crisis to Crisis: Employment and Inequality in the Era of Monetary Integration*, edited by J. E. Dølvik and A. Martin. Oxford: Oxford University Press.

Dribbusch, H. 2004. "Debate on Introduction of Statutory Minimum Wage." Available at www.eurofound.europa.eu/observatories/eurwork/articles/debate-on -introduction-of-statutory-minimum-wage.

Dukelow, F. 2016. "'Pushing against an open door': Reinforcing the Neo-liberal Policy Paradigm in Ireland and the Impact of EU Intrusion." In *The Sovereign Debt Crisis, the EU and Welfare State Reform*, edited by C. De la Porte and E. Heins. UK: Palgrave Macmillan.

Dullien, S., and U. Guérot. 2012. "The Long Shadow of Ordoliberalism: Germany's Approach to the Euro Crisis." European Council on Foreign Relations Policy Brief. February 22, 2012. Accessed July 14, 2020. Available at https://www.ecfr .eu/page/-/ECFR49_GERMANY_BRIEF.pdf.

Dvorakova, Z., and A. Stroleny. 2012. "Social Dialogue and the Public Services in the Aftermath of the Economic Crisis: Strengthening Partnership in an Era of Austerity in the Czech Republic." National report.

ECB (European Central Bank). 2010. "The Impact of the Financial Crisis on the

Central and Eastern European Countries." Monthly Bulletin, July 2010. Available at www.ecb.europa.eu/pub/pdf/other/art3_mb201007en_pp85–96en.pdf.

ECFR (European Council on Foreign Relations). 2012. "Reinventing Europe: Explaining the Fiscal Compact." Available at www.ecfr.eu/article/commentary _reinventing_europe_explaining_the_fiscal_compact.

Economist. 2010a. "Return to Bleak House." Available at http://www.economist.com /node/15497717.

Economist. 2010b. "Czech Politics: A Czech Tea Party?" Available at www.economi st.com/blogs/easternapproaches/2010/12/czech_politics.

Economist. 2011. "Germany's Debt Brake: Tie Your Hands, Please." Available at http://www.economist.com/node/21541459.

Economist. 2013. "Stimulus v Austerity: Sovereign Doubts." Available at www.econ omist.com/news/schools-brief/21586802-fourth-our-series-articles-financial -crisis-looks-surge-public.

Economist. 2014a. "Czech Euroscepticism: The Unloved Union." Available at www .economist.com/news/europe/21602744-ten-years-after-joining-european-uni on-most-czech-parties-are-anti-eu-unloved-union.

Economist. 2014b. "Banning Extremist Ads: A Step Too Far?" Available at www.eco nomist.com/blogs/easternapproaches/2014/05/banning-extremist-ads.

Economist. 2015. "Spain's Regional Elections: Reluctant Partners." Available at www .economist.com/news/europe/21652090-two-party-system-splits-four-party -one-unpredictable-results-hard-interpret.

Economy Watch. 2010. "Sweden Economic Stimulus Package." Available at http:// www.economywatch.com/economic-stimulus-package/sweden.html.

Edlund, J. 2006. "Trust in the Capability of the Welfare State and General Welfare State Support: Sweden 1997–2002." Acta Sociologica 49, no. 4: 395–417.

Eichhorst, W., M. Feil, and P. Marx. 2010. "Crisis, What Crisis? Patterns of Adaptation in European Labor Markets." IZA Discussion Paper No. 5045. Bonn: Institute for the Study of Labour (IZA).

EIRO (European Industrial Relations Observatory). 2008. "Lower Taxes for 2009 in Bid to Boost Employment." EIRO.

EIRO (European Industrial Relations Observatory). 2009a. "New Allowances for Short-Term Work in Bid to Offset Economic Crisis." EIRO.

EIRO (European Industrial Relations Observatory). 2009b. "New Collective Agreement in Metalworking Sector." EIRO.

EIRO (European Industrial Relations Observatory). 2009c. "New Agreement after Brief Bargaining Round in Retail Sector." EIRO.

EIRO (European Industrial Relations Observatory). 2009d. "Working Time Accounts and Short-Time Work Used to Maintain Employment." EIRO.

EIRO (European Industrial Relations Observatory). 2009e. "Young Workers to Substitute for Older Employees." EIRO.

EIRO (European Industrial Relations Observatory). 2009f. "Unemployment Hits Young and Older Workers the Hardest." EIRO.

EIRO (European Industrial Relations Observatory). 2009g. "Government Launches Crisis Package to Tackle Economic Recession." EIRO.

EIRO (European Industrial Relations Observatory). 2009h. "Swedish Government Unveils Measures to Fight Unemployment." EIRO.

EIRO. (European Industrial Relations Observatory). 2009i. "Green Light for New Unemployment Protection Measure." Available at http://www.eurofound.euro pa.eu/eiro/2009/09/articles/es0909029i.htm.

EIRO (European Industrial Relations Observatory). 2010. "Czech Republic: New Government Wants to Reform Labour Code." EIRO CZ1007019I, Available at www.eurofound.europa.eu/eiro/2010/07/articles/cz1007019i.htm, consulted 24/03/11.

El País. 2018a. "Pedro Sánchez Becomes the New Prime Minister of Spain." Available at https://elpais.com/elpais/2018/06/01/inenglish/1527854951_473768. html.

El País. 2018b. "Spain's PM and Podemos Leader Sign Deal for Biggest Wage Hike in 40 Years." Available at https://elpais.com/elpais/2018/10/12/inenglish/15393 32885_013808.html.

Eller, M. 2009. "Fiscal Position and Size of Automatic Stabilizers in the CESEE EU Member States—Implications for Discretionary Measures." Focus on European Integration, Österreichische Nationalbank, Q2:09, 78–84.

Ellison, N. 2016. "The Coalition Government, Public Spending and Social Policy." In The Coalition Government and Social Policy: Restructuring the Welfare State, edited by H. Bochel and M. Powell. Bristol: Policy Press, University of Bristol.

Elster, J., C. Offe, and U. Preuss, eds. 1998. Institutional Design in Post-Communist Societies: Rebuilding the Ship at Sea. Cambridge: Cambridge University Press.

Emerging Europe. 2018. "Pension Reform in the Czech Republic." Available at https://emerging-europe.com/voices/pension-reform-in-the-czech-republic/.

Englund, P. 1999. "The Swedish Banking Crisis: Roots and Consequences." Oxford Review of Economic Policy 15, no. 3: 80–97.

EPSU (European Federation of Public Service Unions). 2011. "50,000 Demonstrate in Prague Against Cuts and Labour Reforms." Available at http://www.epsu.org /a/7655.

Esping-Andersen, G. 1990. Three Worlds of Welfare Capitalism. Princeton, NJ: Princeton University Press.

Esping-Andersen G. 1999. Social Foundations of Postindustrial Economies. New York: Oxford University Press.

ESRC (Economic and Social Research Council). 2015. "Welfare Budget and Benefit Cuts." Available at https://esrc.ukri.org/news-events-and-publications/eviden ce-briefings/welfare-budget-and-benefit-cuts/.

EU Observer. 2014. "Juncker and Schulz in Favour of Eurobonds." Available at https://euobserver.com/eu-elections/123488.

EUCE. 2013. "Policy Area: The Politics of Austerity European Union." Center of North Carolina: EU Briefings. Available at http://europe.unc.edu/wp-content/ uploads/2013/09/Brief1308-austerity.pdf.

Euractiv. 2010. "New Parties 'Re-Write' Czech Political Map." Available at www.eur activ.com/section/central-europe/news/new-parties-re-write-czech-political -map/.

Euractiv. 2014. "European Healthcare First Victim of Social Spending Cuts." Available at www.euractiv.com/section/health-consumers/news/european-healthca re-first-victim-of-social-spending-cuts/.

Euro Intelligence. 2013. "PSOE Turns to the Left." Available at www.eurointelligen ce.com/news-details/article/psoe-turns-to-the-left.html.

Euromanifesto Project. 2016. "European Parliament Election Study 2014, Euromanifesto Study." Available at https://manifesto-project.wzb.eu/information/do cuments/cmp_emp_mapping.

European Commission. 1997. "European Employment Strategy." Brussels, Belgium.

European Commission. 2005. "Working Together for Growth and Jobs: A New Start for the Lisbon Strategy." Available at https://eur-lex.europa.eu/legal-conte nt/EN/TXT/PDF/?uri=CELEX:52005DC0024&from=HR.

European Commission. 2008. "A European Economic Recovery Plan." Available at http://ec.europa.eu/economy_finance/publications/publication13504_en.pdf.

European Commission. 2009a. "The EU's Response to Support the Real Economy during the Economic Crisis: An Overview of Member States' Recovery Measures." Occasional Papers No. 51. Brussels, Directorate General for Economic and Financial Affairs. Available at http://ec.europa.eu/economy_finance/public ations/publication15666_en.pdf.

European Commission. 2009b. "The Swedish Model for Resolving the Banking Crisis of 1991–93. Seven Reasons Why It Was Successful." European Economy. Economic Papers 360. February 2009. Available at http://ec.europa.eu/econo my_finance/publications/publication14098_en.pdf.

European Commission. 2010. "Europe 2020 Initiatives." Available at http://ec.euro pa.eu/social/main.jsp?catId=956.

European Commission. 2012a. "Six-Pack? Two-Pack? Fiscal Compact? A Short Guide to the New EU Fiscal Governance." Economic and Financial Affairs Website. Available at http://ec.europa.eu/economy_finance/articles/governan ce/2012-03-14_six_pack_en.htm.

European Commission. 2012b. "Fiscal Compact Enters Into Force." Available at www.consilium.europa.eu/uedocs/cms_data/docs/pressdata/en/ecofin/134543 .pdf.

European Commission. 2014. "The EU's Fiscal Crisis and Policy Response: Reforming Economic Governance in the EU." Available at www.oecd.org/governance/ budgeting/48871475.pdf.

European Council. 2000. "Lisbon European Council 23 and 24 March 2000 Presidency Conclusions." Available at http://www.europarl.europa.eu/summits/lis1 _en.htm#a.

European Council. 2012. "Treaty on Stability, Coordination and Governance in the Economic and Monetary Union." Available at http://european-council.europa .eu/media/639235/st00tscg26_en12.pdf.

European Parliament. 2009. "Economic Recovery Packages in EU Member States: Compilation of Briefing Papers." Available at www.europarl.europa.eu/RegData /etudes/divers/join/2009/416206/IPOL-ECON_DV(2009)416206_EN.pdf.

European Parliament. 2013. "Is the Semester Hard-Wired for Austerity or Growth?" Interparliamentary Committee Meeting. Available at www.europarl.europa.eu/ RegData/etudes/note/join/2013/492471/IPOL-ECON_NT(2013)492471_EN .pdf.

European Parliament. 2014. "Results of the 2014 European Elections." Available at http://www.europarl.europa.eu/elections2014-results/en/country-results-uk -2014.htmlfetz.

Eurostat. 2011. "The Effect of the Economic and Financial Crisis on Government Revenue and Expenditure." *Eurostat Statistics in Focus* 45: 1–12.

Eurostat. 2015. Eurostat Database. Available at http://ec.europa.eu/eurostat/data/da tabase.

Falkenbach, M., and S. Greer. 2018. "Political Parties Matter: The Impact of the Populist Radical Right on Health." *European Journal of Public Health* 28, no. 3: 15–18.

Farnsworth, K., and Z. Irving. 2011. *Social Policy in Challenging Times: Economic Crisis and Welfare Systems.* Bristol: Policy Press.

Fenger, H. 2007. "Welfare Regimes in Central and Eastern Europe: Incorporating Post-Communist Countries in a Welfare Regime Typology." *Contemporary Issues and Ideas in Social Sciences* 3, no. 2.

Ferrera, M. 1996. "The 'Southern Model' of Welfare in Social Europe." *Journal of European Social Policy* 6, no. 1: 17–37.

Ferrera, M. 2005. *The Boundaries of Welfare: European Integration and the New Spatial Politics of Social Protection.* Oxford: Oxford University Press.

Ferrera, M. 2010. "The South European Countries." In *The Oxford Handbook of the Welfare State,* edited by F. Castles, S. Leibfried, J. Lewis, H. Obinger, and C. Pierson. Oxford: Oxford University Press.

Fetzer, T. 2018. "Did Austerity Cause Brexit?" Working Paper Series. University of Warwick. Available at https://warwick.ac.uk/fac/soc/economics/research/centr es/cage/manage/publications/381-2018_fetzer.pdf.

Financial Times. 2012a. "Merkel Warns on Cost of Welfare." Available at https:// www.ft.com/content/8cc0f584–45fa-11e2-b7ba-00144feabdc0.

Financial Times. 2012b. "Weidmann Considered Quitting, Bild Says." Available at www.ft.com/cms/s/0/50ea0c32-f34b-11e1-9ca6-00144feabdc0.html#axzz28R CMBhX8.

Financial Times. 2013. "Germany Defies Calls for Stimulus." Available at www.ft .com/intl/cms/s/0/8a97c6de-8bff-11e2-b001-00144feabdc0.html#axzz3Wiul r4yR.

Financial Times. 2015. "David Cameron Wants Wage Rises to Replace Benefits." Available at https://www.ft.com/content/caff39f0–18e3–11e5–8201-cbdb03d7 1480.

Finseraas, H., and K. Vernby. 2011. "What Parties Are and What Parties Do: Partisanship and Welfare State Reform in an Era of Austerity." *Socio-Economic Review* 9, no. 4: 613–38.

Foreign Policy. 2015. "Is the Euro Compatible With Democracy? Berlin Doesn't

Seem to Think So." Available at http://foreignpolicy.com/2015/03/06/is-the-eu ro-compatible-with-democracy/.

France-Politique. 2014. "Élections européennes 2014." Available at www.france-pol itique.fr/elections-europeennes-2014.htm.

Freedom House. 2013. "Czech Republic." Available at https://freedomhouse.org/re port/freedom-world/2013/czech-republic.

Frye, T. 2002. "The Perils of Polarization: Economic Performance in the Postcom-munist World." *World Politics* 54, no. 3: 308–37.

Fulcher, J. 1994. "The Social Democratic Model in Sweden: Termination or Restora-tion?" *Political Quarterly* 65, no. 2: 203–13.

Funke, M., M. Schularick, and C. Trebesch. 2015. "Politics in the Slump: Polariza-tion and Extremism after Financial Crises, 1870–2014." Available at http://ec.eu ropa.eu/economy_finance/events/2015/20151001_post_crisis_slump/docume nts/c._trebesch.pdf.

Gardiner, N., T. Bromund, and J. D. Foster. 2010. "The U.K. Budget Cuts: Lessons for the United States." The Heritage Foundation. Available at http://www.herita ge.org/research/reports/2010/10/the-uk-budget-cuts-lessons-for-the-united-st ates.

Garrett, G. 1998. "Global Markets and National Politics: Collision Course or Virtu-ous Circle?" *International Organization* 52, no. 4: 787–824.

Garrett, G. 2001. "Globalization and Government Spending around the World."*Studies in Comparative International Development* 35, no. 4: 3–29.

German Federal Employment Agency. 2009. "Der Arbeitsmarkt in Deutschland: Frauen undMänner am Arbeitsmarkt." Nuremberg. Available at https://ideas.re pec.org/s/iab/iabfob.html.

Gilbert, N. 2002. *Transformation of the Welfare State.* New York: Oxford University Press.

Glassner, V., and M. Keune. 2012. "The Crisis and Social Policy: The Role of Collec-tive Agreements." *International Labour Review* 151, no. 4: 351–75.

Glyn, A., ed. 2001. *Social Democracy in Neoliberal Times: The Left and Economic Policy since 1980.* Oxford: Oxford University Press.

Goodman, J., and L. Pauly. 1993. "The Obsolescence of Capital Controls? Economic Management in an Age of Global Markets." *World Politics* 46, no. 1: 50–82.

Golinowska, S., P. Hengstenberg, and M. Żukowski, eds. 2009. *Diversity and Com-monality in European Social Policies: The Forging of a European Social Model.* Warsaw: Friedrich-Ebert-Stiftung and Wydawnictwo Naukowe Scholar.

Government of Sweden. 2017. "Important Step Towards a More Social Europe." Available at https://www.government.se/opinion-pieces/2017/11/important-st ep-towards-a-more-social-europe/.

Green, J., and S. Hobolt. 2008. "Owning the Issue Agenda: Party Strategies and Vote Choices in British Elections." *Electoral Studies* 27, no. 3: 460–76.

Green-Pedersen, C. 2019. *The Reshaping of West European Party Politics: Agenda-Setting and Party Competition in Comparative Perspective.* Oxford: Oxford Uni-versity Press.

Greer, S. 2017. "Medicine, Public Health and the Populist Radical Right." *Journal of the Royal Society of Medicine* 110, no. 8: 305–8.

Guardian. 2010. "Spanish PM Makes Debt Crisis U-turn with Emergency Cuts." Available at www.theguardian.com/business/2010/may/12/spanish-pm-debt -crisis-emergency-cuts.

Guardian. 2011. "Spanish Election: Convincing Victory for People's Party." Available at www.theguardian.com/world/2011/nov/20/spain-election-polls-rajoy -victory.

Guardian. 2012a. "Mariano Rajoy Announces €65bn in Austerity Measures for Spain." Available at: www.theguardian.com/business/2012/jul/11/mariano-raj oy-spain-65bn-cuts.

Guardian. 2012b. "Spain Given Deadline to Outline Cuts." Available at www.thegu ardian.com/world/2012/jul/11/spain-deadline-outline-cuts.

Guardian. 2012c. "Czechs Stage Mass Rally in Protest against Government." Available at www.theguardian.com/world/2012/apr/21/czech-republic-prague-rally -protest.

Guardian. 2013a. "German Election: Angela Merkel Secures Historic Third Win." Available at http://www.theguardian.com/world/2013/sep/22/angela-merkel -wins-third-term-germany.

Guardian. 2013b. "What Would a Ukip Britain Look Like?" Available at www.theg uardian.com/politics/2013/mar/07/ukip-policies-manifesto-commitments.

Guardian. 2015a. "Iain Duncan Smith Returns to Cabinet to Oversee £12bn Welfare Cuts." Available at www.theguardian.com/politics/2015/may/10/iain-dunc an-smith-conservative-cabinet-david-cameron-welfare-cuts.

Guardian. 2015b. "The Tories' £12bn of Welfare Cuts Could Come Back to Haunt Them." Available at www.theguardian.com/commentisfree/2015/may/08/tories -12bn-welfare-cuts-mythical-scroungers-conservatives.

Guardian. 2017a. "German Elections 2017: Full Results." Available at https://www. theguardian.com/world/ng-interactive/2017/sep/24/german-elections-2017 -latest-results-live-merkel-bundestag-afd.

Guardian. 2017b. "Public Services Face Real-Terms Spending Cuts of Up to 40% in Decade to 2020." Available at https://www.theguardian.com/uk-news/2017/nov /22/public-services-face-real-terms-spending-cuts-of-up-to-40-in-decade-to -2020.

Guardian. 2018. "Welfare Spending for UK's Poorest Shrinks by £37bn." Available at https://www.theguardian.com/politics/2018/sep/23/welfare-spending-uk-poor est-austerity-frank-field.

Guentner, S., S. Lukes, R. Stanton, B. Vollmer, and J. Wilding. 2016. "Bordering Practices in the UK Welfare System." *Critical Social Policy* 36, no. 3: 391–411.

Guillén, A. 2010. "Defrosting the Spanish Welfare State: The Weight of Conservative Components." In *A Long Goodbye to Bismarck? The Politics of Welfare Reforms in Continental Europe*, edited by B. Palier. Amsterdam: Amsterdam University Press.

Guillén, A., and S. Alvarez. 2001. "Globalization and the Southern Welfare States."

In *Globalization and European Welfare States*, edited by R. Sykes, B. Palier, and P. Prior, 103–26. New York: Palgrave.

Haas, E. 1968. *The Uniting of Europe: Political, Social, and Economic Forces, 1950–1957*. Stanford, CA: Stanford University Press.

Hacker, B. 2009. "Hybridization Instead of Clustering: Transformation Processes of Welfare Policies in Central and Eastern Europe." *Social Policy & Administration* 43, no. 2: 152–69.

Haffert, L., and P. Mehrtens. 2015. "From Austerity to Expansion? Consolidation, Budget Surpluses, and the Decline of Fiscal Capacity." *Politics & Society* 43, no. 1: 119–48.

Hall, P. A. 2014. "Varieties of Capitalism and the Euro Crisis." *West European Politics* 37: 1223–1243.

Hassenteufel, P., and B. Palier. 2015. "Still the Sound of Silence? Towards a New Phase in the Europeanisation of Welfare State Policies in France." *Comparative European Politics* 13, no. 1: 112–30.

Häusermann, S., and B. Palier. 2008. "The Politics of Employment-Friendly Welfare Reforms in Post-Industrial Economies." *Socio-Economic Review* 6, no. 3: 559–86.

Häusermann, S,. G. Picot, and D. Geering. 2013. "Rethinking Party Politics and the Welfare State: Recent Advances in the Literature." *British Journal of Political Science* 43, no. 1: 221–40.

Havlík, V. 2015. "Stable or Not? Patterns of Party System Dynamics and the Rise of the New Political Parties in the Czech Republic." *Romanian Journal of Political Science* 15, no. 1: 185–207.

Havlík, V. 2020. "Economy and Political Distrust: Explaining Public Anti-Partyism in the Czech Republic." *Human Affairs* 30, no. 1: 72–85.

Hay, C. 2019. "Does Capitalism (Still) Come in Varieties?" *Review of International Political Economy*. Published online July 2, 2019.

Hemerijck, A. 2013. *Changing Welfare States*. Oxford: Oxford University Press.

Hemerijck, A., B. Knapen, and E. van Doorne. 2009. *Aftershocks. Economic Crisis and Institutional Choice*. Amsterdam: Amsterdam University Press.

Hendrik, Z., A. Schäfer, and P. Manow. 2004. "European Social Policy and Europe's Party-Political Center of Gravity, 1957–2003." MPIfG Discussion Paper, No. 04/6 Available at www.mpifg.de/pu/mpifg_dp/dp04–6.pdf.

Hernández, E., and H. Kriesi. 2016. "The Electoral Consequences of the Financial and Economic Crisis in Europe." *European Journal of Political Research* 55, no. 2: 203–24.

Herwartz, H., and B. Theilen. 2014. "Partisan Influence on Social Spending under Market Integration, Fiscal Pressure and Institutional Change." *European Journal of Political Economy* 34: 409–24.

Heyes, J. 2011. "Flexicurity, Employment Protection and the Jobs Crisis." *Work, Employment and Society* 25, no. 4: 642–57.

Hicks, A., and D. Swank. 1992. "Politics, Institutions, and Welfare Spending in Industrialized Democracies, 1960–1982." *American Political Science Review* 86: 658–74.

Hijzen, A., and D. Venn. 2011. "The Role of Short-Time Work Schemes during the 2008-09 Recession." OECD Social, Employment and Migration Working Papers, No. 115, Paris: OECD.

Hills, J. 2011. "The Changing Architecture of the UK Welfare State." *Oxford Review of Economic Policy* 27, no. 4: 589–607.

HM Government. 2009. *Lisbon Strategy for Jobs and Growth: UK National Reform Programme 2009.* London: HM Treasury.

HM Treasury. 2009. *Budget 2009.* HC 407, London: HM Treasury.

HM Treasury. 2010. Budget Statement by the Chancellor of the Exchequer, The Rt Hon George Osborne MP. June 22. Available at http://webarchive.nationalarch ives.gov.uk/20130129110402/http:/cdn. hm-treasury.gov.uk/junebudget_comp lete.pdf.

Hobolt, S., and J. Tilley. 2016. "Fleeing the Centre: The Rise of Challenger Parties in the Aftermath of the Euro Crisis." *West European Politics* 39, no. 5: 971–91.

Hodson, D., and D. Mabbett. 2009. "UK Economic Policy and the Global Financial Crisis: Paradigm Lost?" *Journal of Common Market Studies* 47, no. 5: 1041–61.

Hooghe, L., and G. Marks. 2001. *Multi-level Governance and European Integration.* Lanham, MD: Rowman & Littlefield.

Hooghe, L., and G. Marks. 2018. "Cleavage Theory Meets Europe's Crises: Lipset, Rokkan, and the Transnational Cleavage." *Journal of European Public Policy* 25, no. 1: 109–35.

Horibayashi, T. 2006. "Central European Welfare System: The Present Characteristics." Available at http://project.iss.u-tokyo.ac.jp/nakagawa/members/papers/4(4)Horibayashi.final.pdf.

Hornát, J. 2014. "A Reflection on Czech Eurosception before the EU Elections." Open Democracy, January 16, 2014. Available at www.opendemocracy.net/can -europe-make-it/jan-horn%C3%A1t/reflection-on-czech-euroscepticism-befo re-eu-elections.

Huber, E., C. Ragin, and J. Stephens. 1993. "Social Democracy, Christian Democracy, Constitutional Structure, and the Welfare State." *American Journal of Sociology* 99, no. 3: 711–49.

Huber, E., and J. Stephens. 2000. "Partisan Governance, Women's Employment, and the Social Democratic Service State." *American Sociological Review* 65, no. 3: 323–42.

Hübner, Kurt. 2013. "Eurozone Crises. Leopard Politics in Action." Vancouver, BC, Amsterdam Paper for the CES Conference in Amsterdam, June 2013.

Huffington Post. 2014a. "Sweden's Turn Left Could Deal a Blow to European Austerity." Available at www.huffingtonpost.com/2014/09/13/sweden-austerity-ele ction_n_5816010.html.

Huffington Post. 2014b. "Sweden Election Results Offer Uncertain Future for Austerity." Available at www.huffingtonpost.com/2014/09/14/sweden-election-resu lts_n_5819612.html.

Hutter, S., H. Kriesi, and G. Vidal. 2018. "Old Versus New Politics: The Political Spaces in Southern Europe in Times of Crises." *Party Politics* 24, no. 1: 10–22.

Hyman, R. 2015. "Austeritarianism in Europe: What Options for Resistance?" In

Social Policy in the European Union: State of Play 2015, edited by D. Natali and B. Vanhercke, 97–126. Brussels: ETUI and OSE.

ILO (International Labour Organization). 2009. *Protecting People, Promoting Jobs.* Geneva, Switzerland.

ILO (International Labour Organization). 2011. "A Review of Global Fiscal Stimulus." EC-IILS Joint Discussion Paper Series No. 5. Geneva, Switzerland.

IMF. 2009. "World Economic Outlook: Sustaining the Recovery." Washington, DC.

IMF. 2012. "Czech Republic: Financial System Stability Assessment Update." IMF Country Report No. 12/177, July 2012. Available at www.imf.org/external/pubs/cat/longres.aspx?sk=26070.0.

IMF. 2013. "Growth Forecast Errors and Fiscal Multipliers." Working Paper No. 13/1. Available at http://www.imf.org/external/pubs/cat/longres.aspx?sk=40200.0.

IMF. 2014. "Redistribution, Inequality, and Growth." Available at http://www.imf.org/external/pubs/ft/sdn/2014/sdn1402.pdf.

Independent. 2015a. "Greek Bailout: Berlin's Stance during the Negotiations Left Greeks Defiant." Available at http://www.independent.co.uk/news/world/europe/greek-bailout-berlin-s-stance-during-the-negotiations-left-greeks-defiant-10060951.html.

Independent. 2015b. "General Election 2015: The Independent Policy Checker—Do You Know What Each Party Actually Stands For?" Available at www.independent.co.uk/news/uk/politics/generalelection/general-election-2015-the-independent-policy-checker—do-you-know-what-each-party-actually-stands-for-10227671.html.

Independent. 2015c. "Thousands of Eastern Europeans Lead Demonstrations against Refugees." Available at www.independent.co.uk/news/world/europe/thousands-of-eastern-europeans-lead-demonstrations-against-migrants-10499692.html.

Independent. 2018. "Jeremy Corbyn Tells EU's Centre-Left Politicians He Wants to Build a 'Socialist Europe.'" Available at www.independent.co.uk/news/world/europe/thousands-of-eastern-europeans-lead-demonstrations-against-migrants-10499692.html.

Iversen, T., and A. Wren. 1998. "Equality, Employment and Budgetary Restraint, the Trilemma of the Service Economy." *World Politics* 50: 507–46.

Iversen, T., and D. Soskice. 2006. "Electoral Institutions and the Politics of Coalitions: Why Some Democracies Redistribute More Than Others." *American Political Science Review* 100, no. 2: 165–81.

Iversen, T., and D. Soskice. 2010. "Dualism and Political Coalitions: Inclusionary Versus Exclusionary Reforms in an Age of Rising Inequality." Paper prepared for presentation at the Annual Meeting of the American Political Science Association, Toronto, 2009.

Iversen, T., D. Soskice, and A. Hope 2016. "The Eurozone and Political Economic Institutions." *Annual Review of Political Science* 19: 163-85.

Jackson, J. 2009. "The Financial Crisis: Impact on and Response by The European

Union." Congressional Research Service. June 24, 2009. Available from www.crs .gov.

Jeong, H. 2010. "Globalization and the Politics of the Welfare State." PhD dissertation, University of Kentucky. Available at http://uknowledge.uky.edu/cgi/viewc ontent.cgi?article=1026&context=gradschool_diss.

Jinsoo, K., and P. Sojeung. 2008. "European Welfare States in Transition: Poland, the Czech Republic, and Hungary." In *Understanding European Social Policy*, edited by P. Abrahamson and C. Aspalter. Casa Verde Publishing.

Junor, P. 2015. "The Rise of the 'Radical' Left in Spain." Contributoria. Available at www.contributoria.com/issue/2015–01/5458108dad18bfb9350000a5/.

Karamessini, M. 2007. "The Southern European Social Model: Changes and Continuities in the Last Decades." Discussion Paper Series No. 174, Geneva: International Institute for Labour Studies, http://www.ilo.org/public/english/bureau/ inst/download/dp17407.pdf.

Kenworthy, L., and J. Pontusson. 2005. "Rising Inequality and the Politics of Redistribution in Affluent Countries." *Perspectives on Politics* 3, no. 3: 449–71.

Kenworthy, L. 2008. *Jobs with Equality*. Oxford: Oxford University Press.

Keskinen, S., O. C. Norocel, and M. B. Jørgensen. 2016. "The Politics and Policies of Welfare Chauvinism under the Sign of the Economic Crisis." *Critical Social Policy* 36, no. 3: 321–29.

Kinderman, D. 2017. "Challenging Varieties of Capitalism's Account of Business Interests: Neoliberal Think-Tanks, Discourse as a Power Resource and Employers' Quest for Liberalization in Germany and Sweden." *Socio-Economic Review* 15, no. 3: 586–613.

Kingdon, J. 1995. *Agenda, Alternatives and Public Policies*. 2nd edition. New York: Harper Collins.

Kirschbaum, E. 2017. "Merkel's Conservatives Rap Her Election Rival Schulz for Eurobonds Talk." Reuters. February 13, 2017. Accessed July 13, 2020. Available at https://www.reuters.com/article/eurozone-eurobonds-germany-election/me rkels-conservatives-rap-her-election-rival-schulz-for-eurobonds-talk-idUSL8 N1FY5PC

Kittel, B., and H. Obinger. 2003. "Political Parties, Institutions, and the Dynamics of Social Expenditure in Times of Austerity." *Journal of European Public Policy* 10, no. 1: 20–45.

Kleider, H., and F. Stoeckel. 2019. "The Politics of International Redistribution: Explaining Public Support for Fiscal Transfers in the EU." *European Journal of Political Research* 58, no. 1: 4–29.

Kok, W. 2004. "Facing the Challenge: The Lisbon Strategy for Growth and Employment." European Commission Report, November, 2004. Available at https://ec .europa.eu/research/evaluations/pdf/archive/fp6-evidence-base/evaluation_st udies_and_reports/evaluation_studies_and_reports_2004/the_lisbon_strategy _for_growth_and_employment_report_from_the_high_level_group.pdf.

Kornai, J. 2001. "The Borderline between the Spheres of Authority of the Citizens and the State: Recommendations for the Hungarian Health Reform." In *Reform-*

ing the State. Fiscal and Welfare Reform in Post-Socialist Countries, edited by J. Kornai, 181–209. Cambridge: Cambridge University Press.

Korpi, W. 1983. *The Democratic Class Struggle*. London: Routledge & Kegan Paul.

Korpi, W. (1989). "Power, Politics, and State Autonomy in the Development of Social Citizenship." *American Sociological Review*, 54, no. 3: 309–29.

Korpi, W. 2003. "Welfare-State Regress in Western Europe: Politics, Institutions, Globalization, and Europeanization." *Annual Review of Sociology* 29: 589–609.

Korpi, W., and J. Palme. 1998. "The Paradox of Redistribution and Strategies of Equality: Welfare State Institutions, Inequality, and Poverty in the Western Countries." *American Sociological Review* 63, no. 5: 661–87.

Korpi, W., and J. Palme. 2003. "New Politics and Class Politics in the Context of Austerity and Globalization: Welfare State Regress in 18 Countries, 1975–95." *American Political Sciences Review* 97, no. 3: 425–46.

Krause, W., and H. Giebler. 2019. "Shifting Welfare Policy Positions: The Impact of Radical Right Populist Party Success Beyond Migration Politics." *Representation* 55: 1–18.

Kriesi, H., E. Grande, M. Dolezal, M. Helbinger, D. Höglinger, S. Hutter, and B. Wüest. 2012. *Political Conflict in Western Europe*. Cambridge: Cambridge University Press.

Kriesi, H., E. Grande, R. Lachat, M. Dolezal, S. Bornschier, and T. Frey. 2008. *West European Politics in the Age of Globalization*. Cambridge: Cambridge University Press.

Kuipers, S. 2006. *The Crisis Imperative: Crisis Rhetoric and Welfare State Reform in Belgium and the Netherlands in the Early 1990s*. Amsterdam: Amsterdam University Press.

Kvist, J. 1999. "Welfare Reform in the Nordic Countries in the 1990S: Using Fuzzy-Set Theory to Assess Conformity to Ideal Types." *Journal of European Social Policy* 9, no. 3: 231–52.

Kvist, J., and J. Sari, eds. 2007. *The Europeanisation of Social Protection*. Policy Press.

Kwon, H., and J. Pontusson. 2010. "Globalization, Labour Power and Partisan Politics Revisited." *Socio-Economic Review* 8, no. 2: 251–81.

Labour Manifesto. 2017. "For the Many Not the Few." Available at https://labour.org .uk/wp-content/uploads/2017/10/labour-manifesto-2017.pdf.

Labour Party. 1994. "Social Justice: Strategies for National Renewal." Commission on Social Justice London.

Labour Party. 1997. "New Labour, New Life For Britain." London.

Labour Party. 2015a. "A Better Plan for Britain's Prosperity." Available at http://acti on.labour.org.uk/page/-/blog%20images/A_better_plan_for_Britains_prosper ity.pdf.

Labour Party. 2015b. "Protecting Better, Demanding More: Labour's Approach to Welfare and Work." Available at http://www2.labour.org.uk/protecting-better -demanding-more-labours-approach.

Labour Party. 2018. "Our Future: Labour's Alternative Budget 2018." Available at https://www.labour.ie/download/pdf/our_future_labours_alternative_budget _2018.pdf.

Laeven, L., and F. Valencia. 2010. "Resolution of Banking Crises: The Good, the Bad, and the Ugly." IMF Working Paper No. 10/146.

Lamartina, S., and A. Zaghini. 2011. "Increasing Public Expenditure: Wagner's Law in OECD Countries." *German Economic Review* 12, no. 2: 149–64.

Lauzadyte-Tutliene, A., T. Balezentis, and E. Goculenko. 2018. "Welfare State in Central and Eastern Europe." *Economics and Sociology* 11, no. 1: 100–23.

LeDuc, L., and J. H. Pammett. 2013. "The Fate of Governing Parties in Times of Economic Crisis." *Electoral Studies* 32, no. 3: 494–99.

Lee, S., and S. McBride, eds. 2007. *Neo-Liberalism, State Power and Global Governance*. New York: Springer.

Lehner, T., and F. Wasserfallen. 2019. "Political Conflict in the Reform of the Eurozone." *European Union Politics* 20, no. 1: 45–64.

León, M. 2011. "The Quest for Gender Equality." In *The Spanish Welfare State in the European Context*, edited by A. Guillén and M. León, 59–74. Farnham: Ashgate.

León, M., and E. Pavolini. 2014. "'Social Investment' or Back to 'Familism': The Impact of the Economic Crisis on Family and Care Policies in Italy and Spain." *South European Society and Politics* 19, no. 3: 353–69.

Leschke, J., and M. Jepsen. 2012. "Introduction: Crisis, Policy Responses and Widening Inequalities in the EU." *International Labour Review* 151, no. 4: 289–312.

Leuffen, D., B. Rittberger, and F. Schimmelfennig. 2012. *Differentiated Integration Explaining Variation in the European Union*. Palgrave Macmillan.

Lewis, J., T. Knijn, C. Martin, and I. Ostner. 2008. "Patterns of Development in Work/Family Reconciliation Policies for Parents in France, Germany, the Netherlands, and the UK in the 2000s." *Social Politics: International Studies in Gender, State and Society* 15, no. 3: 261–86.

Lim, J. 2000. "The Effects of the East Asian Crisis on the Employment of Women and Men: The Philippine Case." *World Development* 28, no. 7: 1285–1306.

Lindqvist, E., and R. Östling. 2010. "Political Polarization and the Size of Government." *American Political Science Review* 104, no. 3: 543–65.

Linek, L. 2011 "Czech Republic." *European Journal of Political Research* 50, no. 7–8: 948–54.

Lipsmeyer, C. 2000. "Reading Between the Welfare Lines: Politics and Policy Structure in Post-Communist Europe." *Europe-Asia Studies* 52, no. 7: 1191–1211.

Lipsmeyer, C. 2011. "Booms and Busts: How Parliamentary Governments and Economic Context Influence Welfare Policy." *International Studies Quarterly* 55, no. 4: 959–80.

Llamazares, I. 2005. "The Popular Party and European Integration: Re-elaborating the European Programme of Spanish Conservatism." *South European Society and Politics* 10, no. 2: 315–32.

The Local. 2014a. "Sweden 'slimmest Nordic welfare state.'" Available at www.thelocal.se/20140121/swedens-welfare-state-most-scaled-back-in-nordics.

The Local. 2014b. "Social Democrats Reveal Election Manifesto." Available at https://www.thelocal.se/20140902/social-democrats-to-reveal-election-manifesto.

The Local. 2018. "Sweden Starts Laying the Groundwork for Snap Election." Available at https://www.thelocal.se/20181214/sweden-starts-laying-the-groundwo rk-for-snap-election.

Lupton R., T. Burchardt, A. Fitzgerald, J. Hills, A. McKnight, P. Obolenskaya, K. Stewart, S. Thomson, R. Tunstall, and P. Vizard. 2015. "The Coalition's Social Policy Record: Policy, Spending and Outcomes 2010–2015." *Social Policy in a Cold Climate: Research Report*. London School of Economics.

Lupton R., T. Burchardt, J. Hills, K. Stewart, and P. Vizard. 2013. "A Framework for Analysing the Effects of Social Policy." *Social Policy in a Cold Climate: Research Note Series*. London School of Economics.

Maatsch, A. 2014. "Are We All Austerians Now? An Analysis of National Parliamentary Parties' Positioning on Anti-Crisis Measures in the Eurozone." *Journal of European Public Policy* 21, no. 1: 96–115.

Magone, J. 2004. *Contemporary Spanish Politics*. New York: Routledge.

Mahoney, J., and K. Thelen, eds. 2010. *Explaining Institutional Change: Ambiguity, Agency, and Power*. New York: Cambridge University Press.

Manifesto Project. 2018. "The Manifesto Data Collection." Version 2018a. Available at https://manifesto-project.wzb.eu.

Manow, P., B. Palier, and H. Schwander, eds. 2018. *Welfare Democracies and Party Politics: Explaining Electoral Dynamics in Times of Changing Welfare Capitalism*. Oxford: Oxford University Press.

Marchal, S., I. Marx, and N. Van Mechelen. 2014. "The Great Wake-Up Call? Social Citizenship and Minimum Income Provisions in Europe in Times of Crisis." *Journal of Social Policy* 43, no. 2: 247–67.

Margalit, Y. 2013. "Explaining Social Policy Preferences: Evidence from the Great Recession." *American Political Science Review* 107, no. 1: 80–103.

Market Watch. 2010. "Germany Targets $97.6 Billion in Budget Cuts Through 2014." Available at www.marketwatch.com/story/germany-plans-976-billion -in-budget-cuts-2010-06-07?siteid=rss&rss=1.

MacLeavy, J. 2011. "A 'New Politics' of Austerity, Workfare and Gender? The UK Coalition Government's Welfare Reform Proposals." *Cambridge Journal of Regions, Economy and Society* 4: 355–67.

Matthijs, M., and K. McNamara. 2015. "The Euro Crisis' Theory Effect: Northern Saints, Southern Sinners, and the Demise of the Eurobond." *Journal of European Integration* 37, no. 2: 229–45.

McCarty, N. 2012. "The Politics of the Pop: The U.S. Response to the Financial Crisis and the Great Recession." In *Coping with Crisis: Government Reactions to the Great Recession*, edited by N. Bermeo and J. Pontusson. Russell Sage Foundation.

McManus, I. 2018. "Political Parties as Drivers of Post-Crisis Social Spending in Liberal Welfare States." *Comparative European Politics* 16, no. 5: 843–70.

McManus, I. 2019. "The Reemergence of Partisan Effects on Social Spending in Europe After the Global Financial Crisis." *Journal of Common Market Studies* 57, no. 6: 1274–91.

McManus, I. 2021. "The Case of the United Kingdom Independence Party (UKIP)."

In *Populist Radical Right and Health: National Policies and Global Trends*, edited by M. Falkenbach and S. Greer. New York: Springer.

Mian, A., A. Sufi, and F. Trebbi. 2014. "Resolving Debt Overhang: Political Constraints in the Aftermath of Financial Crises." *American Economic Journal: Macroeconomics* 6, no. 2: 1–28.

Ministerio de Trabajo y Asuntos Sociales. 1996. *Anuario de Estadísticas Laborales y de Asuntos Sociales 1995*. Madrid: Ministerio de Trabajo y Asuntos Sociales.

Mirror. 2015a. "Where Is the Far Right Most Powerful in Europe?" Available at www.mirror.co.uk/news/ampp3d/far-right-most-powerful-europe-4927430.

Mirror. 2015b. "David Cameron Sharpening the Knife for First Deep Cuts in £12 billion Welfare Savings." Available at http://www.mirror.co.uk/news/uk-news/david-cameron-sharpening-knife-first-5681804.

Mishra, R. 1999. *Globalization and the Welfare State*. Cheltenham, UK: Edward Elgar.

Mladovsky, P., D. Srivastava, J. Cylus, K. Karanikolos, T. Evetovits, S. Thomson, and M. McKee. 2012. "Health Policy Responses to the Financial Crisis in Europe Policy Summary, 5." World Health Organization on behalf of the European Observatory on Health Systems and Policies, Copenhagen, Denmark. Available at www.euro.who.int/en/data-and-evidence/evidence-informed-policy-making/publications/2012/health-policy-responses-to-the-financial-crisis-in-europe.

Möller, J. 2010. "The German Labor Market Response in the World Recession—Demystifying a Miracle." *Zeitschrift für ArbeitsmarktForschung* 42, no. 4: 325–36.

Moreno, L. 2000. "The Spanish Development of Southern Welfare." In *Survival of the Welfare State*, edited by S. Khunle, 146–65. London: Routledge.

Moreno, L., and A. Arriba. 1998. "Decentralization, Mesogovernments, and the New Logic of Welfare Provision in Spain." In *Reforming Social Assistance and Social Services: International Experiences and Perspectives*. European University Institute.

Mudde, Cas. 2007. *Populist Radical Right Parties in Europe*. Cambridge: Cambridge University Press.

Müller-Rommel, F., K. Fettelschoss, and P. Harfst. 2004. "Party Government in Central Eastern European Democracies: A Data Collection (1990–2003)." *European Journal of Political Research* 43, no. 6: 869–94.

Myant, M., J. Drahokoupil, and I. Lesay. 2013. "Political Economy of Crisis Management in East-Central European Countries." *Europe-Asia Studies* 65, no. 3: 383–410.

Myles, J., and P. Pierson. 2001. "The Comparative Political Economy of Pension Reform." In *The New Politics of the Welfare State*, edited by P. Pierson, 305–33. Oxford: Oxford University Press.

The Nation. 2018. "'The Menace Is Inequality': A Conversation With Podemos's Pablo Iglesias." Available at https://www.thenation.com/article/menace-inequality-conversation-podemoss-pablo-iglesias/.

New Statesman. 2017. "What Welfare Changes did Philip Hammond Make in His

Budget 2017?" Available at https://www.newstatesman.com/politics/welfare/20
17/03/what-welfare-changes-did-philip-hammond-make-his-budget-2017.

New York Times. 2009a. "Czech Parliament Vote Clouds U.S. Antimissile Plan."
Available at www.nytimes.com/2009/03/25/world/europe/25czech.html?scp=1
&sq=topolanek&st=cse.

New York Times. 2009b. "European Leader Assails American Stimulus Plan." Available at www.nytimes.com/2009/03/26/world/europe/26czech.html?_r=1.

New York Times. 2010a. "Facing Austerity, Britain Unveils Welfare Cuts." Nov. 11.
Available at http://www.nytimes.com/2010/11/12/world/europe/12britain.html.

New York Times. 2010b. "Britain's Leader Carves Identity as Budget Cutter." July 20.
Available at http://www.nytimes.com/2010/07/21/world/europe/21cameron.ht
ml?pagewanted=all.

New York Times. 2012. "Party Platforms." May 23. Available at http://elections.nyti
mes.com/2008/president/issues/party-platforms/index.html.

New York Times. 2015a. "Eurozone Officials Reach Accord With Greece to Extend
Bailout." Available at www.nytimes.com/2015/02/21/business/international/gr
eece-debt-eurozone-finance-ministers.html?

New York Times. 2015b. "In Spain, Rapid Rise of Leftists Has a Familiar Ring." Available at www.nytimes.com/2015/03/11/world/in-spain-rapid-rise-of-leftists-has
-a-familiar-ring.html?_r=1.

New York Times. 2018a. "In Britain, Even Children Are Feeling the Effects of Austerity." Available at https://www.nytimes.com/2018/09/26/world/europe/uk-au
sterity-child-poverty.html.

New York Times. 2018b. "In Britain, Austerity Is Changing Everything." Available at
https://www.nytimes.com/2018/05/28/world/europe/uk-austerity-poverty.
html.

New York Times. 2018c. "Jeremy Corbyn, in Labour Speech, Vows to Fight Capitalist 'Greed.'" Available at https://www.nytimes.com/2018/09/26/world/europe/je
remy-corbyn-uk-labour-conference.html.

Newman, A. 2015. "The reluctant leader: Germany's euro experience and the long
shadow of reunification." In *The Future of the Euro, eds. Matthijs, M., and M.
Blyth*, pp. 117–35. New York: Oxford University Press.

Obstfeld, M., and K. Rogoff. 2009. "Global Imbalances and the Financial Crisis:
Products of Common Causes." CEPR Discussion Paper No. DP7606.

OECD. 1994. "The OECD Jobs Study: Facts, Analysis, Strategies." Paris.

OECD. 1997. "Implementing the OECD Jobs Strategy: Member Countries' Experience." Paris.

OECD. 2004. "Social Protection Expenditure and Receipts: 1980–2001." Paris.

OECD. 2009. "Economic Outlook Interim Report: Chapter 3. The Effectiveness and
Scope of Fiscal Stimulus." Paris.

OECD. 2010a. "Employment Outlook: Moving Beyond the Job Crisis." Paris.

OECD. 2010b. "OECD Economic Survey—Spain." December 2010, Paris.

OECD. 2010c. "Economic Survey of the Czech Republic 2010." OECD Policy Brief,
April 2010, Paris.

OECD. 2012. "Social Spending during the Crisis: Social Expenditure (SOCX) Data Update 2012." Paris.

OECD. 2014a. "Does Income Inequality Hurt Economic Growth?" Available at www.oecd.org/els/soc/Focus-Inequality-and-Growth-2014.pdf.

OECD. 2014b. "Sweden Should Urgently Reform Its School System to Improve Quality and Equity." Available at http://www.oecd.org/education/school/Impro ving-Schools-in-Sweden.pdf.

OECD. 2015a. "Economic Policy Reforms 2015: Going for Growth." Available at http://www.oecd.org/economy/goingforgrowth.htm.

OECD. 2015b. "Key Short-Term Economic Indicators." Available at http://stats.oe cd.org/index.aspx?queryid=21760#.

OECD. 2021. "Key Short-Term Economic Indicators." Available at https://stats.oecd .org/index.aspx?queryid=60703#.

Offe, C. 1993. "The Politics of Social Policy in East European Transitions: Anteced- ents, Agents, and Agenda of Reform. (The East Faces West; The West Faces East)." *Social Research* 60, no. 4.

Office of Budgetary Responsibility. 2017. "Economic and Fiscal Outlook." Available at https://cdn.obr.uk/March2017EFO-231.pdf.

Oliver-Alonso, J., and J. Valles. 2005. "Spain: Globalization's Impact on Democracy and Inequlity." In *Getting Globalization Right: The Dilemmas of Inequality*, edited by Joseph S. Tulchin and Gary Bland, 183–220. Boulder, CO: Lynne Rienner Publishers.

Open Europe. 2014. "Podemos Gears Up for Next Year's Spanish Elections with Revamped Economic Plan. Available at http://openeurope.org.uk/blog/podem os-economic-proposals/.

Orenstein, M. 1995. "Transitional Social Policy in the Czech Republic and Poland." *Czech Sociological Review* 3, no. 2: 179–96.

Orenstein, M., and M. Haas. 2005. "Globalization and the Future of Welfare States in the Post-Communist East-Central European Countries." In *Globalization and the Future of the Welfare State*, edited by M. Glatzer and D. Rueschemeyer, 130–52. Pittsburgh: University of Pittsburgh Press.

Osborne, G. 2014. "New Year Economy Speech by the Chancellor of the Exche- quer." January 6. Available at www.gov.uk/government/speeches/new-year-eco nomy-speech-by-the-chancellor-of-theexchequer.

OSW (Centre for Eastern Studies). 2018. "Czech Republic: The Government of Babiš and the Left." Available at https://www.osw.waw.pl/en/publikacje/analys es/2018-07-12/czech-republic-government-babis-and-left-0.

Palier, B., and K. Thelen. 2010. "Institutionalizing Dualism: Complementarities and Change in France and Germany." *Politics and Society* 38, no. 2: 119–48.

Palley, T. 2010. "America's Flawed Paradigm: Macroeconomic Causes of the Finan- cial Crisis and Great Recession." *Empirica* 38, no. 1: 3–17.

Palme, J., K. Nelson, O. Sjöberg, and R. Minas. 2009. "European Social Models, Protection and Inclusion." Institute for Future Studies. Accessed August 25, 2014. Available at http://people.su.se/~kennethn/European%20Social%20Mod els,%20Protection%20and%20Inclusion.pdf.

Parsons, C. 2007. *How to Map Arguments in Political Science*. Oxford: Oxford University Press.

Parties and Elections. 2015. "Parties and Elections in Europe: Germany." Available at http://www.parties-and-elections.eu/germany.html.

Parties and Elections. 2018. "Parties and Elections in Europe: Sweden." Available at http://www.parties-and-elections.eu/sweden.html.

Pavolini, E., M. León, A. Guillén, and U. Ascoli. 2016. "From Austerity to Permanent Strain? The European Union and Welfare State Reform in Italy and Spain." In *The Sovereign Debt Crisis, the EU and Welfare State Reform*, edited by C. De la Porte and E. Heins. UK: Palgrave Macmillan.

Petmesidou, M. 2019. "Southern Europe." In *Routledge Handbook of the Welfare State*, 2nd edition, edited by B. Greve. Routledge.

Petrocik, J. 1996. "Issue Ownership in Presidential Elections, With a 1980 Case Study." *American Journal of Political Science* 40, no. 3: 825–50.

Petrocik, J., W. Benoit, and G. Hansen. 2003. "Issue Ownership and Presidential Campaigning, 1952–2000." *Political Science Quarterly* 118, no. 4: 599–626.

Picot, G., and A. Tassinari. 2014. "Liberalization, Dualization, or Recalibration? Labor Market Reforms under Austerity, Italy and Spain 2010–2012." Nuffiled College Working Paper Series in Politics. Oxford University.

Picot, G., and A. Tassinari. 2017. All of One Kind? Labour Market Reforms under Austerity in Italy and Spain." *Socio-Economic Review* 15, no. 2: 461–82.

Pierson, P. 1994. *Dismantling the Welfare State? Reagan, Thatcher, and the Politics of Retrenchment*. Cambridge: Cambridge University Press.

Pierson, P. 1996. "The New Politics of the Welfare State." *World Politics* 48: 143–79.

Pierson, P. 2001. *The New Politics of the Welfare State*. Oxford: Oxford University Press.

Pietras, J. 2009. "Austerity Measures in the EU: A Country by Country Table." European Affairs European Institute. Available at www.europeaninstitute.org/index.php/112-european-affairs/special-g-20-issue-on-financial-reform/1180-austerity-measures-in-the-eu.

Plehwe, D., M. Neujeffski, and W. Krämer. 2018. "Saving the Dangerous Idea: Austerity Think Tank Networks in the European Union." *Policy and Society* 37, no. 2: 188–205.

Policy Network. 2013. "It's All About Tax Cuts: Reinfeldt As a One-Trick Pony." Available at www.policy-network.net/pno_detail.aspx?ID=4469&title=Its-all-about-tax-cuts-Reinfeldt-as-a-one-trick-pony.

Policy Network. 2015. "Targeting Germany's 'Middle Generation.'" Available at www.policy-network.net/pno_detail.aspx?ID=4872&title=Targeting-Germanys-%E2%80%98middle-generation.

Polk, J., and J. Rovny. 2018. "Welfare Democracies and Multidimensional Party Competition in Europe." In *Welfare Democracies and Party Politics: Explaining Electoral Dynamics in Times of Changing Welfare Capitalism*, edited by P. Manow, B. Palier, and H. Schwander. Oxford: Oxford University Press.

Pontusson, J., and D. Rueda. 2008. "Inequality as a Source of Political Polarization."

In *Democracy, Inequality and Representation*, edited by P. Beramendi and C. Anderson. New York: Russell Sage.

Potrafke, N. 2009. "Did Globalization Restrict Partisan Politics? An Empirical Evaluation of Social Expenditures in a Panel of OECD Countries." *Public Choice* 140: 105–24.

Potrafke, N. 2012. "Is German Domestic Social Policy Politically Controversial?" *Public Choice* 53, no. 3: 393–418.

Potůček, M. 2001. "Czech Social Reform after 1989: Concepts and Reality." *International Social Security Review* 54, no. 2–3: 81–105.

Potůček, M. 2009. "The Czech National Model of the Welfare State. Tradition and Changes." In *Diversity and Commonality in European Social Policies: The Forging of a European Social Model*, edited by S. Golinowska, P. Hengstenberg, and M. Żukowski. Warsaw: Friedrich-Ebert-Stiftung and Wydawnictwo Naukowe Scholar.

Potůček, M. 2012 "Discourses on Social Rights in the Czech Republic." In *Social Policy and Citizenship: The Changing Landscape*, edited by A. Evers and A. M. Guillemard, 335–58. Oxford: Oxford University Press.

Pureza, J. M., and M. Mortágua. 2016. "The European Neoliberal Order and the Eurocrisis: Blame It All on Germany?" *World Review of Political Economy* 7, no. 3: 363–81.

Radio Prague. 2007. "Government Approves Public Finance Reform Bill." Available at www.radio.cz/en/section/curraffrs/government-approves-public-finance-reform-bill.

Radio Prague. 2014. "Budget Approved for 2015 Boosts Social Spending But Cuts Investments." Available at www.radio.cz/en/section/business/budget-approved-for-2015-boosts-social-spending-but-cuts-investments.

Radio Prague. 2016. "Anti-Islam, Immigration Protests Take Place in Prague, Brno." Available at www.radio.cz/en/section/news/anti-islam-immigration-protests-take-place-in-prague-brno.

Regan, A. 2012. "The Political and Policy Consequences of the Eurozone Crisis Raises Doubt about the Future of Egalitarian Capitalism and Social Europe." LSE European Politics and Policy (EUROPP). Available at blogs.lse.ac.uk/europpblog/2012/07/18/eurozone-crisis-egalitarian-policies-social-europe/.

Regan, A. 2017. "The Imbalance of Capitalisms in the Eurozone: Can the North and South of Europe Converge?" *Comparative European Politics* 15: 969–90.

Reuters. 2007. "Czech President Names New Govt, PM Seeks Support." Available at www.reuters.com/article/us-czech-government-idUSL0989891520070109.

Reuters. 2010a. "Interview—Czech Social Democrats to Cut Deficit with Tax Hikes." Available at uk.reuters.com/article/czech-politics-idUKLDE63F0EF20100416.

Reuters. 2010b. "Centre-Right Wins Czech Election on Austerity Plan." Available at www.reuters.com/article/us-czech-election-idUSTRE64S0N820100529.

Reuters. 2013. "Analysis: Europe's Austerity-to-Growth Shift Largely Semantic." Available at http://www.reuters.com/article/us-eurozone-austerity-idUSBRE94Q02T20130527.

Reuters. 2014a. "Far-Right National Front Stuns French Elite with EU 'Earthquake.'" Available at http://www.reuters.com/article/us-eu-election-france-idUSBREA4 O0CP20140525.

Reuters. 2014b. "Sweden Social Democrats Will End Tax Cuts If They Win Election." Available at http://uk.reuters.com/article/2014/05/07/uk-sweden-opposit ion-idUKKBN0DN1N620140507.

Reuters. 2015a. "IMF's Lagarde Rules Out Special Treatment for Greece." Available at http://www.reuters.com/article/us-greece-election-lagarde-idUSKBN0KZ0 WT20150126.

Reuters. 2015b. "Merkel Ally Urges ECB Not to Buy Struggling States' Bonds." Available at http://www.reuters.com/article/us-ecb-bonds-germany-idUSKBN 0KB0HE20150102.

Reuters. 2015c. "ECB Launches 1 Trillion Euro Rescue Plan to Revive Euro Economy." Available at http://www.reuters.com/article/2015/01/22/us-ecb-policy-id USKBN0KU2ST20150122.

Reuters. 2015d. "Spain's Ruling PP Gets Worst Local Election Result in 20 Years." Available at www.reuters.com/article/2015/05/24/us-spain-election-idUSKBN 0O90AW20150524#0s2Puuevpcz77IQU.97.

Reuters. 2015e. "Spain's Podemos Says Germany, IMF Put European Project At Risk." Available at https://www.reuters.com/article/us-eurozone-podemos/spai ns-podemos-says-germany-imf-put-european-project-at-risk-idUSKBN0P70 X720150627#KtoErozKJXyZujOd.97.

Reuters. 2018a. "German Parties to Tackle Labour, Healthcare in Extra Round of Coalition Talks." Available at https://www.reuters.com/article/germany-politics /german-parties-to-tackle-labour-healthcare-in-extra-round-of-coalition-tal ks-idUSL2N1PU0FZ.

Reuters. 2018b. "Factbox: Policies of Main Parties Swedish Election." Available at: https://www.reuters.com/article/us-sweden-election-policy-factbox/factbox -policies-of-main-parties-in-swedish-election-idUSKCN1LM27A.

Reuters. 2018c. "Czech Leader's Planned Spending Spree Has Some People Worried." Available at: https://www.reuters.com/article/us-czech-government-fisc al-insight/czech-leaders-planned-spending-spree-has-some-people-worried -idUSKBN1KO0LD.

Reuters. 2021. "IMF urges governments to make fiscal plans to tame pandemic debt." Available at: https://www.reuters.com/business/imf-urges-governments -make-fiscal-plans-tame-pandemic-debt-2021-10-07.

Richardson, D. 2010. "Child and Family Policies in a Time of Economic Crisis." *Children & Society* 24, no. 6: 495–508.

Ripka V., and M. Mares. 2016. "Czech Republic: Awakening of Politics of Welfare." In *Challenges to European Welfare Systems*, edited by K. Schubert, K., P. de Villota, and J. Kuhlmann, 105–31. Springer.

Roberts, K. 2013. "Market Reform, Programmatic (De)alignment, and Party System Stability in Latin America." *Comparative Political Studies* 46, no. 11: 1422–52.

Rodrik, D. 1999. "Where Did All the Growth Go? External Shocks, Social Conflict, and Growth Collapses." *Journal of Economic Growth* 4, no. 4: 385–412.

Rodrik, D. 2011. *The Globalization Paradox: Democracy and the Future of the World Economy*. New York: W. W. Norton.

Royo, S. 2006. "Beyond Confrontation: The Resurgence of Social Bargaining in Spain in the 1990s." *Comparative Political Studies* 39, no. 8: 969–95.

RTE. 2014. "Juncker Cautions on Austerity as New European Commission Backed." Available at http://www.rte.ie/news/2014/1022/653975-european-commiss ion/.

Rueda, D. 2007. *Social Democracy Inside Out: Partisanship and Labor Market Policy in Advanced Industrialized Democracies*. Oxford: Oxford University Press.

Sanchez de Dios, M. 1998. "The Spanish Welfare State under the PSOE Government (1982–1996)." Paper prepared for the 1998 ECPR Conference, Warwick, UK. Available at www.ucm.es/data/cont/docs/862-2014-06-22-1998.pdf.

Sandholtz, W., and A. Stone Sweet, eds. 1998. *European Integration and Supranational Governance*. Oxford: Oxford University Press.

Sandholtz, W., A. Stone Sweet, and N. Fligstein, eds. 2001. *The Institutionalization of Europe*. Oxford: Oxford University Press.

Savage, L. 2019a. "The Politics of Social Spending after the Great Recession: The Return of Partisan Policy Making." *Governance* 32, no. 1: 123–41.

Savage, L. 2019b. "Supplementary Material: The Politics of Social Spending after the Great Recession: The Return of Partisan Policy Making." *Governance* 32, no. 1: 123–41.

Saxonberg, S., and T. Sirovátka. 2009. "Neo-liberalism by Decay? The Evolution of the Czech Welfare State." *Social Policy & Administration* 43, no. 2: 186–203.

Scharpf, F. 2002. "The European Social Model: Coping with the Challenges of Diversity." *Journal of Common Market Studies* 40, no. 4: 645–70.

Scharpf, F., and V. Schmidt, eds. 2000. *Welfare and Work in the Open Economy*. Vols. I and II. Oxford: Oxford University Press.

Schirm, S. A. 2020. "Refining Domestic Politics Theories of IPE: A Societal Approach to Governmental Preferences." *Politics*. Published online January 23, 2020.

Schmidt, V. A. 2002. "Does discourse matter in the politics of welfare adjustment?" *Comparative Political Studies* 35, no. 2: 168–93.

Schmidt, V. A., and M. Thatcher, eds. 2013. *Resilient Liberalism in Europe's Political Economy. Contemporary European Politics*. Cambridge: Cambridge University Press.

Schmitt, C., and P. Starke, 2011. "Explaining Convergence of OECD Welfare States." *Journal of European Social Policy* 21, no. 2: 120–35.

Schmitter, P. 1969. "Three Neo-Functional Hypotheses about International Integration." *International Organization* 23: 562–64.

Schmitter, P. 2002. "Neo-Neo-Functionalism." Available at https://www.eui.eu/Doc uments/DepartmentsCentres/SPS/Profiles/Schmitter/NeoNeoFunctionalismR ev.pdf.

Schulze-Cleven, T., and J. T. Weishaupt. 2015. "Playing Normative Legacies: Partisanship and Employment Policies in Crisis-Ridden Europe." *Politics & Society* 43, no. 2: 269–99.

Scruggs, L., J. Detlef, and K. Kuitto. 2014. "Comparative Welfare Entitlements Dataset 2. Version 2014–03." University of Connecticut and University of Greifswald. Available at http://cwed2.org/.

Seeleib-Kaiser, M., and T. Fleckenstein. 2007. "Discourse, Learning and Welfare State Change: The Case of German Labour Market Reforms." *Social Policy & Administration* 41, no. 5: 427–48.

Seeleib-Kaiser, M., S. Van Dyk, and M. Roggenkamp. 2008. "Polity Politics and Social Welfare: Comparing Christian and Social Democracy in Austria, Germany and the Netherlands." In *Globalisation and Welfare Series*, edited by D. Bouget, J. Lewis, and G. Bonoli Cheltenham: Edward Elgar.

Singer, M. 2011a. "Who Says 'It's the Economy'? Cross-National and Cross-Individual Variation in the Salience of Economic Performance." *Comparative Political Studies* 44, no. 3: 284–312.

Singer, M. 2011b. "When Do Voters Actually Think 'It's the Economy'? Evidence from the 2008 Presidential Campaign." *Electoral Studies* 30, no. 4: 621–32.

Social Europe. 2012. "Spain Is Experiencing a Period of Intense Social Crisis." Available at www.socialeurope.eu/2012/11/spain-is-experiencing-a-period-of-inten se-social-crisis/.

Social Europe. 2015. "Why Podemos Poses a Major Threat to the Spanish Political Establishment." Available at www.socialeurope.eu/2012/11/spain-is-experienci ng-a-period-of-intense-social-crisis/.

Solsten, E., and S. Meditz. 1988. *Spain: A Country Study.* Washington: Government Printing Office for the Library of Congress.

Spáč, P. 2013. "New Political Parties in the Czech Republic: Anti-Politics or Mainstream?" In *Alternative Politics? The Rise of New Political Parties in Central Europe*, edited by G. Mesežnikov, O. Gyárfášová, Z. Bútorová, 127–48. Institute for Public Affairs.

Spectator. 2012. "Sweden's Secret Recipe: Advice from a Successful—and Tax-Cutting–Finance Minister." Available at www.spectator.co.uk/features/7779228 /swedens-secret-recipe/.

Speed, E., and R. Mannion. 2017. "The Rise of Post-truth Populism in Pluralist Liberal Democracies: Challenges for Health Policy." *International Journal of Health Policy and Management* 6, no. 5: 249–51.

Spiegel. 2012a. "A Dose of Its Own Medicine: Schäuble's Secret Austerity Plan for Germany." Available at http://www.spiegel.de/international/germany/berlin-pl an-hints-future-austerity-measures-for-germany-a-874377.html.

Spiegel. 2012b. "Leading By Example: Merkel Bets Austerity Will Result in Re-Election." Available at http://www.spiegel.de/international/business/leading-by -example-merkel-bets-austerity-will-result-in-re-election-a-816464.html.

Spiegel. 2012c. "The Coming EU Summit Clash: Merkel Vows 'No Euro Bonds as Long as I Live.'" Available at http://www.spiegel.de/international/europe/chanc ellor-merkel-vows-no-euro-bonds-as-long-as-she-lives-a-841163.html.

Spiegel. 2012d. "Draghi's Promise: German Opposition to ECB Bond-Buying Plan Mounts." Available at http://www.spiegel.de/international/europe/germany-op poses-draghi-plan-for-ecb-to-purchase-sovereign-bonds-a-847836.html.

Spiegel. 2012e. "Unlimited Bond Purchases: ECB Head Draghi Backs Up Pledge to Save Euro." Available at www.spiegel.de/international/europe/ecb-president-dr aghi-announces-unlimited-bond-buying-program-a-854374.html.

Spiegel. 2013a. "EU Austerity Dispute: How Barroso Let His Opinion Slip." Available at http://www.spiegel.de/international/europe/controversy-simmers-over -eu-austerity-and-growth-remarks-by-barroso-a-896213.html.

Spiegel. 2013b. "'Merkel Must Take Action': SPD Demands a New Europe Approach." Available at www.spiegel.de/international/europe/social-democrats-in-germa ny-demand-more-social-europe-from-merkel-a-924213.html.

Spiegel. 2014. "France and Friends: Merkel Increasingly Isolated on Austerity." Available at http://www.spiegel.de/international/europe/the-anti-austerity-ca mp-is-growing-as-merkel-becomes-more-isolated-a-989357.html.

Spoon, Jay, Sara B. Hobolt, and C. de Vries. 2014. "Going Green: Explaining Issue Competition on the Environment." *European Journal of Political Research* 53, no. 2: 363–80.

Standing, G. 1996. "Social Protection and Eastern Europe: A Tale of Slipping Anchors and Torn Safety Nets." In *Welfare States in Transition: National Adaptations in Global Economics*, edited by G. Esping-Andersen, 225–55. London: G. Sage.

Starke, P. 2006. "The Politics of Welfare State Retrenchment: A Literature Review." *Social Policy & Administration* 4, no. 1: 104–20.

Starke, P., A. Kaasch, and F. van Hooren. 2012. "Comparing Social Policy Responses to Global Economic Crises: Constrained Partisanship in Mature Welfare States." Paper prepared for the ESPAnet annual conference, Edinburgh, September 6–8, 2012.

Starke, P. A. Kaasch, and F. van Hooren. 2014. *The Welfare State as Crisis Manager: Explaining the Diversity of Policy Responses to Economic Crisis*. Palgrave Macmillan.

Starke, P., H. Obinger, and F. Castles. 2008. "Convergence Towards Where: In What Ways, If Any, Are Welfare States Becoming More Similar?" *Journal of European Public Policy* 15, no. 7: 975–1000.

Stoesz, D. 1996. *Small Change: Domestic Policy under the Clinton Presidency*. New York: Longman.

Stoesz, D. 2002. "The American Welfare State at Twilight." *Journal of Social Policy* 31, no. 3: 487–503.

Stoll, Heather. 2010. "Elite-Level Conflict Salience and Dimensionality in Western Europe: Concepts and Findings." *West European Politics* 33, no. 3: 445–73.

Streeck, W., and K. Thelen. 2005. "Introduction: Institutional Change in Advanced Political Economies." In *Beyond Continuity: Institutional Change in Advanced Political Economies*, edited by W. Streeck and K. Thelen, 1–39. Oxford: Oxford University Press.

Swank, D. 2000. "Social Democratic Welfare States in a Global Economy." In

Globalization, Europeanization, and the End of Scandinavian Social Democracy?, edited by R. Geyer, C. Ingrebritsen, and J. Moses. Palgrave Macmillan.

Swank, D. 2002. *Global Capital, Political Institutions, and Policy Change in Developed Welfare States*. New York: Cambridge University Press.

Swedish Ministry of Finance. 2008. Budget Bill 2009. September 22. Stockholm: Ministry of Finance.

Swedish Ministry of Finance. 2009a. 2009 Spring Fiscal Policy Bill. April 15. Stockholm: Ministry of Finance.

Swedish Ministry of Finance. 2009b. Budget Bill 2010. September 21. Stockholm: Ministry of Finance.

Swedish Prime Minister's Office. 2008. The Swedish Programme for Growth and Employment 2008–2010. October 17. Stockholm: Prime Minister's Office.

Tavits, M., and J. D. Potter. 2015. "The Effect of Inequality and Social Identity on Party Strategies." *American Journal of Political Science* 59, no. 3: 744–58.

Taylor-Gooby, P. 2001. "Welfare Reform in the UK: The Construction of a Liberal Consensus." In *Welfare States under Pressure*, edited by P. Taylor-Gooby, 147–70. London: Sage.

Taylor-Gooby, P., ed. 2004. *New Risks, New Welfare: The Transformation of the European Welfare State*. Oxford: Oxford University Press.

Taylor-Gooby, P. 2012. "Root and Branch Restructuring to Achieve Major Cuts: The Social Policy Programme of the 2010 UK Coalition Government." *Social Policy & Administration* 46, no. 1: 61–82.

Taylor-Gooby, P. 2013. *The Double Crisis of the Welfare State and What We Can Do About It*. London: Palgrave Macmillan.

Telegraph. 2015. "Welfare and Pension Policies: General Election 2015 and Where Each Party Stand." Available at www.telegraph.co.uk/news/general-election-2015/11493802/Welfare-and-pension-policies-General-Election-2015-and-where-each-party-stand.html.

Thelen, K. 2009. "Institutional Change in Advanced Political Economies." *British Journal of Industrial Relations* 47, no. 3: 471–98.

Thelen, K. 2012. "Varieties of Capitalism: Trajectories of Liberalization and the New Politics of Social Solidarity." *Annual Review of Political Science* 15: 137–59.

Thelen, K. 2014. *Varieties of Liberalization and the New Politics of Social Solidarity*. Cambridge: Cambridge University Press.

Theodoropoulou, S., and A. Watt. 2011. "Withdrawal Symptoms: An Assessment of the Austerity Packages in Europe." ETUI Working Paper No. 2011.02. Brussels: European Trade Union Institute.

Traber, D., N. Giger, and S. Häusermann. 2018. "How Economic Crises Affect Political Representation: Declining Party-Voter Congruence in Times of Constrained Government." *West European Politics* 41, no. 5: 1100–24.

Trampusch, C. 2005. *Beyond Continuity: Institutional Change in Advanced Political Economies*. Oxford: Oxford University Press.

Trubek, D., and L. Trubek. 2005. "Hard and Soft Law in the Construction of Social Europe." *European Law Journal* 11, no. 3: 343–64.

UK Women's Budget Group. 2010. Report on Budget Proposals in Party Manifestos, May 2010. Available at http://wbg.org.uk/wp-content/uploads/2016/12/RRB_Reports_12_3556891183.pdf.

UKIP. 2015. "Believe in Britain: UKIP 2015 Manifesto." Accessed June 2, 2020. Available at https://d3n8a8pro7vhmx.cloudfront.net/ukipdev/pages/1103/atta chments/original/1429295050/UKIPManifesto2015.pdf.

UKIP. 2017. "Britain Together: UKIP 2017 Manifesto." Accessed June 2, 2020. Available at https://d3n8a8pro7vhmx.cloudfront.net/ukipdev/pages/3944/atta chments/original/1495695469/UKIP_Manifesto_June2017opt.pdf.

UKIP. 2019. "For Brexit and Beyond: UKIP 2019 Manifesto." Accessed June 2, 2020. Available at: https://irp-cdn.multiscreensite.com/f6e3b8c6/files/uploaded/man ifesto_complete.pdf.

UNDP (United Nations Development Programme). 2010. "Social Protection in Fiscal Stimulus Packages: Some Evidence." UNDP/ODS Working Paper, Office of Development Studies, United Nations Development Programme, New York, March 2010. Available at http://www.undp.org/content/dam/undp/library/cor porate/Development%20Studies/socialprotection_fiscalstimulus_march2010.pdf.

Urquijo, L. 2017. "The Europeanisation of Policy to Address Poverty under the New Economic Governance: The Contribution of the European Semester." *Journal of Poverty and Social Justice* 25, no. 1: 49–64.

US Federal Government. 2009. "Stimulus: American Recovery and Reinvestment Act of 2009: Essential Documents (Stimulus American Recovery and Reinvestment Act of 2009)."

Valiente, C. 2013. "Gender Equality Policymaking in Spain (2008–11): Losing Momentum." In *Politics and Society in Contemporary Spain: From Zapatero to Rajoy*, edited by B. Field and A. Botti, 179–95. Basingstoke: Palgrave.

Van de Wardt, Marc. 2015. "Desperate Needs, Desperate Deeds: Why Mainstream Parties Respond to the Issues of Niche Parties." *West European Politics* 38, no. 1: 93–122.

Van der Brug, Wouter, and Joust van Spanje. 2009. Immigration, Europe, and the New Cultural Dimension. *European Journal of Political Research* 48, no. 3: 309–34.

Van Kersbergen, K. 1995. *Social Capitalism. A Study of Christian Democracy and the Welfare State.* London: Routledge.

Van Kersbergen, K., B. Vis, and A. Hemerijck. 2014. "The Great Recession and Welfare State Reform: Is Retrenchment Really the Only Game Left in Town?" *Social Policy & Administration* 48, no. 7: 883–904.

Van Vliet, O. 2010. "Divergence within Convergence: Europeanization of Social and Labour Market Policies." *Journal of European Integration* 32, no. 3:

Vanhercke, B., S. Sabato, and D. Bouget, eds. 2017. "Social Policy in the European

Union: State of Play 2017." Brussels, European Trade Union Institute (ETUI) and European Social Observatory (OSE).

Vidal, G., and I. Sánchez-Vítores. 2019. "Spain—Out with the Old: The Restructuring of Spanish Politics." In *European Party Politics in Times of Crisis*, edited by S. Hutter and H. Kriesi, 75–94. Cambridge: Cambridge University Press.

Vis, B. 2009. "The Importance of Socio-economic and Political Losses and Gains in Welfare State Reform." *Journal of European Social Policy* 19, no. 5: 395–407.

Vis, B., and K. van Kersbergen. 2007. "Why and How Do Political Actors Pursue Risky Reforms?" *Journal of Theoretical Politics* 19, no. 2: 153–72.

Vis, B., K. van Kersbergen, and T. Hylands. 2011. "To What Extent Did the Financial Crisis Intensify the Pressure to Reform the Welfare State?" *Social Policy & Administration* 45: 338–53.

Wagner, M. 2012. "Defining and Measuring Niche Parties." *Party Politics* 18, no. 6: 845–64.

Wagner, M., and T. Meyer. 2014 "Which Issues Do Parties Emphasise? Salience Strategies and Party Organisation in Multiparty Systems." *West European Politics* 37, no. 5: 1019–45.

Wall Street Journal. 2012a. "Total Global Losses From Financial Crisis: $15 Trillion." Available at http://blogs.wsj.com/economics/2012/10/01/total-global-losses-from-financial-crisis-15-trillion/.

Wall Street Journal. 2012b. "How ECB Chief Outflanked German Foe in Fight for Euro." Available at http://online.wsj.com/article/SB10000872396390443507204578020323544183926.html.

Wall Street Journal. 2012c. "Madrid Austerity Plan Boosted to $80 Billion." Available at www.wsj.com/articles/SB10001424052702303919504577520213420179248.

Wall Street Journal. 2012d. "Czech Opposition Left Tightens Hold on Upper House." Available at http://blogs.wsj.com/emergingeurope/2012/10/22/czech-opposition-left-tightens-hold-on-upper-house/.

Wall Street Journal. 2014. "Sweden's Left Victorious in Elections: Social Democrat Leader Stefan Lofven Defeats Incumbent Prime Minister Fredrik Reinfeldt." Available at www.wsj.com/articles/swedes-go-to-the-polls-1410695627.

Wall Street Journal. 2015a. "Podemos and Ciudadanos Punish Spain's Ruling Popular Party in Regional Elections." Available at http://www.wsj.com/articles/spanish-incumbent-party-tested-as-voters-go-to-polls-1432460241.

Wall Street Journal. 2015b. "Syriza Victory in Greek Election Roils European Debate Over Austerity." Available at http://www.wsj.com/articles/syriza-victory-in-greek-election-roils-european-debate-over-austerity-1422236014.

Washington Post. 2013. "An Amazing Mea Culpa from the IMF's Chief Economist on Austerity." Available at www.washingtonpost.com/news/wonk/wp/2013/01/03/an-amazing-mea-culpa-from-the-imfs-chief-economist-on-austerity/.

Washington Post. 2017. Czech Elections Have Become Really Volatile. This Year Was No Exception." Available at https://www.washingtonpost.com/news/monkey-cage/wp/2017/10/24/czech-elections-have-become-really-volatile-this-year-was-no-exception/?noredirect=on&utm_term=.ece1ccb4e90d.

Watt, A., and M. Nikolova. 2009. "A Quantum of Solace? An Assessment of Fiscal Stimulus Packages by EU Member States in Response to the Economic Crisis." ETUI Working Paper No. 209.05. Brussels: European Trade Union Institute.

Wendler, F. 2014a. "Justification and Political Polarization in National Parliamentary Debates on EU Treaty Reform." *Journal of European Public Policy* 21, no. 4: 549–67.

Wendler, F. 2014b. "Debating Europe in National Parliaments: Justification and Political Polarization in Debates on the EU in Austria, France, Germany and the United Kingdom." OPAL Online Paper Series No. 17.

Wonka, A. 2016. "The Party Politics of the Euro Crisis in the German Bundestag: Frames, Positions and Salience." *West European Politics* 39, no. 1: 125–44.

World Bank. 2014. "World Development Report 2014: Risk and Opportunity— Managing Risk for Development." Available at http://siteresources.worldbank. org/EXTNWDR2013/Resources/8258024–1352909193861/8936935–1356011 448215/8986901–1380046989056/WDR-2014_Complete_Report.pdf.

Zeitlin, J. 2008. "The Open Method of Co-ordination and the Governance of the Lisbon Strategy." *JCMS: Journal of Common Market Studies* 46, no. 2: 436–50.

Zeitlin, J., and Vanhercke, B. 2017. Socializing the European Semester: EU Social and Economic Policy Co-ordination in Crisis and Beyond." *Journal of European Public Policy* 25: 1–26.

Zohlnhöfer, R., and Herweg, N. 2012. "Expanding Paradigmatic Change in German Labour Maket Policy: A Multiple Streams Perspective." Paper prepared for the Workshop "The Politics of Labour Market Policy in Times of Austerity" at the ECPR Joint Sessions of Workshops. Antwerp, April 11–13, 2012.

Żukowski, M. 2009. "Social Policy Regimes in the European Countries." In *Diversity and Commonality in European Social Policies: The Forging of a European Social Model*, edited by S. Golinowska, P. Hengstenberg, and M. Żukowski. Warsaw: Friedrich-Ebert-Stiftung and Wydawnictwo Naukowe Scholar.

INDEX

Note: Page numbers in italics indicate a figure.

Printed and bound by CPI Group (UK) Ltd, Croydon, CR0 4YY

09/06/2025

14686108-0001